LE CORDON BLEU

Kitchen ESSENTIALS

LE CORDON BLEU

ESSENTIALS

**THE COMPLETE ILLUSTRATED REFERENCE TO
THE INGREDIENTS, EQUIPMENT, TERMS AND TECHNIQUES
THAT ENSURE CULINARY SUCCESS**

CARROLL & BROWN PUBLISHERS LIMITED

This edition published in 2006 in the United Kingdom by

Carroll & Brown Publishers Limited
20 Lonsdale Road
London NW6 6RD

Text, illustrations and compilation
copyright © Carroll & Brown Limited, 2000, 2006

A CIP catalogue record for this book is available from
the British Library.

ISBN-10 1-904760-34-1
ISBN-13 978-1-904760-34-4

10987654321

First published in the UK in 2000 under the title
Good Housekeeping Complete Cook's Book

Reproduced by Colourscan in Singapore
Printed and bound by Everbest in China

contents

FOREWORD 7

1 ESSENTIAL KNOW-HOW 8

BATTERIE DE CUISINE 10
• Knives and cutters • Other essential equipment • Stovetop pots and pans
• Pastry and cake equipment

COOKING TERMS AND TECHNIQUES 18
• Pastry making • Cake making • Blanching and tenderising • Stuffing • Boiling
• Poaching • Steaming • Braising and stewing • Roasting and baking • Grilling
• Barbecuing • Frying • Carving • Garnishing

2 INGREDIENTS 54

FISH AND SHELLFISH 57
• White fish • Oily fish • Freshwater fish • Exotic fish • Preserved fish • Squid
• Shrimps and prawns • Lobster • Crab • Molluscs • Garnishes for fish and shellfish

MEAT 81
• Beef • Veal • Lamb • Pork • Ham and bacon • Offal • Sausages • Cured meats

POULTRY AND GAME 101
• Chicken • Turkey • Duck • Goose • Game birds • Furred game

DAIRY PRODUCTS 117
• Milk • Cream and yogurt • Butter and other fats • Cheese • Eggs

PULSES AND GRAINS 133
• Pulses • Grains • Rice • Flours • Breads and yeast • Pasta and noodles

VEGETABLES 155
• Onions • Leeks and spring onions • Garlic • Shoots and stems • Globe artichokes
• Potatoes • Other root vegetables • Unusual and exotic roots • Leafy greens • Pods,
seeds and beans • Squashes • Peppers and chillies • Tomatoes • Other vegetable fruits
• Salads • Herbs • Mushrooms • Seaweed and sea vegetables • Olives and capers

FRUITS AND NUTS 203
• Apples and pears • Stone fruits • Berries • Citrus fruits • Exotic fruits
• Other fruits • Dried fruits • Preserves and condiments • Nuts and seeds

FLAVOURINGS 227
• Spices • Oils • Vinegars • Storecupboard extras • Salt and pepper • Sweeteners
• Chocolate • Coffee and tea

INDEX 252
ACKNOWLEDGEMENTS 256

foreword

It is with great pleasure that we introduce our new millennium book: *Le Cordon Bleu Kitchen Essentials*. I will not call it a cookbook because it is more than that. It is a guide that can be useful to both amateurs and professionals alike. With an ordinary cookbook, we could try to help everyone be better cooks by giving them recipe after recipe, but after more than a century of culinary education, Le Cordon Bleu has learned that the secret to success in the kitchen is more than just a good recipe, but a solid understanding and knowledge of the ingredients, techniques, and processes. A recipe is but a guide that can lead to the creation of a delectable meal that also serves to nourish the body, the spirit, and the conviviality between friends.

Ingredients and the tools of the kitchen are the keys that most people take for granted. How to check for freshness in fish, how to select a ripe melon: these are mysteries that have intimidated cooks the world over. *Kitchen Essentials* provides you with the information to make the most of your purchases and also introduces you to new ingredients from around the globe. It not only explains but shows you how to select and store fresh produce, and advises on standard preparations such as peeling, cutting, and cooking.

Today's cooks have more professional-style equipment available to them than ever before. Avid gourmets can outfit their kitchens to resemble a miniature of their favorite restaurants. *Kitchen Essentials* is unique in that it goes into the same detail in explaining and selecting the right tools as it does for ingredients.

Le Cordon Bleu's team of over 50 international Master Chefs pass on their savoir-faire to amateurs, aspiring chefs, and experienced professionals. During their training, our students are exposed to new ingredients and new tools that they learn to adapt to their own style of cooking, taking home with them a new-found sense of confidence both in the market and in the kitchen. We hope that *Le Cordon Bleu Kitchen Essentials* can do the same for you.

From our kitchen to yours,

André J. Cointreau
President, Le Cordon Bleu International

knives and cutters

other essential equipment

stovetop pots and pans

pastry and cake equipment

pastry making

cake making

blanching and tenderising

stuffing

boiling

poaching

steaming

braising and stewing

roasting and baking

grilling

barbecuing

frying

carving

garnishing

essential know-how

knives and cutters

A well-equipped kitchen will contain a range of different knives. Quality knives are made of high-carbon stainless steel and should have tangs (a narrow metal part at the base of the blade), that go right through the handles. Many cooks prefer the heavier weight of a cleaver's rectangular blade when cutting through bone and meat.

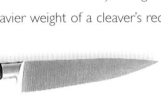

Paring knife Used for cutting fruits, vegetables, meat and cheese, similar in shape to a chef's knife with a 6–9 cm (2½–3½ in) blade.

Chef's knife Essential for chopping, slicing, dicing and mincing, this knife has a long triangular-shaped blade that ranges in length from 15 to 30 cm (6–12 in). The edge is slightly curved so you can rock the knife for easy chopping.

Serrated knife Sold in various sizes, the smaller knives – 13 cm (5 in) long – are ideal for slicing through fruits and vegetables while the large ones cut cakes and breads evenly.

Carving knife (and fork) This knife has a long, narrow blade, ideal for slicing hot cooked meats. The double-pronged fork is used to hold the meat steady during carving.

A knife with a scalloped blade and rounded tip cuts cold meats better than a carving knife.

Sharpening and storing knives

Use a sharpening steel to keep knives sharp. To use, rest the steel on your worktop and position the widest part of the knife blade at a 20° angle on the underside of the steel near the fingerguard. Draw your knife downward, pulling the handle gradually toward you until you have sharpened the full length of the blade. Repeat this action on the other side and then make alternate strokes until both sides are sharp.

Knives should be stored in a wooden block or in a drawer on their own to prevent dulling.

Knife chopping

Hold the tip of your knife firmly against the board with one hand and use your other hand to raise and lower the handle working the blade over the food.

Chopped Food is cut into small, irregular pieces about the size of peas.

Finely chopped Ingredients are cut into tiny, irregular pieces less than 3 mm (⅛ in) in size.

Dice Small, uniform cubes of about 5 cm (2 in) in length. First cut food into matchsticks and then slice crosswise into cubes.

Julienne Food is cut into thin matchsticks. First cut the food into 5 x 3 cm (2 x 1¼ in) slices and then cut lengthwise into 3 mm (⅛ in) wide strips.

Slicers, peelers and graters

A mezzaluna has a curved steel cutting blade with a vertical wooden handle at each end. You rock it across the ingredient to cut.

▶ **A vegetable peeler** is easier to use than a paring knife for potatoes, apples, carrots and other fruits and vegetables. A swivel blade conforms more to the shape of the ingredient than a fixed blade so less of the item's flesh is removed.

▶ **Graters** most often consist of a hollow box with different perforations on each side. Other types are: rotary graters with different blades; single-sided graters for citrus zest and Parmesan cheese; and concave nutmeg graters which can hold the whole spice.

▶ **A zester** has a stainless steel rectangular head with five holes that are designed to remove fine shavings of citrus zest when dragged along the surface of the fruit.

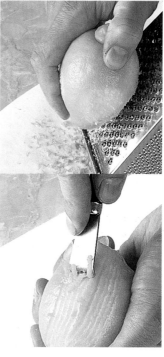

knives and cutters

11

other essential equipment

There is a wide range of specialist equipment that can make specific techniques easier to master, and many of these will be demonstrated throughout the book. Here we concentrate on the 'work horses' of the kitchen.

Mixing bowls
These have many uses in the kitchen and a well-equipped one will have bowls in various sizes. Stainless steel bowls are durable and good conductors of heat and cold; glass and ceramic bowls are heavier so will sit firmly on a counter while ingredients are beaten. The latter may also be suitable for use in ovens and microwaves.

Whisks
Available in different sizes, from giant balloon whisks used for whipping cream, light batters and eggs to tiny ones for mixing dressings or cups of hot chocolate, a good whisk should feel comfortable in your hand and all wires should be solidly anchored. Flat whisks are good for reaching into the corners of a saucepan and for deglazing.

Spoons and scoops
Essential for mixing, stirring and serving, wooden spoons are strong, inflexible and poor conductors of heat, which make them ideal for beating and creaming. Metal or plastic spoons are used for basting, stirring and mixing. Because they don't absorb strong flavours as wooden spoons do, they are more suitable for general use. A slotted spoon is used for lifting and draining foods out of hot liquid or oil and also for skimming – though a purpose-made flatter tool is also sold. Ladles come with various capacity bowls and are essential for serving liquids; the better ones have a lip on one side to make pouring easier. A melon baller (see page 221) usually has two bowl-shaped blades and is used to cut ball-shaped pieces from potatoes and other vegetables and fruit and for garnishes. An ice-cream scoop can be useful or else use a dessertspoon.

Sieves and strainers
These are used with both wet and dry ingredients, and are made of metal, plastic or wood, with different-sized mesh. Conical shapes are ideal for straining liquid ingredients into jugs and jars; bowl and drum sieves are the best for dry ingredients. A colander's

perforated holes make it easy to drain cooked pasta and vegetables, and to wash fruits and vegetables. Single-handled ones with feet are the most useful.

Kitchen devices and machines

In addition to the electrical appliances described below, there is a number of manual devices that you can use to make accomplishing particular tasks that much easier.

- Mortars and pestles (see page 229) – small stone or marble bowls and their hand-held grinders – have multiple uses in the kitchen. They grind spices, nuts and seeds, anchovies and other ingredients to form pastes and sauces.
- Timers range from simple sand-in-glass vial devices to battery-operated bell ringers, and are vital for keeping track of important preparation and cooking stages.
- Deep-fat, sugar and meat thermometers are frequently essential for ensuring ingredients reach their optimum cooking temperatures.
- Pasta machines are purpose-made devices that both roll and cut out dough. They are sold with a variety of cutters to make noodles and ribbons of various widths.
- Rotary beaters are hand-held mixers that can beat eggs, whip cream and other light liquids.

Electrical equipment There is a variety of electrical devices for the kitchen that can make quick and easy work of food preparation.

- A food processor is a multi-purpose machine that can chop, mince and purée a wide range of ingredients. Most models come with extra shredding and slicing attachments and blades for making and kneading dough.
- Though not as versatile as a food processor, a blender comes in handy when liquefying food for soups, sauces, drinks and purées. The more substantial blenders can chop ice as well.
- Mixers are available as both hand-held and worktop models. They are essential for mixing doughs and batters, whipping cream, whisking egg whites and creaming cake mixtures. The worktop models often come with other useful attachments, such as pasta makers, grinders and even juice extractors.
- Deep-fat fryers have their own thermostats to regulate the temperature of oil, which makes them safer than using a frying basket and pan.
- Ice-cream makers are sold as small models which churn the mixture in the freezer and larger, free-standing ones, which have an integral stirring and cooling mechanism.

Measures and measuring

For successful cooking, the right amount of ingredients must be used. Although ingredients in the UK and Europe are measured metrically by weight and volume, an American cookbook would use cup measures.

Measuring spoons are ideal for small amounts of dry ingredients. Unless heaped spoonfuls are called for, these must be levelled off (see below).

Measuring jugs are necessary for the volume measurement of liquids. They must be checked at eye level to ensure the required depth is reached (see below).

Scales, whether balance or digital, must be used when recipes call for ingredients by weight.

▶ **Measuring a level spoon** Over a bowl or a plate, fill your spoon so the ingredient stands proud. Place the straight edge of a knife blade across the spoon at the handle end and push the knife away from you and over the spoon to level the surface.

▶ **Checking a liquid measure** Stand the jug on a flat surface and wait for the liquid to stop moving. Look at it at eye level to check the measurement; the liquid should be exactly on the required volume line.

▶ **Checking volume** As well as the ingredients, the pan or dish should be the correct size. If you want to check the volume, fill it with water from a measuring jug using 500 ml (17 fl oz) at a time. Keep filling and taking note of the measures until the water reaches the brim.

stovetop pots and pans

Any well-equipped kitchen will have a wide selection of saucepans, for cooking different foods. Buying a new set of pans can be a big investment so bear the following points in mind before buying and also check whether they feel comfortable in your hand. If you are investing in a whole new set of pans, you could buy just one from the range you have chosen in order to check it out. And remember that the base of the pan should be of a similar size to the ring you will be cooking on.

How many saucepans are necessary?

- Three or four saucepans ranging from 1 to 5 litres (1¾ to 8¾ pints) for everyday cooking of sauces and vegetables.
- One 8 litre (14 pints) two-handled pot for bulky foods such as corn on the cob and lobster.
- One or two deep, wide 5 litre (8¾ pints) two-handled pots for stocks, soups and cooking pasta and rice.
- It is also worth investing in a steamer – steamed foods are cooked by a gentle, moist heat and have a wonderful flavour. There are many types available, from electric to hob-top models which consist of a base pan topped with two or three inserts that fit together and a close-fitting lid.

Materials should conduct heat evenly from the base up to the sides. Pans with straight sides that are reasonably deep, 7.5–10 cm (3–4 in), contain heat the best.

Handles should be sturdy, heatproof and fitted securely. If they are too heavy the pan may tip over.

A hole in the end of the handle for hanging is a plus.

Bases should be thick and heavy. If too thin, the food is likely to burn and the pan may buckle.

Lids should fit snugly with the knob attached securely.

Weight is important, so lift the pan to check that it is not too heavy.

Materials

- Aluminium pans conduct and hold heat well and do not dent easily. They can, however, affect the taste and colour of acidic or egg dishes if cooked slowly.
- Cast-iron pans distribute heat evenly and cool slowly. They need to be seasoned before use to create a non-stick finish (see box, below) and are not suitable for cooking vegetables as the iron destroys vitamin C.
- Copper pans are expensive but conduct heat perfectly. Do not use them to make pickles because vinegar can react with the metal and cause poisoning. Avoid cooking any vegetables in them as the copper destroys vitamin C. To prevent this, ensure the pan is lined with stainless steel – these pans are expensive, but if you can afford them they are much the best buy and will last forever.
- Enamelled cast-iron pans are sturdy and distribute heat well. They can, however, be very heavy and slow to heat and cool, so they are not good for delicate sauces. The enamel may crack if the pan is dropped and the inside can also be scratched. These pans don't need to be seasoned.
- Stainless steel is a hard-wearing material. Most pans have a layer of copper or aluminium to aid the transfer of heat.
- Glass and porcelain pans are suitable only for gentle cooking over a low heat. Glass is an average conductor.
- Non-stick pans are vital for low-fat cooking as they require no extra fat to prevent the base from burning.

Seasoning a cast-iron pan

Regular (not enamelled) cast-iron pans require seasoning before use in order to create a non-stick finish. Wash the pan in hot, soapy water, then dry thoroughly. Using a cloth soaked in vegetable oil, rub the entire surface – even the exterior and lid. Heat upside down in a 180°C (350°F/gas 4) oven for 1 hour. Turn off oven and allow the pan to cool in the oven.

Volume equivalents

600 ml	1 pint	0.5 quart
1.2 litres	2 pints	1 quart
1.75 litres	3 pints	1.5 quarts
2.3 litres	4 pints	2 quarts
3.4 litres	6 pints	3 quarts
4.5 litres	8 pints	4 quarts
6.8 litres	12 pints	6 quarts
9.1 litres	16 pints	8 quarts

BAINS-MARIE

A bain-marie is a 'water bath' made by placing a pan or bowl of food above a larger pan of hot water. A double boiler (right), consisting of a set of two stacking pans, is an ideal bain-marie for the hob. This gentle method of cooking is often used for delicate sauces and melting chocolate.

Care and cleaning

Aluminium is relatively easy to clean; scrub with a mild abrasive cleanser. If the pan has darkened, fill it with water and vinegar or lemon juice; boil for 15 minutes.

Cast-iron needs to be cleaned carefully in boiling water using a paper towel or soft cloth (without soap); use a nylon pad to scrub off any food. Dry thoroughly after each use to prevent rusting; wiping with oiled paper helps.

To rescue burnt pans spread a teacup of any biological washing powder over the burnt surface of the pan. Add two teacups of water and simmer for 10 minutes. Pour the contents away and scrub.

Enamelled cast-iron should not be scoured; if food sticks, soak in warm water then use a plastic pad to loosen.

Copper should be washed in hot, soapy water with a soft cloth; dry immediately. These pans need relining occasionally (large kitchen equipment shops can arrange this); reline if you see copper through the lining. Copper tarnishes quickly so the outside needs to be polished regularly; clean by rubbing with a cut lemon dipped in salt.

Stainless steel is easy to clean as it does not scratch when scoured. Wash in hot, soapy water with a nylon pad. Polish the outside with newspaper for extra shine.

Glass and porcelain are easy to clean and dishwasher safe. To remove grease, soak in hot, soapy water.

Non-stick finishes must be cleaned using a soapy sponge.

pastry and cake equipment

There are a number of specialist items that will make the production of perfect pies, tarts, biscuits and cakes a reality for every cook. If you invest in a new tin every time a recipe calls for one, you'll gradually build up a good collection.

Baking sheets

These are used to cook biscuits, strudels and choux pastry shapes. Heavy gauge aluminium baking sheets with a dull finish produce the most evenly browned cookies and pastry. The best air circulation results if the sheets are at least 5 cm (2 in) smaller in length and width than your oven and if they have only one or two turned-up edges. A turned-up edge enables you to remove the sheet easily and the bare sides means that delicate items can be slid off instead of being lifted. Grease the sheet only if the recipe calls for it as some mixtures already have a high fat content.

Greasing and flouring

To prevent sticking, evenly spread a little butter using crumpled greaseproof paper, then coat with 15 ml (1 tbsp) flour by tilting and tapping the sides of the baking sheet.

Tins

Cake tins are metal and may be square, round or rectangular of different sizes and volumes (see right). The size of the tin should be matched to the amount of cake mixture. Ideally, the tin should be the same height as the cake at its highest point, so when adding your mixture, make sure that the tin is filled at least halfway.

▼ **Measuring tins** For cake tins, turn the tin over and place a ruler across to check size. If you have a sloping pie dish, measure across the top of the dish from inside edge to inside edge. Measure depth on the inside of the tin as well, from the bottom to the top.

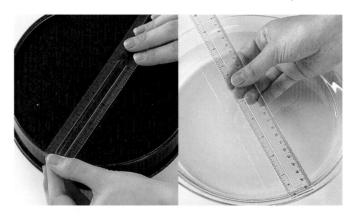

► **Lining a cake tin** As with baking sheets, greasing and flouring a pan prevents sticking. Some mixtures, however, also call for a greaseproof lining. Place your tin on greaseproof paper and trace around the base. Cut out the circle. Grease your tin, add the paper, grease the paper, then lightly dust with flour. Tap to remove excess.

PIE TINS

Pie 'tins', which may be made of glass, porcelain or metal, are round, shallow and slope-sided. Choose one sufficiently deep so your filling and juices won't overflow. For tarts, quiches and flans, it is best to use a flat tin with a removable base to make extraction easier. Small tartlet tins are also available, often with decoratively shaped edges. A glass pie plate, or a metal one with a dull finish, will produce a crisp, well-browned crust. Choose a deep-dish plate when your filling is substantial.

A springform cake tin is shallower than a standard tin and has a removable base and a spring-clipped side that makes extraction easier. Funnel and decorative bases are also generally available.

A Swiss roll tin is a shallow, rectangular tin designed for cooking sponge sheets.

Flan tins used for tarts, quiches and flans, are often fluted with removable bases to make extraction easier while small tartlet tins also are often fluted and decoratively shaped.

Cake rack

This open metal grid can be round or rectangular; the best ones are footed to allow air to circulate underneath the food so it cools once removed from the oven.

▶ **Baking beans** These ceramic or metal shapes are used to weight down pastry in its tin when you are baking the pastry 'blind' (without a filling), to prevent it from bubbling.

Cake tin equivalents

Tin called for	Substitution
15 cm (6 in) square	18 cm (7 in) round
18 cm (7 in) square	20 cm (8 in) round
20 cm (8 in) square	23 cm (9 in) round
23 cm (9 in) square	25 cm (10 in) round
25 cm (10 in) square	28 cm (11 in) round
2 × 18 cm (7 in) sandwich tins	18 paper cake cases

Tin volumes

Tin size	Approximate volume
Each 7 × 3 cm (2¾ × 1¼ in) muffin tin	90 ml (6 tbsp)
21 × 11 cm (8½ × 4¼ in) loaf tin	1.2 litres (2 pints)
20 cm (8 in) square baking tin	1.2 litres (2 pints)
22 cm square (8¾ in) baking tin	2 litres (3½ pints)
23 cm (9 in) pie plate	1 litre (1¾ pints)
30 × 18 cm (12 × 7 in) baking tin	1.75 litres (3 pints)
33 × 20 cm (13 × 8 in) baking tin	3 litres (5 pints)
39 × 27 cm (15½ × 10½ in) Swiss roll tin	1.5 litres (2½ pints)

Biscuit and pastry cutters

Sold individually or in sets, these are thin, metal, straight-sided cutters of varying sizes that come in a wide range of shapes – from plain round to novelty.

Rolling pin

Choose a plain, smooth, heavy hardwood roller. You can choose between no handles, integral handles or handles that attach to a central rod in the roller.

Pastry wheel

A wooden-handled cutter that has a fluted wheel. Use it to decoratively trim the edges of pies.

◀ **Pastry brush** Round or flat-headed, this brush may have plastic or hog's head bristles. Use it to apply glazes to your pastry before baking.

pastry making

Delicious pies and cakes depend on the mastery of a variety of techniques. There is also a range of special equipment that can help make these tasks easier.

Perfect pies and tarts

Tender, flaky pastry is well within the scope of the average home cook. Some tips to bear in mind include:

- All ingredients should be cold when beginning (use butter from the refrigerator and iced water) and the kitchen shouldn't be warm, either.
- Dough should be handled as little as possible. It also should be chilled 30 minutes before rolling.
- A mixture of butter and white vegetable fat produces a better result – the butter adds flavour and colour and the vegetable fat adds flakiness.

Rubbing in

Most pastry recipes call for rubbing the fat into the flour. This is done to incorporate the butter into the flour and to aerate the mixture; it can be done by hand or with a special tool, a pastry blender.

Rolling out

To prevent sticking, roll dough on a lightly floured surface, sprinkling additional flour as necessary.

Roll the dough from the centre forwards and then back; rotate the dough a quarter-turn and repeat rolling and rotating to make an even circle.

Using your hands Cut the butter into small pieces and place in the bowl with the flour. Pick up some flour along with each butter piece and rub your thumbs over your fingertips to combine the two together.

Using a pastry blender The sharp steel wires attached to the blender handle will mix the fat into the flour when you move the utensil up and down in the mixture.

Placing the lining Take the pastry round and roll it gently onto a rolling pin. Ease the pastry into the pie dish. Press it to the bottom of the dish with your fingertips or a small ball of dough. Take care to press out air pockets. Don't stretch or pull the pastry. If it tears, moisten the edges and press together.

Baked to perfection

- To make handling your pie easier and to catch any drips, place it on a baking sheet before putting it in the oven.
- To prevent double-crust pies from becoming soggy, cut slits in the top crust before putting them in the oven; these allow steam to escape during cooking.
- Bake in the lower third of the oven so the bottom crust becomes crisp and the top doesn't overbrown. If the pie starts to brown too quickly, cover it loosely with foil.
- Before removing the pie from oven, check for doneness. Fruit pies will be ready when they bubble in the centre; with custard pies, a knife inserted 2–3 cm (¾–1¼ in) from the centre should come out clean.

Recipes

Shortcrust pastry A rich, flaky dough with a high proportion of fat to flour. Also called pâte brisée, this is used for flans, tarts and quiches and for single and double-crust pies.

Choux pastry A twice-cooked dough that produces crisp, airy shells for buns and éclairs, and savoury appetizers. It also can be deep-fried for fritters.

Puff pastry A light, buttery dough raised to many times its original thickness by the action of steam, used for sweet and savoury tarts, vol au vents, bouchées and feuilletés.

Pâte sucrée This is identical to shortcrust pastry except that it contains sugar and produces a more crumbly dough. It is especially good for desserts such as tarts.

Decorative pastry edges

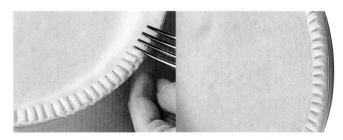

Forked edge Pastry should be even with the edge of the plate; if necessary remove excess with kitchen scissors. Using a floured four pronged fork, work all around the rim pressing pastry to plate.

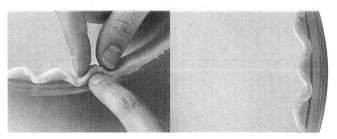

Fluted edge Push one index finger against the outside edge of the rim; using thumb and index finger of the other hand, gently pinch to form ruffles. Leave 5 mm (¼ in) space between each ruffle.

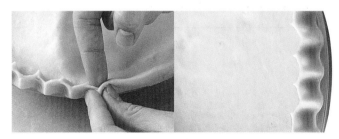

Sharp fluted edge Push the index finger of one hand against the inside edge of the rim; using thumb and index finger of the other hand, pinch firmly to form flutes. Leave 5 mm (¼ in) space between each flute.

Rope edge Press thumb into pastry edge at an angle, then pinch pastry between thumb and knuckle of index finger. Place thumb in groove made by index finger, then pinch as before; repeat all round the edge.

cake making

There are two basic types of cake: creamed and whisked. Success with creamed cakes depends on beating the sugar and butter together to produce a pale mixture of a fluffy consistency and on ensuring that all the other dry ingredients are evenly dispersed within the batter. A light and airy whisked cake is achieved when eggs or egg whites alone are beaten to create sufficient volume.

In order to turn out perfect cakes, you need to:
- Beat eggs when they are at room temperature if you want the best volume.
- Use softened, not melted, butter for easier blending.
- Gently tap tins on the worktop after filling to prevent air bubbles.
- Preheat the oven properly. Ensure the oven is at the correct temperature before you put the cake in; an oven thermometer is invaluable.
- Bake cakes in the centre of your oven. If making more than two layers, switch the position of the tins halfway through cooking.
- Do not open the oven door during the first 15 minutes of baking or your cake may sink.
- Unless the recipe specifies otherwise, use granulated sugar; coarser sugars don't blend in with the mixture as well.

All cakes must be left to cool before unmoulding them; creamed cakes need to cool on a rack for approximately 10 minutes; then remove them immediately to prevent sogginess. Whisked cakes should be allowed to cool completely in their tins. Chiffon and angel cakes must be cooled upside-down.

With many recipes, cake tins need to be greased and floured, and sometimes lined (see page 16) for a perfect result. There are also ways of cutting layers that will ensure a neater finished result and of rolling up sponges successfully. Make sure you test for doneness, and let the cake cool completely, before adding any fillings or icings.

◄ Testing for doneness
Sponge and whisked cakes should spring back if you lightly press their centres with your fingertips. The sides of a cooked cheesecake must have shrunk away from the sides of its tin and a skewer inserted into its centre should come out clean.

► Unmoulding cakes
Carefully run a small knife around the edge to loosen it. Then place a cooling rack over the tin and carefully invert it. Remove tin then flip the cake onto another rack.

Preparing a Swiss roll
Sponge mixtures can be formed into different shapes as well as rolling it round a filling. The mixture is baked, then turned out and cooled before rolling. Using baking parchment to roll up the sponge will produce a neater finish.

Transfer a cooked sponge to baking parchment paper dusted with caster sugar. Peel off the lining paper. Add your filling.

Fold over approximately 2 cm (¾ in) of one of the longer sides and begin to roll. Pull on the baking parchment to help you roll up the sponge evenly.

Filling and layering cakes

For a neat finish, cakes must be cut accurately and the layers matched. The base of the cake often has the flattest surface, so use it as the top layer. A palette knife makes spreading icing in an even layer much easier.

▶ **Cutting layers** Place two mixing spoons of identical size on either side of your cake, parallel to one another. Make a notch down the side of the cake with a small knife. Using a serrated knife, saw across the cake with the knife resting on both of the spoons.

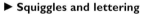

◀ **Spreading filling/icing** Using a palette knife, place icing on one layer. Add the next layer, lining up the notches. Spread with icing. Place the last layer cut-side down on the previous layer, then spread the top and sides with the icing, using a warm palette knife.

Recipes

Whisked sponge cake A light and airy mixture of eggs, sugar, flour and salt. Butter can also be included for an added richness and a filling of apricot or strawberry jam to sandwich the cakes together.

Victoria sandwich cake The basic creamed cake, it is a mixture of flour, butter, sugar and eggs usually with a filling of strawberry jam.

Traditional baked cheesecake Cream and soft or curd cheeses, sugar, sultanas and soured cream are baked in a pre-cooked pastry case.

Icing and decorating cakes

A piping bag and nozzles make short work of creating decorative finishes. To make it easier to fill the bag with icing, stand it in a measuring jug or heavy glass. Fold the bag over to make a cuff and fill halfway with icing.

▶ **Rosettes** Holding star nozzle at a 90° angle just above the cake, squeeze the bag moving the tip up in a circular motion. Stop squeezing and lift the tip of the bag up.

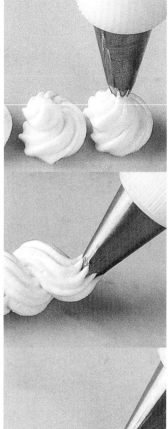

▶ **Ropes** Holding star nozzle at a 45° angle, pipe a 'C'. Tuck the tip under bottom portion of C; repeat, overlapping curves to form a rope.

▶ **Squiggles and lettering** Using writing nozzle and thinned icing, hold nozzle at a 45° angle, just touching the cake. Squeeze the bag gently as you go and lift it slightly to form squiggles.

▶ **Dots** Hold writing nozzle at a 90° angle just above the cake. Squeeze bag gently until the dot forms, then stop squeezing and lift the nozzle.

blanching and tenderising

Some foods have to be treated in particular ways before final cooking. Blanching can be a useful technique with several different functions. It is used to prepare raw vegetables for later final cooking – say if you are going to stir-fry or sauté them and want to do some of the preparation ahead – and for freezing. Blanching inhibits the enzyme action that can occur during freezing, ensuring that the vegetables will be safe for later cooking. Blanching also can be used to remove the skin of particular fruits and vegetables, to enhance the colour, to reduce the bitterness of vegetables used for hors d'oeuvre and to draw out excess salt from salt pork and bacon. If you want to tenderise food, this also has to be done before it is finally cooked.

Blanching

You blanch foods by boiling them briefly in water and letting them set in cold water until completely cold. Most vegetables can be blanched successfully in boiling water and many can be blanched over steam, which preserves their shapes better and conserves more nutrients. You can also blanch in a microwave oven, which will maintain colour and nutrients. Times will depend on the specific vegetables and what you will use them for; if you simply want to make peeling easier, 1–2 minutes will be all that's needed.

Water blanching Bring lightly salted water to a rolling boil in a large pot. Prepare your vegetables and place them in a strainer, basket or colander that fits your pot. The food should be able to move around in the strainer. Lower the vegetables into the water, cover and return the water to the boiling point as quickly as possible. Stir the vegetables again once boiling resumes. Boil for the required time then place vegetables in iced water or hold under cold running water until completely cooled; drain immediately.

Steam blanching Use a large saucepan with a tight-fitting lid and fill with 5 cm (2 in) water. Place a rack in the pan and bring to the boil (make sure water does not touch rack). Add the vegetables, loosely packing them into a single layer no more than 5 cm (2 in) deep, and cover the pot. Steam for the required time then place vegetables in iced water or hold under running water until cooled; drain immediately.

Microwave blanching Put 450 g (1 lb) vegetables into a microwave-proof casserole and add 75 ml (5 tbsp) water. Cover and cook at 100 per cent power for 4–6 minutes, until evenly cooked. Cool and drain.

Parboiling

When you parboil foods, you cook them for longer than blanching – almost halfway. You parboil older vegetables to tenderise them so they cook in the same amount of time as fresher ones. For a better result when making roast potatoes, you should parboil them before roasting (see page 165). You can also parboil vegetables ahead of time to save time on later preparation. This is particularly useful if you are going to stir-fry or sauté them later on.

Removing skin

Peaches, apricots, and tomatoes all can have their skins removed by cooking them very briefly in boiling water – for no more than a minute. They need to be removed from the cooking pot with a slotted spoon and put immediately into a bowl of cold water to stop further cooking. Fruit or vegetables can be dropped directly into boiling water. You will find it easier to remove the skin of tomatoes if you cut a shallow 'x' into the bottom end of each one. You can also use the technique for skinning almonds. These should be put into a strainer, lowered into boiling water and cooked for 2–3 minutes. Pinch the softened skin between your thumb and index finger to slip it off.

Tenderising

Many meat and poultry cuts and some fish need softening before they can be finally cooked. There are a number of methods that can be employed; the easiest is to sprinkle a proprietary meat tenderiser over the cut. However, this often just treats the surface and the interior of the meat can remain tough. Another method is physical; you simply pound the meat and this breaks down muscle bundles. A third way is to steep the meat in either a wine or vinegar-based marinade. This not only flavours and moisturises the meat but both wine and vinegar contain acids which can denature surface proteins and soften fibres. This is also why you should use a non-reactive container such as glass, porcelain or glazed earthenware to hold the marinade.

Marinating The length of time you keep food in a marinade depends on the nature and size of the item. Small cuts of meat that will be grilled or fried need to be marinated only for an hour or two; even 30 minutes can be sufficient for kebabs. A large pot roast, however, can be marinaded for 1–2 days. If you are marinating for more than 30 minutes, place the food in the refrigerator. You should turn the food from time to time with a slotted spoon to ensure that the marinade covers the meat entirely. Before cooking, the food should be brought to room temperature, removed from the

Pounding This not only breaks up connective tissues but can be used if you need to thin meat so that it cooks quicker or you require a flatter shape. You can use a rolling pin, cleaver or purpose-made tool.

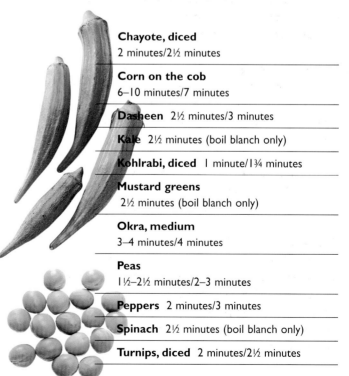

marinade and thoroughly drained. If you are using sugar in your marinade, the browning temperature will be lowered and you will need to be vigilant to ensure that the caramelising sugars do not burn.

Quick marinating When time is of the essence you can quickly coat food in a liquid or spice-based marinade by placing all the ingredients in a plastic bag and shaking it to coat. This works best if food is cut into small pieces.

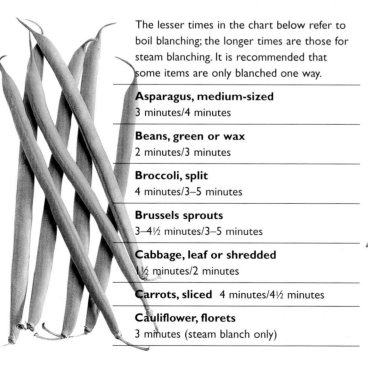

The lesser times in the chart below refer to boil blanching; the longer times are those for steam blanching. It is recommended that some items are only blanched one way.

Asparagus, medium-sized
3 minutes/4 minutes

Beans, green or wax
2 minutes/3 minutes

Broccoli, split
4 minutes/3–5 minutes

Brussels sprouts
3–4½ minutes/3–5 minutes

Cabbage, leaf or shredded
1½ minutes/2 minutes

Carrots, sliced 4 minutes/4½ minutes

Cauliflower, florets
3 minutes (steam blanch only)

Chayote, diced
2 minutes/2½ minutes

Corn on the cob
6–10 minutes/7 minutes

Dasheen 2½ minutes/3 minutes

Kale 2½ minutes (boil blanch only)

Kohlrabi, diced 1 minute/1¾ minutes

Mustard greens
2½ minutes (boil blanch only)

Okra, medium
3–4 minutes/4 minutes

Peas
1½–2½ minutes/2–3 minutes

Peppers 2 minutes/3 minutes

Spinach 2½ minutes (boil blanch only)

Turnips, diced 2 minutes/2½ minutes

stuffing

Poultry, fish and shellfish, meat and many vegetables benefit from the addition of a savoury filling before being cooked. Sometimes the stuffing can be placed just on top of the ingredient, as with mussels, or in a hollowed out space, as with artichokes. In the case of an escalope or fillet, you can wrap the chicken, fish or meat around the stuffing. Other times you may have to cut a pocket in the food.

Poultry

Both whole birds and breasts benefit from a filling; it can add flavour and extra moistness. Before stuffing a whole bird, make sure you rinse the fowl inside and out and pat dry. Stuff a bird just before cooking; if you are using a cooked stuffing, make sure this is cool before using unless you are roasting right away; bacteria forms quickly in tepid fillings. Stuffing expands during cooking so don't pack it in too tightly. The legs and tail flap need to be tied together to hold the stuffing in the body cavity. Stuffing temperature in a roasted bird should be 74°C (see page 35 for details).

▶ Stuffing a whole bird

Place the bird, breast-side up in a bowl so it is held upright. Lightly spoon the stuffing into the body cavity.

Tie string around the legs and under the skin flap at the tail to secure the stuffing. If you like, you can add more stuffing to the neck cavity and use a skewer to secure.

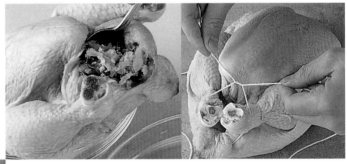

◀ Stuffing a whole breast

Gently push your fingers between the skin and meat of the chicken breast to form a pocket. Be careful not to tear the skin.

Using your fingers or a spoon, push the filling inside and smooth the skin over it.

▶ Stuffing a breast fillet

You either can cut a pocket 3–4 cm (1¼–1½ in) deep in the side of the breast and fill with stuffing or take a flattened fillet and carefully roll it around your filling.

In the latter case, to hold the stuffing in place, tie the roll with kitchen string at 4 cm (1½ in) intervals.

Fish and shellfish

As fish flesh is delicate, you should ensure your filling is not too robust. Make sure all ingredients are chopped finely and use very small breadcrumbs. You can treat a fish fillet in the same way as a poultry fillet, rolling it around your stuffing. In this case, you might like to secure it with a few strands of chives, which not only look pretty but add flavour.

Although you can stuff the stomach cavity, it is better to stuff the back cavity of a whole fish as this enables it to keep a good shape.

Shellfish such as mussels, clams, oysters, lobster and crab can have a filling added directly on top of their meat to fill the available space in the shell.

Meat

Some cuts, like a crown roast of pork or lamb, make magnificent settings for a stuffing. Check your recipe as to when to add the stuffing. It is usual to add the stuffing to the meat once it has been partially roasted because if added at the same time, the high heat of this cooking process will make it overdone. You can transform plain cuts like fillets or veal breasts by cutting pockets in them and adding a filling.

Cut lengthwise along the centre of the fillet cutting almost, but not quite all the way, through. Ease the meat open and spoon in the stuffing mixture. Use kitchen string to tie the fillet securely.

With a veal breast, work a boning knife between the two main muscle layers. Extend the space until the pocket is deep and wide. Spoon in the stuffing loosely, and thread with a metal skewer to secure.

Vegetables

Many vegetables, such as potatoes, peppers, squash, chillies and tomatoes, can have their centres hollowed out to make attractive settings for fillings. Other, more leafy vegetables such as cabbage and lettuce, can be rolled around a filling. In the case of cabbage it can also have its centre removed and be used as an attractive container.

You can hollow out vegetables such as artichokes and peppers, removing all seeds and cores before you add your filling. Whole cabbages, too, can have their centres removed to form a 2.5 cm (1 in) thick shell that can be filled. Reserve two leaves to place over your stuffing, and secure with string before cooking.

Individual leaves of cabbage or lettuce can be used to wrap around a filling. Cabbage usually needs to be blanched before using (see page 24). Ensure the leaves lie flat (you may need to trim any thick ribs) and place the filling in the centre of each leaf. Fold the sides over the filling, then roll up the leaf from one end to form a neat package.

boiling

This is an efficient way of cooking ingredients without them browning – and it is quick. When you boil food, its entire surface is in contact with water (or other liquid) and the water molecules are therefore able to rapidly impart their energy to the food. Also, it is easy to reach and maintain water's boiling point, unlike oil where you need to monitor the temperature continuously with a thermometer. Boiling brings out the natural flavour of vegetables and can help to retain their colour and maintain their nutrients. It softens meat by breaking down the protein collagen that forms its connective tissue. It is also used to cook pasta, crustaceans and eggs, and to reduce sauces.

Types of boil
Once water reaches 100°C, it has reached the boiling point and all of the liquid will be in motion with bubbles rising and breaking on the surface all the time. With a moderate boil, the water surface will be agitated but not moving on top of itself whereas in a rolling boil, there is a great deal of turbulence. Simmering is just below boiling point, and there is a stream of small bubbles just visible on the surface.

Boiling vegetables
Most vegetables should be cooked as briefly as possible to retain the best colour, texture and flavour. Unless the recipe directs otherwise, cook in the minimum amount of lightly salted water so you don't drain away nutrients. The fresher the vegetable and the smaller the size, the quicker it will cook. Vegetables cut to a similar size will also cook more evenly. If you are serving them cold or reheating them later, put straight into cold water to halt the cooking.

Boiling crustaceans
Lobsters, crabs, shrimps, prawns and crayfish should be cooked in a large, deep pot filled with a minimum of 2 litres (3½ pints) of water or other liquid. For each 500g (1¼ lb) of shellfish, use 1 litre (1¾ pints) water and 15 ml (1 tbsp) salt.

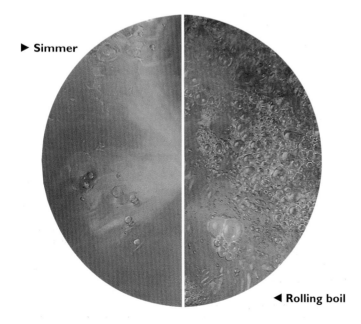

▶ Simmer

◀ Rolling boil

Root vegetables, like potatoes, turnips and parsnips, should be added to cold water and slowly brought to the boil.

Green vegetables, including leaf spinach and broccoli, should be plunged immediately into rapidly boiling water.

Recipes

Court bouillon An aromatic cooking liquid that is a mixture of fish trimmings, water, carrots, onions, bouquet garni, salt and white peppercorns.

Crab bouillon The traditional fiery broth in which crab can be cooked. It can contain allspice, peppercorns, chillies and other spices and herbs.

Bouillon à la nage Cooking liquid boiled until it is reduced by half and used to moisten small lobster, prawns and crayfish.

Add the live shellfish as the water comes to a rolling boil. Simmer for the appropriate time (see below, right) then drain and cool. Crustaceans should always be boiled in their shells.

Boiling eggs

Use a small pan so your eggs don't move around too much and fill with just enough water to cover them completely. Bring the water to simmering point before adding the eggs. Start timing when the water returns to the boil. Simmer gently, reducing the heat, if necessary, for the desired time. If you're using the egg as a garnish and want the yolk centred, spin the egg in the pan as it cooks. If the egg cracks while it's cooking, add a little salt or vinegar to the water to coagulate the white and stop it running out.

Reducing sauces

Boiling a sauce or stock to evaporate some of the liquid and reduce the volume thickens and concentrates it. This makes the sauce more flavourful, smoother and more consistent. How long you boil depends on the quantity of liquid and how concentrated you want the sauce. Reducing a liquid so that it coats the back of a spoon takes the longest time.

Cooking time

As the water temperature will be lowered by the addition of the vegetables, seafood or eggs, cooking time (see the charts, right) generally is measured from the point at which the water returns to a boil after the food has been added.

Beans, cut up	5–10 minutes
Broccoli florets	3–5 minutes
Broccoli spears	7–10 minutes
Cabbage, wedges	10–15 minutes
Carrots, cut up	10–20 minutes
Cauliflower florets	5–10 minutes
Cauliflower head	15–20 minutes
Cauliflower slices	3–5 minutes
Corn on the cob	5 minutes
French beans	5 minutes
Parsnips, cut up	8–15 minutes
Parsnips, whole	20–30 minutes
Peas	3–5 minutes
Potatoes, medium	25–30 minutes
Potatoes, small	15–20 minutes
Spinach	1–3 minutes

Eggs, hard-boiled	10–12 minutes
Eggs, soft-boiled	3½–5½ minutes

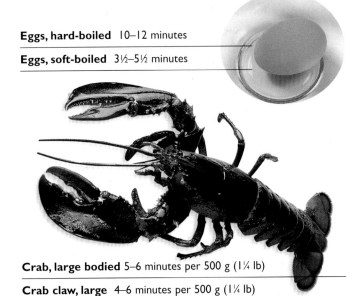

Crab, large bodied	5–6 minutes per 500 g (1¼ lb)
Crab claw, large	4–6 minutes per 500 g (1¼ lb)
Crayfish	6–8 minutes
Lobster	5 minutes first 500 g (1¼ lb); 3 minutes each subsequent 500 g (1¼ lb)
Prawns, jumbo	5–8 minutes
Prawns, medium	3–5 minutes

poaching

This is a gentler method of cooking ingredients in water; the water is hot but not quite boiling, and is suited to the delicate flesh of chicken, fish and fruit, and produces a softly cooked egg. During poaching, flavourings in the water seep into the food and vice versa. Therefore food gains from being poached in a flavoured liquid. Some cuts of meat are also poached and produce a delicious stock. Food should be poached in large pieces so it remains moist, and bones can be left on as they add flavour to the liquid. All you need is a saucepan large enough to hold the food and enough liquid to cover; too large a pan and too much liquid produces less tasty food.

Using a fish kettle
Measure the thickest part of the fish before placing it on the rack and lowering it into the kettle. Cover with cold water or court bouillon, bring to simmering point and for each 2.5 cm (1 in) in width, cook for 10 minutes.

Poaching fish
Fish and shellfish should be added to cold water which should be heated just until the surface moves. This prevents the outside of the fish cooking before the inside and helps prevent it falling apart and any skin splitting. If you want to cook whole fish, you will need to invest in a fish kettle (see right). Small fish, fillets and steaks can be cooked successfully in a saucepan. All fish must first be trimmed, scaled and gutted before poaching.

Poaching steaks and fillets Lower the fish into a pan of cold water or court bouillon, using a slotted spoon. Bring to simmering point and cook for the required time.

Poaching smoked fish To help rid preserved fish of excess salt and to mellow its smoky flavour, cook in milk or an equal mixture of milk and water. Place the fish in the milk with one or two bay leaves and a few peppercorns and bring to a simmer over a moderate heat. Remove from the heat, cover tightly and let stand for 10 minutes.

Poaching eggs
An egg poacher makes easy work of cooking eggs, but you also can slip them very gently into a wide shallow pan filled with simmering water. Adding 5–10 ml (1–2 tsp) vinegar will help the eggs set. Use very fresh eggs and, as soon as they are in the water, swirl them around in a circular motion to contain the shape. When the whites are set and yolks begin to thicken, remove them using a slotted spoon and drain on kitchen roll. For best results, cook only one egg at a time; to ensure proper timing, don't cook more than four at any one time. For a neat edge, trim with scissors, if desired.

Poaching chicken
Whole birds and breasts when poached are succulent and tender and, if cooked with vegetables, produce a delicious stock. To keep the breast meat moist, you may have to bard the bird, see pages 34–35. Whole birds are done when you pierce the thigh with a skewer and the juice runs clear. Keep the cooking liquid to use as stock.

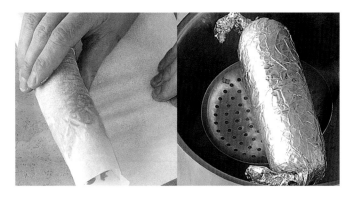

To make a pinwheel Flatten a chicken breast, place it on a piece of baking parchment then spoon the filling down along the centre. Roll up the breast into a cylinder, roll the parchment around the chicken cylinder and twist the ends to seal.

Wrap the chicken in foil then add the roll to a pan of boiling water. Cover, reduce the heat and poach until a metal skewer feels warm to the touch when withdrawn from the centre (about 15 minutes).

Eggs	3–5 minutes
Fish, fillets	5–10 minutes
Fish, steaks	10–15 minutes
Fish, whole	10 minutes for each 2.5 cm (1 in) in width (see using a fish kettle, left)
Fruit in red wine	15–25 minutes
Fruit in sugar syrup	10–15 minutes
Poultry, whole bird	20 minutes per 450 g (1 lb)
Poultry, breasts	6–7 minutes
Stuffed chicken pinwheels	15 minutes

Whole birds To help the bird maintain its shape, truss the chicken (see page 106). Place with any vegetables in the pan and pour over enough cold water to cover. Bring the liquid to a boil over a moderate heat. The chicken will produce some scum; this should be skimmed off with a slotted spoon and you should time cooking once it has been removed.

Pinwheels Plain poached chicken breast meat is ideal for use in sandwiches and salads but cooking it as a pinwheel also enables you to add a filling of your choice.

Poaching fruit

Simmering fruit in a sugar syrup, plain or flavoured, or in wine can produce a juicy delicious dessert. Fruit should be firm and not too ripe to keep its shape. Peel hard and citrus fruits and core pears and apples before cooking; you can remove the stones and skin of soft fruit when poached. Once cooked, let the fruit cool in the saucepan then remove. Reduce the cooking syrup or wine by boiling, strain and use as a sauce.

Cooking in sugar syrup Prepare the sugar syrup in a saucepan and then add the fruit. Poach until it is tender. Remove cooked fruit with a slotted spoon.

Cooking in wine Heat red wine with sugar and any flavourings until sugar dissolves. Add fruit and bring slowly to a simmer. Poach until tender. Remove from heat, cover and leave to cool.

steaming

An efficient cooking method and one in which the most nutrients are preserved, steaming also preserves the colour of vegetables and the texture and taste of delicate ingredients, like fish. While steaming, the food has no contact with water, unlike boiling which may put physical stress on the food, tearing and toughening it, but it is cooked by the intense moist heat of steam swirling around it. The food is placed on a rack above the water in the pan and the pan is kept covered to keep the steam from escaping. Because there is a boiling layer at the bottom of the pot while the top remains cooler, this is the ideal method for cooking asparagus, with its delicate tops and much hardier stalks. To ensure successful steaming, it is important that the steam circulates freely in the pan and that the liquid never actually touches the food – as this can deliver a sudden burst of extra heat – or boils dry. Keep on hand a separate pot of boiling water in order to replenish the steaming water; this also will ensure that the temperature is maintained.

Bamboo steamers

Using these stacking baskets means that you can cook many different foods at once over the same heat source. If cooking in a wok, pour in enough water just to cover the bottom and bring to the boil. On top of a trivet, stack your baskets so the firmest vegetables are on the bottom and more delicate ones on top. Cover and steam until they are tender.

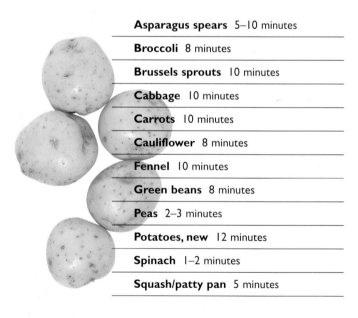

Asparagus spears	5–10 minutes
Broccoli	8 minutes
Brussels sprouts	10 minutes
Cabbage	10 minutes
Carrots	10 minutes
Cauliflower	8 minutes
Fennel	10 minutes
Green beans	8 minutes
Peas	2–3 minutes
Potatoes, new	12 minutes
Spinach	1–2 minutes
Squash/patty pan	5 minutes

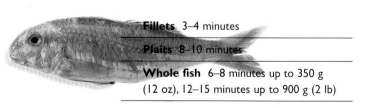

Fillets	3–4 minutes
Plaits	8–10 minutes
Whole fish	6–8 minutes up to 350 g (12 oz), 12–15 minutes up to 900 g (2 lb)

Steaming vegetables

A basket steamer makes it easy to lift the vegetables out for draining. The water should be at simmering point, not a rolling boil when you add the vegetables. Do not add salt as this can discolour the vegetables and draws out moisture. When the vegetables are tender, remove the basket; refresh under cold running water then reheat and season. Asparagus is traditionally boiled upright so that the thick ends of the stalks cook in simmering water while the tender tips gently steam above. Special asparagus steamers are available specifically for the job. Alternatively, cook the stalks horizontally in a deep sauté pan.

Steaming fish

There is no better way to cook delicate fish – steaming is suitable for whole fish, steaks and fillets as well as scallops and shrimps. It also can preserve the colour of certain fish, such as red snapper. Use a flavoured broth, such as a court bouillon (see page 27), or alternatively you can add more robust seasonings, such as spring onion and ginger, to the cooking water. If using a conventional steamer, arrange fish in a single layer in the basket; it is cooked when it is opaque and the flesh feels moist and tender when pierced with a fork. If using a bamboo steamer and a wok, you can add further flavourings to the fish, such as spring onion and carrots, which can be served as an accompaniment.

Steaming mussels

Contrary to other shellfish, mussels are steamed directly in a flavoured cooking liquid – usually white wine with herbs. Once the cooking liquid is hot, the cleaned, tightly closed mussels are tossed in and cooked. They will open upon being steamed and can be served with their cooking liquid if strained and reduced.

Steamed puddings

A number of traditional desserts are cooked by steaming, the most famous of all being Christmas pudding. Steaming the pudding makes it moister, softer and heavier than if baked. Traditionally, it is placed into a basin and covered with greaseproof paper and then pleated foil (to let out steam) before being placed in a steamer.

braising and stewing

Both these methods are ideal for cooking tougher cuts of meat, older birds and fibrous vegetables. Braising and stewing are almost identical techniques, the main difference being that braising calls for less liquid and the meat is cooked whole or as large pieces. A stew contains more liquid and the meat is usually cut into small pieces.

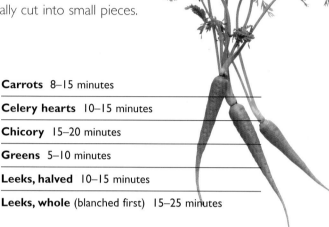

Braising
The ingredients are first sautéed or browned (see page 44) to add colour and flavour, and are then cooked slowly in a small amount of liquid – about 5–10 mm (¼–½ in) of water, stock, wine, cider or tomato sauce – in an airtight pot. This moist, steamy cooking gently breaks down meat and poultry's tough connective tissue and releases the food's own juices. Browned meat is often placed on a mirepoix (a bed of chopped aromatic vegetables). This is then later puréed and used as a sauce.

Carrots 8–15 minutes	
Celery hearts 10–15 minutes	
Chicory 15–20 minutes	
Greens 5–10 minutes	
Leeks, halved 10–15 minutes	
Leeks, whole (blanched first) 15–25 minutes	

Vegetable braising Although usually cooked along with meat and poultry, vegetables can be braised separately and served as an accompaniment. Root and leafy green vegetables taste delicious when braised. They can be cooked simply in butter or with a little water, stock or wine added plus some herbs and seasoning. Adding sugar will produce an attractive shiny surface.

CASSEROLES

Use a casserole with a tight-fitting lid that is not much larger than the meat plus its liquid; this ensures that heat is directed to the food and not empty spaces. Enamelled cast-iron or clad metal (a mixture of several metals) pots will conduct heat evenly and efficiently to prevent hot spots and scorching.

Mirepoix and brunoise

Two popular vegetable dices used to used to enhance soups, stews, sauces, meats, game and fish, and as a garnish. The former is a mixture of diced vegetables (carrot, onion, celery). The latter is minute dice of carrot, celery, leek or courgette used singly or as a mixture.

Casseroling poultry
Older chickens and some small game birds, such as quail and grouse, which can be dry and tough, benefit from slow, moist methods of cooking. Poultry pieces are tenderised by being steeped and slowly simmered in a concentrated cooked red wine marinade. It is essential to use a good-tasting wine, as the flavour in the bottle will be passed on to the final dish. To avoid a sharp, raw taste, boil the wine to reduce it by at least half; this evaporates the alcohol and concentrates the wine, creating a mellow flavour.

For a fuller flavour, the casserole can be refrigerated and reheated a day later. To give the poultry meat added moistness, you can wrap smaller birds in bacon (see pages 34–35) and then let them marinate before cooking them in a flavourful liquid.

Stewing meat
In this technique, small pieces of meat are completely covered with water, stock, wine or a combination to which vegetables and seasonings are added. The meat may or may not be browned first. Browning seals in the delicious juices

and adds colour to the sauce. The meat is done when the point of a small knife inserted into the meat pieces slides easily through the fibres.

On completion, the meat is very flavourful and, if reduced by boiling (see page 26) or by the addition of thickeners, the cooking liquid becomes a rich, delicious sauce. The most successful stews are those that contain ingredients of a similar cooking time; hardy root vegetables such as potatoes, carrots, parsnips and onions can withstand long cooking times. If you are using more delicate vegetables, add them near the end of cooking time or when you reheat.

Preparing meat for stews As many stews use extra fat to flavour the tougher cuts of meats, you should remove any visible fat before serving. Also, in order for the gelatinous tissues to break down and for tough muscle to soften,

producing the rich and velvety texture of stewed meat, meat needs to be cut into even-sized cubes that will cook evenly.

- Discard any excess fat and sinew from the meat.
- Cut across the grain into 3–4 cm (1¼–1½ in) wide slices. Cut these slices in half lengthwise and then across to produce even-sized cubes.
- Brown the cubes of meat in batches to seal in the juices.
- If the dish is hot, you will have to skim the fat (which appears as shiny, surface patches) from the sauce using a slotted spoon. If left to cool overnight in the refrigerator, it is quite easy to remove the layer of white fat that congeals on the surface.

Recipes

Veal in tomato and wine sauce A dish in which coated and seasoned veal is browned, then braised in a thickened dry white wine sauce with fried garlic and vegetables.

Hearty chicken stew A traditional favourite in which seasoned and coated chicken is browned and casseroled with fried vegetables.

Daube de boeuf A dish of marinated beef seared with flaming brandy and then braised with vegetables in a red wine stock and well seasoned with a bouquet garni. Can be served either hot or cold.

roasting and baking

These processes both refer to cooking raw food with currents of hot, dry air – roasting generally refers to the cooking of whole meats and poultry, often with added fat. Baking, on the other hand, is used when referring to other oven-cooked foods such as fish, bread or cut-up poultry. Roasts are usually cooked in a shallow pan so the air circulates evenly and there is good heat penetration. They are placed fat side up, so the fat melts during cooking and bastes the food as it drips. Lean cuts may need to be larded, barded (have fat added to keep them tender and succulent) or basted regularly. The resulting drippings form the basis for delicious sauces and gravies.

Meats
Tender, large cuts of meat with some internal fat are recommended as they remain succulent. Popular beef cuts include standing rib roasts, sirloin, fillet and whole rib-eye; shoulder, loin, rump and breast make good veal roasts; pork choices include rib crown roast, rolled hand roast, leg, whole tenderloin, bone-in and boneless loin; while best lamb cuts are leg of lamb, leg shank end, shoulder and rack. Extra flavour can be imparted to your roast by adding stuffing (see page 25) or a seasoned paste, or by inserting herbs directly into the meat.

When roasting boneless joints, place the meat on a rack in the tin so that the heat circulates, preventing the meat from cooking in its own juices. The bones of rib roasts act as a built-in rack.

Flavouring roasts
Strong-tasting ingredients such as herbs, mustard and other spices, garlic and anchovies can be mashed into a paste with a mortar and pestle and used to coat the outside of roasts. You also can insert slivers of garlic, and sometimes fresh herbs, directly into slits cut into the meat.

Larding and barding meat
Well-chilled pork fat can be inserted into lean roasts or wrapped round them to help keep the meat moist as it cooks. Lean birds such as pheasant also benefit from having fat added to their breasts. In this case, use bacon strips. The bacon can be served with the bird, but remove any barding fat from meat roasts before bringing to the table.

Inserting flavourings
Make slits by cutting directly into the flesh then add herbs and garlic.

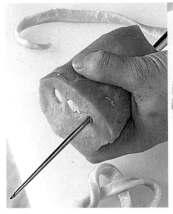

Larding Add pork fat to the centre of a lean roast by threading it through a large larding needle. Insert the needle into the meat, following the grain, and pull it through.

Barding Wrap a thin layer of pork fat around the outside of the meat and secure it in position with string.

Poultry

Fatty birds such as duck or goose will drip a lot of fat which you may need to remove during cooking. With drier birds, such as turkey and pheasant, you will need to add fat – by barding or by placing softened butter on or under the skin – to ensure moistness. Most other birds will need to be basted regularly to ensure moist meat and crisp skin. If the skin becomes too brown, cover it with a sheet of foil.

▶ Preparing a fatty bird
Cut away excess fat from the tail and cavity. Place the bird breast-side up on a rack in a roasting tin and prick the skin in several places to drain the fat during roasting.

◀ Barding birds Loosely drape some bacon rashers over the breast and thighs.

Basting

Most recipes call for the roast to be placed on a rack or trivet over the roasting tin. This ensures that the cooking juices drain and that the meat is not cooked by the drippings or a crisp brown crust develops. The drippings, however, should be used for moistening the meat during cooking.

Basting Using a spoon or a bulb baster, scoop up some of the cooking juices and pour these over the meat.

Bulb baster This giant syringe-like object can be used to suck up the fat from meat juices and gravy.

Testing for doneness

All meat and poultry needs to be cooked carefully to kill any disease organisms. You also need to ensure that the degree of doneness is as you like it. Using a meat thermometer will help. Beef will be medium–rare at 59.5°C (139°F) and medium at 67°C (153°F). Small pork roasts should have an internal temperature of 67°C (153°F) and large ones, like leg of pork, 77°C (170°F). Pork cooked to medium 67°C (153°F) will have a pink-tinged centre and be slightly deeper pink near any bone. Well-done pork is less pink. Pork roasted too highly will be tough and dry. Lamb will be medium–rare at 67°C (153°F), medium at 77°C (170°F) and well done above that. Poultry should be roasted to 80–83°C (176°F–181°F); stuffing should reach 74°C (165°F).

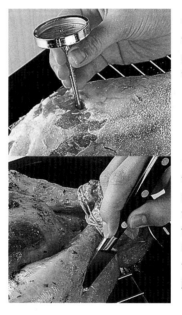

◀ Meats Insert the thermometer into the thickest part of the roast without touching the bone.

◀ Poultry Insert the thermometer into the thickest part of the inner thigh without touching the bone and so it faces the body. You also can insert a small knife into the thickest part of the thigh; the juices should run clear.

▶ Making gravy
Remove the bird or roast from the tin and pour off almost all the fat except about 15 ml (1 tbsp). Put the tin over a low heat, sprinkle in 15 ml (1 tbsp) flour and stir well, until all the browned bits are loosened. Gradually whisk in 500 ml (17 fl oz) hot stock or water. Increase the heat and bring to the boil. Simmer, whisking for

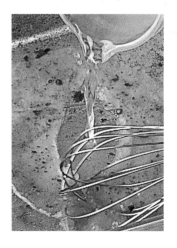

roasting times

The following charts provide guidelines on how long to roast a variety of cuts. All meats and poultry are calculated from room temperature. Meat and poultry should be removed from the oven when they reach 2–5°C (35–41°F) below desired doneness; their temperatures will rise as they stand.

BEEF

Type and weight	Oven temp.	Cooking time (medium rare)	(medium)
Rib roast (chine bone removed) 1.8–2.75 kg (4–6 lb)	180°C (350°F/gas 4)	1¾–2¼ hours	2¼–2¾ hours
2.75–3.6 kg (6–8 lb)		2¼–2½ hours	2¾–3 hours
Rib eye roast 1.8–2.75 kg (4–6 lb)	180°C (350°F/gas 4)	1¾–2 hours	2–2½ hours
Whole fillet 1.8–2.25 kg (4–5 lb)	220°C (425°F/gas 7)	50–60 mins	60–70 mins
Half fillet 900 g–1.3 kg (2–3 lb)	220°C (425°F/gas 7)	35–40 mins	45–50 mins
Silverside 1.3–1.8 kg (3–4 lb)	160°C (325°F/gas 3)	1¾–2 hours	2¼–2½ hours
2.75–3.6 kg (6–8 lb)		2½–3 hours	3–3½ hours
Topside 900 g–1.3 kg (2–3 lb)	160°C (325°F/gas 3)	1½–1¾ hours	2–2¼ hours

VEAL

Type and weight	Oven temp.	Cooking time (per 450 g/1 lb)
Boneless shoulder roast 1.3–2.25 kg (3–5 lb)	160°C	35–40 mins
Leg rump roast (boneless) 1.3–2.25 kg (3–5 lb)	160°C	35–40 mins
Boneless loin roast 1.3–2.25 kg (3–5 lb)	160°C	25–30 mins
Middle or best end of neck 1.3–2.25 kg (3–5 lb)	160°C	30–35 mins

LAMB

Type and weight	Oven temp.	Cooking time (per 450 g/1 lb) (med. rare)	(medium)	(well done)
Whole leg 2.25–3.1 kg (5–7 lb)	160°C	15 mins	20 mins	25 mins
3.1–4.1 kg (7–9 lb)		20 mins	25 mins	30 mins
Leg shank end 1.3–1.8 kg (3–4 lb)	160°C	30 mins	40 mins	45 mins
Leg fillet 1.3–1.8 kg (3–4 lb)	160°C	25 mins	35 mins	45 mins
Leg roast (boneless) 1.8–3.1 kg (4–7 lb)	160°C	20 mins	25 mins	30 mins
Rib roast or rack 800 g–1.2 kg (1¾–2½ lb)	190°C	30 mins	35 mins	40 mins
Crown roast (unstuffed) 900 g–1.3 kg (2–3 lb)	190°C	25 mins	30 mins	35 mins
Shoulder roast 1.8–2.75 kg (4–6 lb)	160°C	20 mins	25 mins	30 mins
Shoulder roast (boneless) 1.6–2.75 kg (3½–6 lb)	160°C	35 mins	40 mins	45 mins

PORK

Type and weight	Oven temp.	Cooking time (per 450 g/1 lb)
Crown roast 2.7–3.6 kg (6–8 lb)	180°C	20 mins
Loin roast (with bone) 1.3–2.25 kg (3–5 lb)	180°C	20 mins
Boneless loin roast 900g–1.8 kg (2–4 lb)	180°C	20 mins
Whole leg 5.4 kg (12 lb)	180°C	25–30 mins
Leg half, fillet or knuckle end 1.3–1.8 kg (3–4 lb)	180°C	40 mins
Rolled hand 1.3–2.75 kg (3–6 lb)	180°C	45 mins
Tenderloin 225–750g (8 oz–1 lb 10 oz)	220°–230°C	25–35 mins total
Whole ham 6.3–7.3 kg (14–16 lb)	180°C	15–18 mins

POULTRY

Type and weight	Oven temp.	Cooking time (unstuffed)	(stuffed)
Chicken	180°C		
1.2–1.3 kg (2½–3 lb)		1¼–1½ hours	1¼–1½ hours
1.3–1.8 kg (3–4 lb)		1½–1¾ hours	1½–1¾ hours
1.8–2.75 kg (4–6 lb)		1¾–2 hours	1¾–2 hours
Capon	160°C		
2.25–2.75 kg (5–6 lb)		2–2½ hours	2½–3 hours
2.75–3.6 kg (6–8 lb)		2½–3½ hours	3–4 hours
Poussin	180°C		
450g (1 lb)		1–1¼ hours	1–1¼ hours
Turkey	160°C		
3.6–5.4 kg (8–12 lb)		2¾–3 hours	3–3½ hours
5.4–6.3 kg (12–14 lb)		3–3¾ hours	3½–4 hours
6.3–8.2 kg (14–18 lb)		3¾–4¼ hours	4–4¼ hours
8.2–9.1 kg (18–20 lb)		4¼–4½ hours	4¼–4¾ hours
9.1–10.8 kg (20–24 lb)		4½–5 hours	4¾–5½ hours
Duck	180°C		
1.8–2.25 kg (4–5 lb)		2½–2¾ hours	2½–2¾ hours
Goose	180°C		
4.5–5.4 kg (10–12 lb)		2¾–3¼ hours	3–3½ hours
Grouse	200°C		
per 450 g (1 lb)		35 mins	
Partridge	200°C		
per 450 g (1 lb)		40 mins	
Pheasant	230°C		
per 450 g (1 lb)	for first 10 mins, then 200°C for 35 mins		
Quail	190°C		
per 450 g (1 lb)		15–20 mins	
Guinea Fowl	200°C		
per 450 g (1 lb)	15 mins plus extra 15 mins		

Whole smoked hams

Those labelled 'fully cooked' can be eaten as is, but additional heating will improve their flavour and texture. Bake ham at 160°C (325°F/ gas 3) until a thermometer inserted in the centre registers 52–57°C (126–135°F). For a whole ham of 6.3–7.3 kg (14–16 lb), this will take 1–1¾ hours total and for half a ham of 2.75–3.6 kg (6–8 lb), 1 hour in total. Smoked hams that are not marked 'fully cooked' must be cooked to an internal temperature of 67°C (153°F).

baking

Fish

Large and medium-sized whole fish and thick steaks and fillets can all be baked successfully, but certain techniques will help keep the fish moist. Wrapping in foil will seal in juices and keep any stuffing in place. Baking en papillote (in a paper bag) protects fish and, if cooked with flavourings, allows them to permeate the fish. Vine and banana leaves also keep fish moist. Baking with a salt crust will produce a crispy skin and moist flesh – but will not be over salty.

▶ **Salt crust** Spread a 5 cm (2 in) layer of sea salt evenly over the bottom of a heavy-based casserole. Lay the fish on top of the salt and cover with another salt layer (1.3 kg/3 lb salt will cover a 900 g/2 lb fish). Sprinkle the salt with water and bake the fish at 220°C (425°F/gas 7) for 30 minutes.

   When cooked, chip through the top layer of salt with a small hammer. Remove the fish in one piece and brush away the excess salt.

▲ **En papillote** Cut a heart-shaped piece of baking parchment, foil or greaseproof paper 5 cm (2 in) larger than the fish. Oil it and place the fish and any flavourings on one half of the oiled side of the paper.

Fold over the other half and twist to seal. Bake until puffed – about 15–20 minutes at 180°C (350°F/gas 4).

Vegetables

Most vegetables can be baked or roasted; fibrous roots and tubers and vegetable fruits are particularly suitable for being cooked on their own or with a sauce. They keep their shapes during long cooking and need little additional liquid. The long cooking time intensifies their flavours. Potatoes and other large root vegetables and squashes can be cooked whole, or cut vegetables into chunky pieces, mix them with oil and seasonings and turn them once or twice as they roast. Potatoes and other unpeeled root vegetables should be pricked before they are baked in order to let some steam escape; beetroot should be left intact.

   Potatoes bake best if placed on a special gadget consisting of several metal spikes attached to a central handle. The spikes conduct heat from the oven to the centre of each potato to ensure that the insides cook thoroughly.

Roasting times for vegetables (at 200°C/400°F/gas 6)

Aubergines	30 minutes
Carrots	45 minutes
Parsnips	30–45 minutes
Potatoes	1–1¼ hours
Sweet potatoes	45 minutes
Turnips	30–45 minutes
Winter squash	30–45 minutes

◀ **Beetroot** This needs cooking before it can be used in salads. Leave it unpeeled otherwise the colour will bleed. Cut off the tops, leaving the stalks intact and wrap in foil. Roast at 150°C (300°F/gas 2) for 1–1½ hours. Let cool slightly before peeling.

◀ **Baking halved fruit** Cut the fruit in half and, if desired, slice a little from the base of each half so fruit sits flat in the dish. Remove any stone or core and spoon in the filling. Bake for around 45–50 minutes at 200°C (400°F/gas 6). The fruit is done when the flesh

▶ **Potatoes** For perfect baked potatoes, scrub each one clean and pat dry. Prick all over with a fork. For crisp skins, brush with some olive oil. The potato is cooked when the tip of a small sharp knife inserted into the centre goes through without any resistance.

▶ **Baking apples** Score around the middle to allow the fruit to expand during baking. Remove core, spoon filling inside and place in a baking dish. Top with butter and bake – about 45–50 minutes at 200°C (400°F/gas 6).

Fruit

Roasting brings out the natural sweetness of fruit and gives them a soft, luscious texture. Firm, ripe fruits are the best choice. Large fruits are ideal containers for sweet stuffings. Fruit should be cored or stoned, depending on the type and the filling added. Fruit that discolours easily, such as peaches and apples, should be sprinkled first with a little lemon juice.

Bread

Successful bread baking depends in large part on how well you've made your dough and allowed it to rise (see page 147). Bake breads on the centre rack in your oven and, if baking several pans at once, allow at least 5 cm (2 in) between each pan. If your bread is too pale, place the loaf directly on the oven rack and bake for 5–10 minutes longer. If the bread has cracks, there was too much flour in the dough or too much dough in the pan. If the bread has holes in it, it wasn't kneaded enough. Bread is done when it pulls away from the sides of the pan and is nicely browned. When you tap the bottom it should sound hollow.

Quick breads

Muffins, scones and tea loaves all need the same treatment to bake successfully. Be sure the rising agent is fresh and unless cold butter is called for, start with the ingredients at room temperature. Don't over-mix the dough or the end product will be too tough. If using baking tins, fill only about two-thirds full and smooth the top of the mixture with a rubber spatula. If using muffin pans, fill these two-thirds to three-quarters full and half fill any empty ones with water. Bake in the centre of the oven and, if baking two loaves at once, leave some space between the tins to let air circulate. To test for doneness, insert a cocktail stick into the centre of the loaf: it should come out clean. If not, bake the dough for a few minutes longer.

Desserts

See pages 18–21 for information on cooking pastry and cakes. The trick when baking custards is not to overbake them or the dessert will become watery and start to separate. Cooking custards in a bain-marie ensures they cook evenly. To do this, divide the custard mixture into ramekins, and place these in a roasting tin. Then, carefully pour boiling water into the roasting tin to come halfway up the sides of the ramekins. Transfer the roasting tin to the oven and bake.

grilling

A quick and simple method of cooking, grilling uses dry radiant heat to produce outwardly browned food with a succulent interior. For the food to be moist and tender, you have to maintain a delicate balance between rapid surface cooking and slower internal heat transfer. The further you keep the food from the heat source, the longer it can stay under the grill before becoming overcooked. For food to cook quickly and evenly, items should be uniform in size and at room temperature. Thin fillets or skewered foods can be placed on a high shelf while larger pieces of meat, which will require a longer grilling time, should be set on a low oven rack. Where you are not sure, and as a general rule of thumb, place food about 10–15 cm (4–6 in) from the grill element. Always remember to preheat your grill.

Meat

Lean, tender cuts work best for grilling. Because success in grilling relies on so many variables – the shape of the meat, the amount of bone and fat, the temperature when put under grill, even the accuracy of your oven – timing guidelines can only be estimates. To determine doneness, don't depend just on the meat's colour and texture. Make a small cut (near the bone if meat contains one or near the centre if it is boneless) and look at the inside.

When grilling steak, trim away most of the fat, leaving about 5 mm (¼ in), and slash the fat to keep it from curling. Trim any excess fat from all meats since this can ignite under a very hot grill. Very lean meat can be brushed lightly with oil or a marinade. If you are using an oil-based marinade, pat meat dry before grilling to prevent any chance of it igniting. To avoid piercing meat (which will release its juices and become dry), use tongs rather than a fork to turn it over.

▲ **Trimming fat** Cut off all but 5 mm (¼ in) of fat, then cut through remaining fat at regular intervals with a chef's knife.

▲ **Brushing with oil** Add some chopped garlic and ground black pepper to olive oil and brush lightly over meat.

▶ **Doneness** Always use a meat thermometer for thicker cuts and make sure it registers 59.9°C (139°F) for medium-rare and 67°C (153°F) for medium, but a visual check is usually sufficient for steaks. Starting from the top, the meat is very rare (1–2 minutes each side); rare (2–3 minutes each side); medium (3–4 minutes each side); and, finally, well done (seared for 3 minutes each side then cooked at a lower heat for 6–10 minutes, turning once).

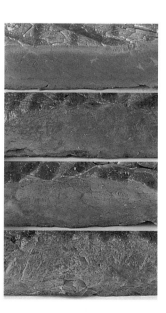

essential know-how

Fish

Oily fish like salmon, trout, bass, tuna and swordfish remain moist and tender when quickly cooked under a grill. Skin and bones help keep fish moist so it's best to grill smaller fish whole. Trim, scale and gut the fish first (see page 65) and score to prevent the skin from splitting. You can add flavour by brushing on a sauce. Place the fish on a grill pan, about 10–15 cm (4–6 in) from the heat source, and cook for 8–10 minutes per 2.5 cm (1 in) thickness. Fish is done when the meat is opaque. Insert the point of a small knife into the thickest part and gently separate the flesh to check.

▲ **Scoring fish** Make two or three slashes in one side of the fish, cutting through to the bones. Repeat for other side.

▲ **Adding flavourings** Herbs and lemon or lime slices can be tucked into the slashes before the fish is grilled.

Poultry

The intense dry heat of a grill crisps poultry skin and gives it a unique flavour. Whole birds, joints and small pieces all can be grilled, though dark meat produces the juiciest results. White meat is easily overcooked and can become dry. For the moistest results, leave poultry unskinned or marinate (see page 23) beforehand. When grilling whole birds, you will need to use a spit for large chickens and turkeys or spatchcock smaller birds such as poussins. Make sure you preheat your grill and place the rack about 12 cm (4½ in) from the heat source. If the rack cannot be placed far enough from the heat, grill chicken with the oven set at 180°C (350°F/gas 4). Do not line the rack of the grill pan with foil – this can catch fat and cause flare-ups during the cooking process.

Rotisserie grilling Many ovens come with a rotisserie grill that rotates at a slow speed under or over the heat source and is ideal for cooking larger birds. A long square rod goes through the bird and you use two pronged 'forks' at either end to hold the bird in place. Quick and easy to use, this technique enables the bird to self-baste as it turns around.

Spatchcocking

This technique is ideal for smaller birds. The bird is flattened so that it becomes the same thickness overall, which is much better for cooking methods like grilling.

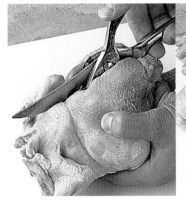

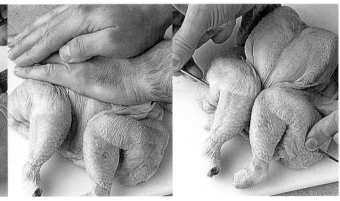

Using a pair of poultry shears, cut along each side of the backbone and then remove it. Tuck the wings under and remove the wishbone.

Push down firmly on the bird, flattening it against the chopping board, until you feel the breastbone break.

Keeping the bird flat, push a metal skewer through the wings and breast. Push another through the thighs.

barbecuing

Identical to grilling except that the food is cooked outdoors by direct heat over wood or charcoal and sometimes over a gas grill with lava rocks or porcelain-coated metal bars. Generally, barbecued food has a smoky flavour and is served more plainly than grilled food. Barbecuing can be done in two ways: in direct heat barbecuing, food is placed directly over heat and turned to expose both sides to the glowing charcoal. In indirect heat barbecuing, slower cooking foods are done on a covered barbecue. They are placed over the fire, the lid is closed and there is no need to turn the food.

Creating kebabs Make sure all foods to be cooked on the same skewer take the same amount of time to cook. Leave a little space between each piece so it cooks evenly. Alternate meat with cubed or sliced vegetables to add colour and make the meat go further.

Barbecue equipment

Long handled tongs are necessary both for handling food and for moving hot briquettes. You need two, one for each job. Because they won't pierce food, tongs are better than forks for handling food.

Basting brush A long handled, twisted-wire brush can be used to brush food with oil or a marinade while it is cooking.

Spatula An offset (angled-neck) stainless steel one with a 12–15 cm (4½–6 in) blade will slide under most chops and fish fillets and stop them tearing and sticking to the grill.

Mitts Heavy-duty fireproof mitts, particularly if they are elbow length, are ideal for working near a barbecue.

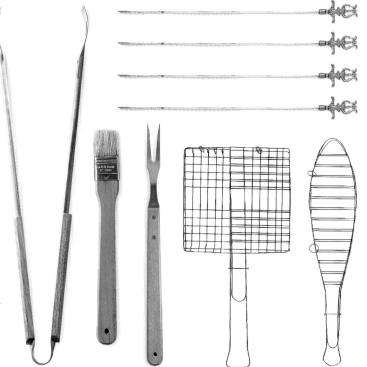

Skewers Metal and bamboo skewers are essential when cooking kebabs and satays. Soak the bamboo ones in water for at least 30 minutes (to prevent them from burning) and discard them after use.

Mesh racks Ideal for cooking fish, meat patties, and other small items, they should be hinged and secured with a latch. Brush with oil before using.

Instant-read thermometer Well-suited for the fast pace of grill cooking, these give very accurate readings within seconds of insertion and are often necessary to ensure larger pieces of meat and poultry have reached their correct internal temperatures.

essential know-how

42

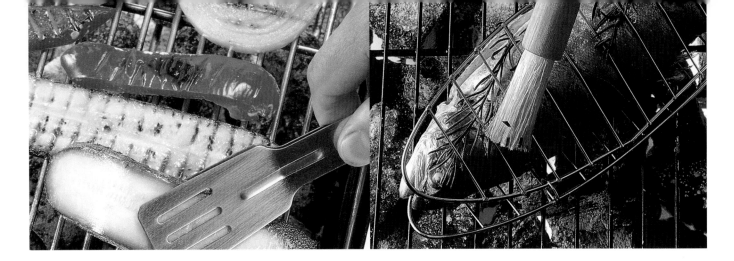

Vegetables

Squash, aubergine, mushrooms, peppers, onions and tomatoes all barbecue well but as they have no way of staying moist when exposed to a high heat, they need to be brushed with oil before being placed on the grill. They also benefit from added flavourings. If you cook them as kebabs, make sure they are cut in pieces that will cook in the same time as the meat, poultry or fish; otherwise, cook them separately. Some longer cooking vegetables, such as carrots, may need to be blanched (see page 22) before barbecuing. Potatoes can be wrapped in foil and cooked directly on the coals. Corn is often barbecued in its husk. Soak cobs in cold water for 15 minutes; this keeps them from burning on the barbecue. Drain and gently pull back husks to about three-quarters of the way down. Remove the silk. Brush with 15 ml (1 tbsp) olive oil. Tuck several sprigs of herbs into each cob. Replace the husks, and cook for 30–40 minutes, turning occasionally, until tender when pierced with a knife.

Meats

Most meat cuts should be marinated before cooking in order to tenderise them (see page 23) and to add extra flavour. Tender cuts of beef, however, can be cooked directly over a high heat without any marinade. Steaks should be at least 2–2.5 cm (¾ –1 in) thick, otherwise they will dry out. Trim off excess fat and slash the fat edges at intervals to prevent curling (see page 40). Hamburgers should be 2.5 cm (1 in) thick otherwise they, too, will be dry. Turn meat occasionally during cooking to prevent it from burning.

Fish

Because they have little internal fat, most fish benefit from a marinade to keep them from drying out on the grill. Also oil the grill to keep the delicate flesh from sticking to it, or use a rack. Don't move the fish too much and only turn it once; too much movement will cause the flesh to tear. If you don't have a barbecue tray, cook seafood in a foil parcel using a double layer of heavy-duty foil. Close parcel with a double fold on top and ends, leaving space for steam expansion. To avoid punctures, use tongs when turning. The flesh of fish and seafood should feel firm to the touch when done.

Poultry

Unless making kebabs or satay, use poultry on the bone as it will remain moister. As with fish, chicken pieces will taste more delicious and remain more juicy if used with a marinade or flavoured coating. Poultry is done when the juices run clear when pierced with a knife.

frying

Frying means cooking in hot fat. Its appeal lies in the wonderful flavour and crisp brown appearance of the food. When done properly, fried food is light and not at all greasy. There are various kinds of frying – pan-frying, shallow-frying, sautéeing, stir-frying and deep-frying. Ingredients for frying should always be at room temperature: cold food lowers the temperature of the fat. The surface of the food should be as dry as possible, as surface moisture converts to steam, causing the fat to bubble and lowering the temperature.

It is important to choose the correct oil. Most Chinese stir-frying is done with peanut oil. When deep-frying, use an oil that can be heated to a high temperature without smoking. Safflower, soya bean and corn oils have higher smoke points and so are preferable for deep-frying.

- Corn oil is a bland unsaturated oil, excellent for frying.
- Olive oil is ideal for sautéeing or stir-frying, but is unsuitable for deep-frying as it tends to smoke at high temperatures.
- Peanut oil is ideal for stir-frying, and can also be heated to high temperatures.
- Safflower oil is ideal for all types of frying, including deep-frying.
- Soya bean oil has a bland flavour and can be heated to high temperatures.

Sautéeing and pan-frying

These quick-cooking methods are virtually the same, although sautéeing is a French technique. Small cuts (steaks, breasts or escalopes) of meat, calves' liver, fish fillets, prawns, scallops and eggs are all suitable for pan-frying and sautéeing. The high temperature and hot fat seal the meat or fish, keeping it moist and succulent. Guidelines for successfully sautéeing meat are as follows:

- Cut the meat into slices about 1½ cm (½ in) thick.
- Use a mixture of oil and melted butter for the best results.
- Add the meat, and cook on each side over a medium heat until the meat is just tender.
- If you wish to make a sauce, remove the meat and set aside. Add the sauce ingredients to the pan, reducing if necessary, then put the meat back in and spoon over the sauce.

Frying escalopes

For chicken or turkey escalopes, slices of breast are placed between sheets of baking parchment or clingfilm and pounded to a uniform thickness to tenderise the meat and ensure even cooking. Veal escalopes also require a light pounding. Pat the meat dry after pounding. These delicate cuts are often coated in flour, egg and breadcrumbs before being quickly fried in hot oil. For moist, tender veal do not cook the meat beyond medium done.

Adding the coating Escalopes are usually dipped in seasoned flour then into milk, beaten egg or water, and finally into bread-crumbs; this helps protect the delicate flesh and adds flavour.

Don't overcook Once the escalope is lightly browned on both sides, remove it from the pan. Overcooking will make meat and poultry tough.

Dry-frying duck breasts

Fatty foods such as duck breasts can be pan-fried in their own fat, with no extra oil added. For successful results, trim and score the skin first, to help release the fat during cooking. Place the breast skin-side down in the pan over a moderate heat, so that the fat runs into the pan. Cook for about 5 minutes, pressing down with a palette knife, before turning to cook the other side.

Scoring a pattern By cutting diamond shapes in the skin, you not only allow excess fat to be released but also make the breast more attractive for serving.

Extracting juices Place the breast skin-side down, and as you cook press with a palette knife to keep it flat and to help extract the juices.

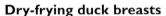

FRYING/SAUTÉEING PANS

A good frying pan has a thick base, so that the heat is distributed evenly, low sides and a heatproof handle. Stainless steel, anodised aluminium and cast-iron are all very good materials for conducting heat. Sauté pans (as shown below) are straight-sided, heavy and 6–10 cm (2½–4 in) deep.

Shallow-frying eggs

The perfect fried egg has a runny yolk and a set white. Heat oil or butter in a frying pan until it is hot before you add the eggs. Fry over moderate heat and baste frequently with the hot fat. For a neatly shaped egg, place a metal pastry cutter in the frying pan with the oil and heat until hot. Slide the egg into the cutter and fry until it is done to your liking, basting with the hot fat. Carefully remove the cutter from the pan before lifting out the egg.

stir-frying

Stir-frying is a quick and easy way of cooking bite-sized pieces of food over high heat, with the minimum of fat. It is an ideal way of preserving the colour, flavour and texture of food, as well as maintaining its nutritional value. The food is cooked both by the heat of the pan and the heat of the oil, and as it is stirred constantly, it cooks evenly. This was originally a Far Eastern technique, as reflected by the spices, flavourings and ingredients most often used.

Stir-frying is a very quick cooking method, but it does entail lengthy preparation. The meat, fish and vegetables to be cooked must all be prepared in advance. All the food is cut into small strips or slices of equal size and thickness, and the ingredients are then grouped together in bowls according to the time taken to cook. It is essential to assemble all the tools, sauces and spices before the wok is heated. If any ingredients are stored in the fridge, bring them out 30 minutes before you start cooking. For best results, heat the wok first, then add the oil in a thin stream round the sides of the wok. Make sure the oil is very hot before you add food: test with a small strip of onion; if it sizzles, the oil is hot enough. Don't add too much food at once, or it will stew rather than fry, and remember to stir continuously so that the food cooks evenly.

Stir-frying equipment

Cleaver The Chinese use cleavers for chopping and slicing ingredients. Cleavers are available in Chinese supermarkets, but a large, very sharp cook's knife is probably a bit easier to use.

Accessories A metal spatula, wok ring, wire strainer, and a set of cooking chopsticks for stirring are useful tools for stir-frying.

Wok The round, slope-sided wok is the traditional pan for stir-frying. The traditional shape has a round bottom, for cooking over a flame, but flat-bottomed ones are available for electric hobs. They either have a long wooden handle, or two metal or wooden ones. They come in several sizes: the 35 cm (14 in) is most common. Steel or cast-iron ones are best. Stainless steel is a poor heat conductor and food often tends to stick to it.

Stir-frying greens	Prepare	Blanch	Stir-fry time
Batavia (curly lettuce)	Wash; tear leaves	No	5 minutes
Bok choy	Wash; slice stalks	No	5 minutes
Chicory (curly endive)	Wash; tear leaves	No	5 minutes
Chinese cabbage	Wash; thinly slice	No	3 minutes
Kale	Wash; discard stalks; tear leaves	5 minutes	5 minutes
Mustard greens	Wash	5 minutes	5 minutes
Spinach	Wash	No	3 minutes
Spring greens	Wash; discard stalks; slice leaves	3 minutes	5 minutes
Sprouting broccoli	Wash; trim stalks	5 minutes	5 minutes
Swiss chard	Wash; slice stalks; slice leaves	No	3 minutes
Watercress	Wash	No	3 minutes

Preparing vegetables for stir-frying

It is important that vegetables for stir-frying are cut into small, uniform pieces so that they can be tossed easily and cooked quickly in the high heat of the wok. Long vegetables such as cucumbers, leeks and spring onions are cut into julienne strips. Carrots, mushrooms and courgettes are thinly sliced. Broccoli and cauliflower are divided into tiny florets.

Choosing and preparing meat for stir-frying

Meat to be stir-fried is either cut into small thin strips, or wafer-thin slices. Choose lean, tender cuts of meat that cook quickly, such as beef fillet, pork tenderloin, chicken breast or turkey breast. To tenderise and add flavour, the meat or poultry is often marinated for 1–2 hours before cooking in a mixture of oils, garlic, soy sauce, ginger and flavourings.

Stir-fried cabbage
Cut out the hard core, then separate the leaves and cut into matchbox-sized pieces. Heat the oil in a wok, add the spices and flavourings, then add the cabbage and stir-fry for 2–3 minutes. You can add soy sauce or sugar to taste, and sprinkle with a little sesame oil to finish.

Stir-fried noodles with vegetables To cook this classic dish, the dried egg noodles are first soaked, then drained and tossed with soy sauce. The sliced vegetables are stir-fried and the noodles are then added for the last 2–3 minutes. Soy sauce and oyster sauce can be added at the end.

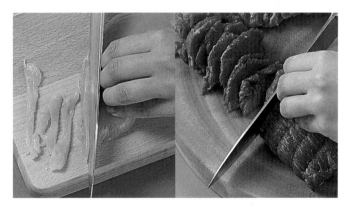

Cutting chicken for stir-fries
With a small sharp knife, cut away the white stringy tendon underneath the breast and detach the fillet. Cut the breast and fillet on the diagonal into thin strips about 5 mm (¼ in) wide. To make this easier, you can freeze the chicken for about 1 hour beforehand.

Cutting beef for stir-fries
Cut the beef into matchstick-sized shreds. If you freeze the beef for 1 hour beforehand, it will be easier to slice. Cut any vegetables, such as celery and leeks or spring onions, into julienne strips the same size as the beef. Cut fresh ginger into julienne, too.

deep-frying

Deep-frying means cooking food in hot, deep fat. There is a wide range of foods that can be deep-fried, from chipped potatoes and other vegetables to seafood, chicken and even fruit. It is a quick way of cooking, and not unhealthy, in spite of its bad image. When done properly, deep-frying does not involve a lot of oil absorption. The important points are to use a good quality oil, to have the oil at the correct temperature and to coat foods before cooking when necessary. The food to be cooked should be cut into pieces of equal size and thickness, and should be as dry as possible. After lifting the food out of the pan, drain on kitchen paper so that it stays dry and crisp.

The right temperature

If the oil is too hot it will burn the outside of the food before the inside is cooked. Oil will begin to burn at over 200°C (400°F). To make sure the oil is at the right temperature, you can use a thermostatically controlled deep-fryer, or a thermometer. For best results the oil should be at 180–190°C (350–375°F). If you don't have a thermometer, heat the oil in a deep pan or wok until it is almost smoking, then drop in a cube of bread. If the bread browns in 30 seconds, the oil is at the right temperature. To keep up the temperature during frying, do not fry too much food at a time.

Coatings and batters

Coatings shield food from the hot oil and help to prevent over-absorption of fat. Flour is the simplest coating, forming a thin, crisp crust. For extra insulation, for example when deep-frying chicken or fish, the food can be dipped in flour, then egg, then breadcrumbs. Another kind of coating is a batter made of flour and milk or water, sometimes with beaten egg added. Sieve the batter to make sure there are no lumps, or whizz in an electric blender. Use beer instead of milk for added colour, and for extra flavour add cayenne, chilli or curry powder to the flour. Tempura batter is ultra-light and crisp, so that the colour of the food shows through. Use it for a crisp and light coating on prawns, sliced vegetables or small pieces of fruit.

Safety notes

- Use a deep, heavy pan or wok.
- Fill deep-fryers no more than half full of oil, and woks no more than one-third full.
- Dry food well before frying to avoid spattering.
- Lower food into the hot oil gently to avoid splashing.
- Use a slotted spoon, wire skimmer or basket to remove food from the pan.
- Keep pan handles pushed back.
- Never leave the pan unattended.
- Clean up spills immediately and ensure that no fat is on the outside of the pan.
- Keep a fire blanket close to the stove.

Deep-frying potatoes

Potatoes can be cut into many different shapes for deep-frying, from ordinary chips to gaufrettes. They are always peeled first, and must be uniform in size and thickness. Drop the pieces into acidulated water (see page 169) as you cut them to avoid discoloration. This also removes some of the starch and helps to make them crisp. Drain and dry thoroughly before deep-frying.

French method of deep-frying potatoes This method twice-fries the potatoes, to give an ultra-crisp finish. The chips are deep-fried until tender, left to cool, then fried again at a higher temperature. Heat the oil to 160°C (325°F) and deep-fry the potatoes for 5–6 minutes. Remove, drain and allow to cool. Increase the temperature to 180°C (350°F) and deep-fry again for 1–2 minutes until crisp.

Fritters

Fruit fritters are wonderfully crisp on the outside, yet sweet and juicy inside. You can use any firm fruit, such as apples, bananas or pineapple. Peel the fruit first and remove all pips and stones before dipping in batter.

Fruit fritters Peel the fruit and pat dry. Use a two-pronged fork to dip the pieces of fruit into a light batter, allowing the excess to drip off. Heat the oil to 190°C (375°F) and fry the fritters for 2 minutes or until golden brown. Drain the fritters thoroughly on kitchen paper, then dip in caster sugar to give an even coating.

Deep-frying fish

For best results, a high cooking temperature is necessary: 180–190°C (350–375°F). In Chinese cooking, a whole fish can be deep-fried in a wok. For safety's sake, use a wok with two handles. Choose a whole, firm-fleshed fish such as red snapper, sea bass or grey mullet. The fish is first deep-fried until golden brown on both sides, then braised in sauce.

Prawns are coated with tempura batter to give a light, crisp coating.

For fish pieces, batter provides a protective coating which keeps the fish succulent and moist. Cut the fish into even-sized pieces, or use steaks or fillets, and cook large pieces of fish one at a time to ensure even cooking. For goujons, cut the fish into thin strips. Put the strips into a plastic bag containing seasoned flour and shake well to coat evenly.

carving

Even if you have roasted a bird or joint to perfection, sloppy carving will ruin your effort. Your carving knife (see page 10) should have a blade long enough to carve the breast of large birds or sides of large roasts into neat slices, so it should extend about 5 cm (2 in) beyond the meat on both sides to accommodate the sawing action. Letting the bird or roast rest covered with foil for 10–15 minutes after cooking, results in firmer, juicier meat that is easier to carve. Always carve across the grain of the meat not parallel to its fibres. This produces more tender slices. Make sure your serving platter is warm.

▶ **Carving a chicken or turkey**

Cut each leg from the body. Separate the thigh from the drumstick and remove to a warm plate.

Make a deep horizontal cut just above the wing through the breast until the knife touches the breastbone.

Then make a series of vertical cuts through the breast meat, going all the way down to the first horizontal cut.

Overlap the slices of white meat on a platter next to the drumsticks and thighs.

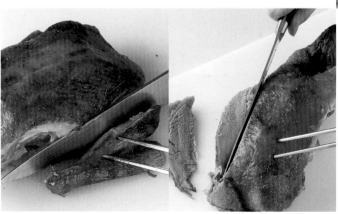

◀ **Carving a duck**

Remove each wing by cutting through the joint between the wing and body. To remove each leg, cut through the skin around the leg, then cut down between the thigh and body to reveal the joint; cut through the joint to separate. If you like, cut the drumstick from the thigh through the centre joint.

Hold the knife blade at a 45° angle to the duck and cut long, thin slices from one side of the breast. Repeat on other side.

Arrange the slices, wings and legs on a platter.

▶ Carving a rib roast

Your butcher should remove the chine bone so you can carve the roast between the rib bones.

Place the roast, rib-side down on a cutting board. Holding the knife about 5 mm (¼ in) in from the edge, slice towards the ribs.

Cut along the edge of the rib bone to release the slice. Transfer the slice to a warm platter.

Continue to make slices as above. As each rib bone is exposed, cut it

◀ Carving a veal breast roast

Steadying the roast with a two-pronged fork, cut down through the meat following the line of the rib bone.

Cut away the exposed rib and continue working along the breast, carving even slices of meat. Remove the slices to a warm platter.

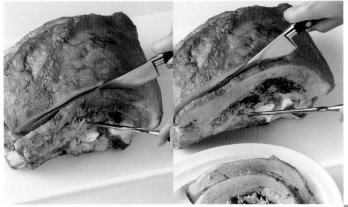

▶ Carving lamb

Leg Cut a slice from the thin side of leg and turn the leg cut-side down. Make a vertical cut to the bone about 2–3 cm (¾–1¼ in) from the shank. From the shank end, make a horizontal cut parallel to bone to release the wedge of meat. Cut even slices of meat, slicing perpendicular to the bone and working away from the shank. Turn leg over and cut long slices following line of bone.

Carving a rack Place the rack, ribs facing down, on a chopping board. Holding it steady, cut between the ribs using a sawing action.

◀ Carving a whole ham

Place the ham on a chopping board. Steadying the ham with a two-pronged fork, cut a few slices from the thin side of the ham so that it will lie flat.

Turn ham over onto cut surface, then cut a small wedge of meat at the shank end. Cut even slices along the ham right to the bone.

Release the slices from the bone by working the blade under the slices and using a sawing action. Transfer the slices to a warm platter.

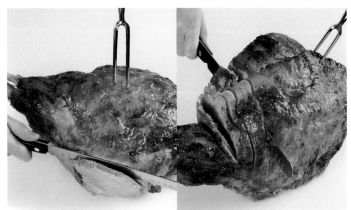

garnishing

The presentation of food not only makes it look more appetising by adding colour and interest, but can also improve the taste and texture – a few chosen herbs can transform a plain omelette into something much more interesting and a light drizzle of sauce can lift a simple dessert for a special occasion. Here are just a few ways to make food look as good as it tastes. A simple dessert of poached pears (see right) can be made into something more special with the addition of a swirl of chocolate sauce and a few berries.

◀ Piping ricotta into figs

For a decorative variation on the traditional Italian combination of Parma ham and figs, ricotta cheese is mixed with herbs and seasoning and then piped into the centre of each fig.

▶ Spring onion tassels

Used to garnish cold meats, steaks, salads and Chinese dishes, prepare these tassels a couple of hours in advance. Make several cuts into the stem of the onion to within 2.5 cm (1 in) of the bulb, place the onion in iced water and leave until the tassels open out.

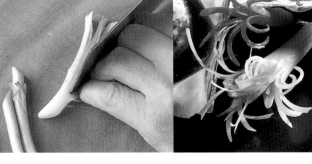

◀ Timbales

Cooked, puréed vegetables or rice mixtures look impressive served as timbales. Press chosen filling into an oiled mould, invert onto a plate and remove the mould. If it doesn't come out first time, run a knife around the inside to loosen it. To finish, arrange tiny pieces of vegetables, in a contrasting colour, on top of the timbale.

Finishing touches for soups

From a swirl of cream or yogurt, or a sprinkling of spice, to crispy croutons or finely grated cheese, there are lots of different ways you can make a plain bowl of soup more appetising. Make sure you match the flavour of the garnish to the flavour of the soup, so that they will complement each other.

Fresh sage leaves Fresh herbs, either chopped or whole, depending on the herb, go particularly well with cream of vegetable soups. A sprinkling of sage leaves on courgette soup finishes it off perfectly.

Toasted almonds Garnishes can be used to add texture and flavour as well as colour. A few toasted, flaked almonds look wonderful and add a nutty crunch to apple and almond soup.

Garnishing meat and poultry

There is a variety of traditional herb garnishes. These include fresh sage for roast pork, fresh mint for roast lamb, watercress sprigs for roast beef, parsley sprigs for roast veal and chives or fresh coriander sprigs for chicken. A sprinkling of chopped fresh herbs adds a special touch to a casserole or stew. Lemon slices or twists are often used to garnish chicken or turkey salads, while orange slices are traditional with duck.

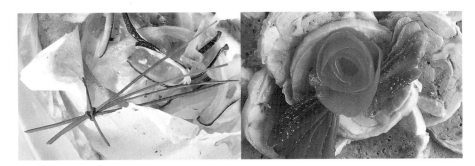

Chive knot Chives go very well with chicken – this impressive-looking chive knot adds colour and a touch of style to chicken en papillote. To make the knot, take a few strands of fresh chives and tie them together near the base with another strand.

Carved vegetables With a sharp knife and a little time you can create a wonderful array of vegetable 'flowers'. Peel a long strip of your vegetable (carrots, cucumber and radishes all work well) then spiral the strip into a flower shape and secure at the base with cocktail sticks.

Decorating desserts

A rosette of piped cream or a dusting of icing sugar or cocoa powder can add interest for a special occasion. Frosted fruits take a little longer, but a few grapes or redcurrants coated in sugar look good on soufflés, mousses and other cold fruit desserts. Wash and dry clusters of grapes or currants and coat in beaten egg white. Dip into a bowl of caster sugar, shake off any excess and leave to dry on a wire rack.

Half coated fruits Chocolate decorations are always popular – melt some chocolate over hot water and then dip in whole, small fruit (such as cherries, strawberries or grapes) until half coated. Leave to set on greaseproof paper and then serve with fruit or chocolate puddings (see page 249 for more chocolate decorations).

Contrasting coulis Smooth fruit sauces or coulis add a delicious flavour as well as a contrasting colour to desserts. To prepare a serving plate for a slice of dessert (as above), you will need two sauces of the same consistency. Spoon a little of each sauce onto each half of the plate, and when they meet, use a cocktail stick to swirl the two sauces together.

garnishing

ingredients

fish and shellfish

meat

poultry and game

dairy products

pulses and grains

vegetables

fruits and nuts

flavourings

INGREDIENTS This section of the book looks at ingredients in detail, providing you with the information you need to become familiar and confident with the vast range of ingredients available today. Each chapter covers a major food group, featuring the most versatile varieties, with information on how to choose, prepare and cook them. Nutritional values, specialist equipment, step-by-step techniques and recipes are included.

fish and shellfish

white fish

White fish largely fall into two main groups: flat fish, which include plaice, sole, halibut and turbot; and round fish and the cod family, which also includes haddock, whiting, hake and coley. Also included in the round, white fish group are sea bass, grey mullet and monkfish. Most white fish are gutted at sea immediately after they are caught, to ensure that their flesh remains white.

Although the availability of fresh fish is no longer strictly governed by the seasons, due to deep-freezing, there is still nothing to beat the flavour of fish when it is in season and at the peak of its condition – particularly white fish. White fish are saltwater fish, and those from the colder waters around the British coast and the North Atlantic have the firmest flesh and the best flavour.

Choosing

To ensure that the fish is absolutely fresh, always buy from a reliable source, preferably on the same day that you want to cook it. When you need something special, be sure to order it well in advance from a good traditional fishmonger, or from the fish counter of one of the larger supermarkets, which have a quick turnover. Buy only fish that is displayed on ice in a refrigerated cabinet.

Fish fillets and steaks should look fresh and translucent, rather than have a milky-white appearance. Any that are discoloured or dried around the edges should be rejected. The texture of the flesh tends to vary from one fish to another, but generally the flakes should be dense – if loose, it is a sign of deterioration.

Frozen fish, whether whole, fillets or steaks, should be sealed in undamaged packaging and have a minimal amount of ice crystals, preferably none. Prawns are more prone to have ice crystals in the packet, but filleted fish and steaks should be crystal free.

When buying fish from open freezer cabinets at the supermarket, always gently feel the fish to ensure that it is frozen solid, especially those packets on the top of the pile. Any fish that has a dry, white or discoloured appearance – which indicates freezer burn – should also be rejected. Fish that has been cut into steaks or fillets tends to deteriorate more rapidly than whole fish because the exposed surface is more vulnerable to bacteria.

A CLOSER LOOK AT FRESH FISH

Appearance and odour are the best guide to the condition and freshness of all fish.

Flesh
If possible, press the flesh to test that it is firm and stiff, not limp or floppy.

Eyes
The eyes should be bright with black pupils and transparent corneas, not sunken or cloudy.

Tail
The tail should look fresh and moist, not dried out or curled.

Skin
The skin of the whole fish should be bright and shiny, with the scales tightly in place.

Gills
The gills should be bright pink or red.

58

Flat white fish Flat fish are two-sided and the backbone runs through the centre of the fish, with two lines of bones fanning out on either side, separating the top and bottom fillets. They range in size from very large halibut, which can be 2 m (6½ ft) in length, to the smaller turbot, brill, sole and plaice. Very large halibut are sold cut into steaks, but smaller halibut and all other flat fish can be cleaned and cooked whole, or filleted. When being cooked whole, the dark upper skin is usually removed, but the more delicate, white skin on the underside may be left on.

Type	Season	Substitute	Cooking methods
Brill	June to February	Turbot	Bake (wrapped and unwrapped), steam, poach, grill, pan-fry
Flounder	March to November	Plaice	Bake, steam, poach, grill or sauté
Halibut	June to March	Turbot	Bake, poach, grill, pan-fry or steam
Plaice	All year	Sole	Bake, steam, poach, grill or sauté
Sole	All year	Plaice	Bake, steam, poach, grill or sauté

Round white fish These are plump, rounded fish with eyes that lie on either side of the head. They have the same coloured skin all over. The backbone runs along the centre of the fish, with rounded bones curving downwards, separating the two thick fillets on either side. Round fish can be cleaned and cooked whole, or filleted or cut into steaks before cooking.

Type	Season	Substitute	Cooking methods
Bass	August to March	Grey mullet, sea trout	Bake, steam, poach, barbecue
Black sea bream	July to December	Red sea bream, bass	Bake, braise
Red sea bream	June to February	Black sea bream, bass	Bake, braise
Catfish	February to July	Cod, huss, haddock	Stew, braise, grill
Cod	June to February	Haddock, hake, halibut	Bake, grill, poach, pan-fry, deep-fry
Conger eel	March to October	Monkfish, halibut	Bake, stew
Coley	August to February	Cod, haddock	Steam, poach
Haddock	May to February	Cod	As for cod
Hake	June to March	Cod, haddock	Bake (wrapped), steam, pan-fry
Huss (dogfish)	All year	Cod, haddock, whiting	Bake, grill, stew
Monkfish	All year	Conger eel, halibut	Bake, grill, pan-fry, barbecue
Whiting	June to February	Cod, haddock	Bake or fry

white fish

59

STORING

FRESH FISH After purchasing, fresh fish should be taken home immediately, preferably packed in a cool-bag with ice packs – particularly when the weather is hot (if you ask, some fishmongers and supermarkets will provide you with ice).

Once home, rinse fish and pat dry with kitchen paper. Then place in a dish, cover with a lid or foil and store in the coldest part of the refrigerator, 1–5°C (34–41°F), for no longer than one day.

Ungutted fish, such as mackerel, trout, and herrings should be gutted immediately you get it home, then rinsed, dried and stored as above. If stored ungutted, the bacteria in the guts will multiply and cause the fish to deteriorate rapidly.

Whole fish and fish portions bought in controlled atmosphere packs from the chiller cabinet should be stored in the pack, in the refrigerator, and not opened until ready to cook. Use within the time specified on the pack.

Fish must be kept cold until you are ready to cook it – never leave it standing around at room temperature.

FROZEN FISH After purchasing, take frozen fish home immediately, preferably in a cool-bag. Put it straight into the freezer. Generally, frozen fish should be stored for no longer than three months – but always use by the use-by date on the packet.

To prevent the texture and structure of fish from breaking down, thaw frozen fish slowly in the refrigerator overnight before cooking. Place, in the original packaging, on a plate to catch any drips. When thawed, unwrap, drain well and pat dry with kitchen paper. Never defrost under water, as the flavour and texture of the fish will be affected, and many of its nutrients will also be lost. Fish can be thawed at room temperature, but as this can cause naturally occurring bacteria in fish to multiply, it must be used immediately it is thawed out. Once thawed, frozen fish should never be re-frozen.

Fish fillets and steaks can be cooked from frozen, but will require a few more minutes cooking time.

SKINNING A WHOLE FLAT FISH

If serving the fish whole, only the dark skin needs to be removed. The white skin will help to hold the fish together while cooking. The fish can be cooked whole with the head or the head can be removed.

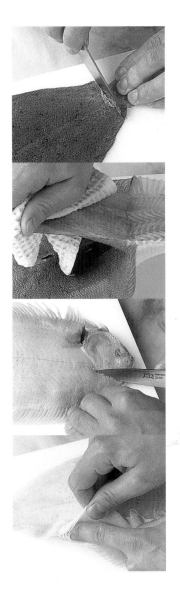

▶ Remove dark skin first. Make a small incision at the tail end to loosen the skin. Then work the knife just under the skin, to loosen it enough to get hold of.

▶ Grip the loosened skin with one hand and the tail with the other, using a tea towel. Firmly pull the skin away from the tail end and over the head.

▶ Detach the black skin completely, then turn the fish over to the white side. If you are removing the white skin too, cut around the head with a sharp knife to loosen the skin.

▶ Insert a finger under the skin at the head end and work all the way to the tail, ensuring it is well loosened. Repeat on the other side. Grasp the skin at the tail end as before and pull off.

fish and shellfish

YIELD PER SERVING				
WHOLE FISH, UNPREPARED	**WHOLE FISH, PREPARED**	**PREPARED WHOLE FISH, HEAD REMOVED**	**STEAKS, WITH OR WITHOUT BONES**	**FILLETS, BONELESS**
500 g (1¼ lb)	450 g (1 lb)	225–450 g (8 oz–1 lb)	175–275 g (6–10 oz)	175–275 g (6–10 oz)

FILLETING A WHOLE FLAT FISH

Depending on its size, a flat fish will yield two large double fillets, or four single fillets, as shown right with a large brill. Always trim the fish before filleting, cutting around the outside of the fish where the flesh meets the fins. The skin is often left on fish fillets to help them keep their shape.

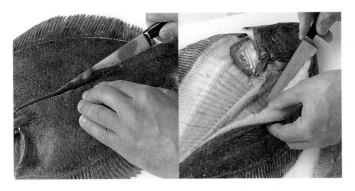

▲ **Preparing single fillets** Using a sharp filleting knife, make a cut down the centre of the fish from head to tail, cutting right down to the central backbone.

▲ Starting at the head end, insert the knife under the flesh and work your way down the fish with long, firm strokes, holding the knife flat and as close to the bones as you can. Turn and repeat on the other side.

DOUBLE FILLETS

Cut around the outside of the fish with a filleting knife where the flesh meets the fins, following the shape of the fillets. Carefully insert the knife under the flesh at one side and work it right across the fish, up and over the backbone as you come to it. Turn the fish over and repeat the action on the other side.

Single fillets

Double fillet

SKINNING FLAT FISH FILLETS

After removing the fillets from a flat fish, it is preferable to remove the skin, particularly the dark skin. Depending on the fish, the white skin may be left on. It is an easy task, but one that must be done properly if the fillet is to look neat and retain its shape. A sharp filleting knife is essential.

FILLETING KNIFE

When filleting a whole fish it is preferable to use a special, flexible filleting knife. Be very careful when handling these knives – the blades are razor-sharp. Dip your fingers in salt to help get a grip on the skin.

▲ **Skinning a fillet** Lay the fillet skin-side down on a board and, with the knife held at a slight angle, make a small cut through the flesh at the tail end of the fillet, just down to the skin, and taking care not to cut through the skin.

▲ Hold the skin tightly with one hand and slightly angle the blade between the flesh and skin. Keep the blade as close to the skin as possible and use a gentle sawing action to work the knife under the flesh until you come to the end.

white fish

USEFUL TECHNIQUES

After skinning, fillets of sole or plaice can be fried in butter, perhaps coated first with breadcrumbs or batter, or poached. Or they can be transformed into impressive, classic shapes such as goujons or paupiettes.

▼ **Goujons** These are thin strips of fish, cut diagonally down the fillet for long ones, or across for short, coated with flour, egg and breadcrumbs and deep-fried. Goujons are usually served with a tartare sauce.

▲ **Paupiettes** This is a rolled fillet of fish, usually sole or plaice. It may be stuffed or unstuffed, and can be steamed, baked or poached. Spread with filling, roll up skinned side inwards and secure it with a cocktail stick.

PREPARING A WHOLE ROUND FISH

Most round fish have scales and fins that should be removed before cooking. This is usually a messy job, so work outside or near the kitchen sink. Once the fish has been scaled and gutted, it can also be filleted. Two fillets, one from each side, can be cut from round fish. Use a filleting knife and leave as little flesh on the bones as possible.

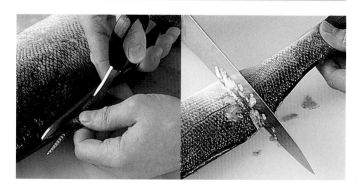

▲ **Removing fins** Trim off the fins on the back and stomach. Cut close to the skin with a pair of sharp kitchen scissors.

▲ **Removing scales** Hold the tail firmly and scrape off the scales with a fish scaler, serrated knife or the back of a chef's knife.

REMOVING FILLETS FROM A ROUND FISH

Place the cleaned fish on a board and make a diagonal cut behind the head, cutting right down to the backbone. With the back of the fish towards you, cut along one side of the backbone from the head to the tail.

To remove the top fillet, insert the knife into the cut at the head and cut the flesh away from the rib bones.

Hold the knife flat, parallel with the fish, and make short strokes, supporting the fillet with your other hand. Turn the fish and repeat for the second fillet.

SKINNING AND BONING MONKFISH

Only the tails of monkfish are used. These are often skinned and baked whole, or they may be filleted. After filleting, remove the dark membrane from the underside of each fillet. The fillets can then be cooked whole, or cut into cubes for kebabs, stews or stir-fries. The backbone can be used to make fish stock.

▲ **Skinning** Loosen the skin at the head end. Grasp the skin firmly and pull back towards the tail.

▲ **Boning** Using a chef's knife, cut the fillets from each side of the backbone and remove the membrane.

TESTING FISH FOR DONENESS

Fish should be cooked for the shortest time possible, as overcooking will make it tough and dry. The fish is cooked when the flesh is no longer translucent, but has turned opaque virtually all the way through. The flesh should flake easily.

MAKING A FISH STOCK

Cooking fish in a stock enhances the flavour. Fish stock also enriches sauces, stews and casseroles. A fish stock, also known as fish fumet, is made with white fish trimmings, such as heads and bones, including prawn heads and shells.

The trimmings are cooked in water and wine, with aromatic vegetables and herbs. Simmer for no longer than 20 minutes or the stock may start to taste bitter. Oily fish is too strongly flavoured.

Fish sauces

Mayonnaise A creamy blend of egg yolk, lemon juice or white wine vinegar, mustard and olive oil.

Tartare sauce (Served with fried fish) Mayonnaise, with finely chopped gherkins, capers, lemon juice and some finely chopped fresh herbs, such as parsley and chives or tarragon.

Béchamel sauce A white sauce made by adding warmed milk to a butter and flour roux. The milk can be flavoured by infusing it with vegetables and bay leaves.

Mornay sauce (Served with any white fish) A béchamel sauce flavoured with grated Gruyère or Parmesan cheese. Can be used as an accompaniment or for a gratin, where it is poured over fish, such as fillets of sole, and placed under the grill until golden brown.

Velouté sauce (As used for Sole Veronique and Sole Bonne Femme.) Can be served with any white fish (including a whole poached sea bass). Made like a béchamel sauce, but with fish stock (see left) and cream instead of infused milk.

Hollandaise sauce A hot emulsified sauce based on egg yolks and unsalted butter. It is often served with fish cooked in a court bouillon.

Fish quenelles

Quenelles are minced fish or meat shaped into balls or ovals. Small fish quenelles can be used to garnish clear soups. Larger ones may be poached, then coated with a rich cheese sauce and browned in the oven or under the grill. Whiting, plaice or sole fillets are all perfect for making flavourful fish quenelles.

FISH CAKES

Fish cakes can be made with a variety of raw fish: white fish such as cod, haddock, whiting or hake, or oily fish such as salmon or mackerel. A mixture of fresh and smoked fish gives a very good flavour.

For light cakes, chop or flake the fish by hand – minced fish tends to make heavy cakes. Leftover cooked fish can also be used in fish cakes – use equal quantities of cooked fish and potatoes in the mixture.

▲ **Making cakes** Remove all bones from raw fish and chop finely. Mix with fresh breadcrumbs, herbs, beaten egg, lemon juice and seasoning. You can also add Tabasco or mayonnaise.

▲ **Cooking cakes** Shape the mixture into neat patties and chill until firm. Coat the cakes with breadcrumbs and fry in hot oil for 5–6 minutes on each side. Drain on kitchen roll.

white fish

oily fish

Oily fish differ from white fish in that their oil is distributed throughout their flesh, whereas in white fish the oil is retained in the liver. Oily fish therefore have a stronger flavour, and darker flesh with a meaty texture. Because of the fat content, the flesh remains moist and tender when grilled or fried, and is less delicate than white fish.

Choosing

The same rules for buying and storing white fish (see page 58 and 60) also apply to oily fish. More often than not, oily fish are sold whole and require scaling and cleaning before cooking. A fishmonger will do this for you, but it is also quite simple to do yourself.

NUTRITIONAL INFORMATION

Fish is a naturally low-fat food, oily fish having the highest concentration of fat – from 6 to 20 per cent – but this is a 'good' kind of fat. Eating foods like fish that are rich in omega-3 fatty acids is a natural way to help maintain a balanced, healthy diet. Fish such as mackerel, herring, trout, sardines and salmon are the richest sources of omega-3 fatty acids. Unlike the saturated fats found in meat, these fatty acids are polyunsaturated, and thus can actually help to protect us against coronary heart disease.

Type	Season	Substitute	Cooking methods
Anchovy	June to December	Sardines, sprats	Deep-fry
Herring	May to December	Mackerel, pilchards	Bake, grill, souse
Mackerel	All year	Herring, pilchards	Bake, grill, steam, barbecue
Pilchards	January, February, April, November, December	Small herring, small mackerel	Bake, grill, pan-fry, barbecue
Sardines	As for pilchards	Pilchards	As for pilchards
Tuna	All year	Swordfish	Bake, pan-fry
Whitebait	February to July	None	Deep-fry

BONING SMALL OILY FISH

Small oily fish such as sardines have very soft bones which can easily be removed with your fingers.

▼ Holding the head of the fish just behind the gills, break it off and discard. Insert your forefinger into the head end of the fish and run it down the belly to slit it open. Pull out the innards and discard.

▲ Gently open the fish out and pull out the backbone, starting at the head end. Nip it off with your fingers at the tail end. Rinse the fish thoroughly under cold running water and pat dry.

SCALING, GUTTING AND BONING A HERRING

Some oily fish need to be scaled before cooking. The many small bones in oily fish often cause problems. Small fish can be boned with your fingers (see below left), while larger fish such as herring and mackerel are boned by a different technique. When boned they can be filled with a stuffing and baked, or grilled. They can also be rolled and soused, or opened out flat, coated with oatmeal and pan-fried. The skin of oily fish is usually left on during cooking, to help hold the flesh together.

Marinating

To counteract the richness of the flesh, oily fish, whole or cut into strips, is often marinated and cooked in a mixture of vinegar and cider or water, with spices and flavourings such as onion and bay leaves.
Sushi is made with rice and vinegar rolled in seaweed, with strips of raw fish such as tuna and mackerel in the centre. Sashimi is simply raw sliced fish served along with wasabi.

In spite of their rich flesh many oily fish are good pan-fried or grilled, since this seals in the flavour and helps to dissolve the fat under the skin. Baby herring and sprats (whitebait) are often served deep-fried.

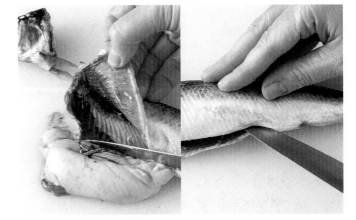

▲ Cut off the head, slit along the belly and pull out the innards. Remove the black membrane inside the fish and rinse it well.

▲ Turn the fish over and run your thumb under the rib bones, along each side of the backbone.

First, remove the scales with a fish scaler or serrated knife, working from tail to head. Scale fish inside a polythene bag, or outdoors.

▲ Cut all the way to the tail. Open the fish out flat and lay it skin-side up. Press firmly along the backbone to loosen the bones.

▲ Lift out the loosened backbone and rib bones, freeing them with a knife if necessary. Cut off at the tail.

oily fish

freshwater fish

Most wild freshwater fish are caught in lakes and rivers. Some, such as salmon, sea trout and eels, spend part of their lives at sea but are caught in lakes and rivers. Sea trout, although they are larger and look different, are the same species as brown trout, but because they resemble a small salmon they are sometimes called salmon trout. Carp and bream are found only in fresh water.

Unless you are a keen fisherman, wild freshwater fish such as brown trout are now virtually unobtainable. However, farmed fish is available all year round at most fishmongers and in larger supermarkets. And, when in season, it is still possible to buy wild salmon, although it is expensive. The flavour of freshwater fish can range from delicate to strong. It can also have an 'earthy' taste, depending on where it is bred. The most delicate freshwater fish is trout, which is best cooked simply. Salmon is very versatile as it combines equally well with spicy seasonings, rich sauces such as hollandaise, and simple toppings such as crème fraîche flavoured with fresh herbs.

YIELD

4.5 KG (10 LB) SALMON = serves up to 25 people*
* for trout – allow one for each person, with an average weight of 350–450 g (12 oz–1 lb), after gutting and cleaning

Choosing

The rules found on page 58 also apply to freshwater fish – but be extra sure that it smells really fresh. Newly caught fish should be gutted immediately. You should gut and clean fish from the supermarket as soon as you get it home.

Type	Season	Substitute	Cooking methods
Carp	Farmed: all year	Bream	Bake, pan-fry, deep-fry
Char, arctic	Farmed: all year. Wild (from Coniston Water or Lake Windermere): 15 March to 30 September	Trout	Bake, grill, poach
Eel	Farmed: all year	None	Stew, grill, barbecue
Pike	All year	Grey mullet	Bake, grill
Salmon	Farmed: all year. Wild: February to October	Large trout, sea trout	Bake, grill, poach, pan-fry
Trout, wild and brown	England and Wales: available only in the open season, which varies from season to season. Scotland: 1 April to 30 September	Rainbow trout	Bake, grill, poach, pan-fry, barbecue

GUTTING THROUGH THE GILLS

Round fish served with their heads on, such as trout, look better if they are gutted through their gills.

▼ Lift up the gill flaps behind the head, snip them out with scissors and discard. Holding the fish belly up, make a small cut at the bottom of the stomach.

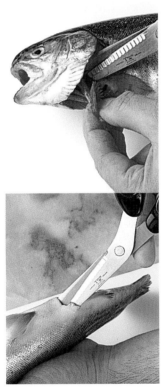

▲ Insert the points of the scissors and cut through the innards to loosen them. Grasp hold of the innards through the gill opening, pull them out and discard. Rinse thoroughly under cold running water. Dry well.

BONING THROUGH THE STOMACH

When stuffing whole large fish, it is best to bone the fish through the stomach.

Place the gutted fish on its back and extend the opening up to the tail. Insert a filleting knife under the rib bones at one end and slowly work the knife along to free them from the flesh.

To loosen the backbone, carefully work the knife along the spine on both sides, taking care not to cut through the skin.

Using kitchen scissors, cut the backbone away from the head and the tail.

Remove the fine pin bones from the flesh with a pair of tweezers, checking for bones with your fingers.

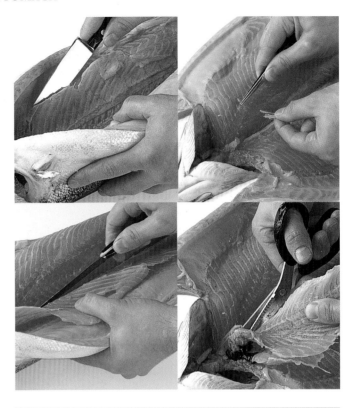

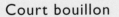

Court bouillon

This is an aromatic liquid used for poaching fish, such as a whole salmon or sea bass. It is made with vegetables, such as onion, carrot, leek and celery, and fresh herbs, cooked briefly in salted water, just long enough to draw out the flavours. White wine can be added after 20 minutes (if you add it before, it will prevent the release of flavours). Alternatively, a little red or white vinegar can be added to taste. Allow to cool before use.

HOW TO SERVE A WHOLE COOKED FISH

With a sharp knife, slit the fish from head to tail along the backbone, then remove the skin (if still on). Carefully turn the fish, and remove the skin from the underside. Using a sharp knife, split the top fillet of the fish and lift away. If the fish is stuffed, scoop the stuffing out before removing the bones from the lower fillet.

To remove the bones, lift up and pull the tail forward to free the bones and the head from the lower fillet, cutting it from the tail with scissors. Lift the top fillets back into place. The fish is now ready to be served in portions. Alternatively, the fish can now be coated with a sauce, or with aspic, and garnished before serving.

exotic fish

Unlike the availability of our native fish, which is strictly governed by the seasons, exotic fish (generally those from tropical waters) are available virtually all year round. However, precisely which exotic fish will be available in the fishmongers each week is determined entirely upon what is being imported at the time.

Although exotic fish often look a little different, they are just as easy to prepare and cook as any other round fish (see page 59), and can be equally delicious.

PREPARING EXOTIC FISH

Many have large, sharp, bony fins, which are best removed before gutting and cooking, and particularly when cooking them whole.

Type	Texture and flavour	Cooking methods	Substitute
Emperor fish	May have a strong flavour	Is best baked	Parrot fish
John Dory	Has delicate yet firm flesh which resembles sole and turbot when filleted	Poach, grill, pan-fry, bake	Sole, turbot
Parrot fish (usually sold frozen)	Bland flavour	Best cooked whole – baked or steamed	Emperor fish
Red gurnard	Has firm, tasty flesh	Often included in stews, particularly in the Mediterranean	Red mullet
Red mullet	Firm, white flesh, well-flavoured. Prized for its liver, which is regarded as a delicacy	Bake, fry, grill	Red snapper
Red snapper	Firm to soft-textured, white/off-white flesh. Mild flavour	Bake, grill, pan-fry, braise	Red mullet
Red strawberry grouper (quite difficult to get)	Firm textured flesh. Delicate flavour	Stew, poach, bake or treat as sole or turbot. Traditional ingredient of bouillabaisse	Mullet, sole, turbot
Shark (sold cut into steaks)	Pink to ivory flesh. Very meaty texture. Mild flavour	Barbecue, grill, pan-fry, braise	Swordfish
Sturgeon (freshwater fish – mainly available farmed)	Oily, firm-textured fish with delicate flavour. Valued for its eggs which are eaten as caviar. Has cartilage instead of bones and can be used instead of chicken	Grill, barbecue, poach, pan-fry	Tuna
Swordfish (mainly sold as steaks)	Oily fish with tough skin and off-white flesh. Rich and juicy	Barbecue, grill, bake, poach	Shark

preserved fish

The ancient methods of preserving fish by salting and smoking are still used today, but more to satisfy our appetites for their delicious flavours than for long-term keeping.

When salted or smoked, the texture and flavour of fish changes. Textures become firmer, oily fish become richer, and their flavours can vary from mild to strong. But all still have to be prepared before they can be used or eaten.

Dried salt cod One of the most commonly used ingredients in cuisines all around the world, particularly in Europe and the Caribbean, salt cod is readily available from ethnic stores and many delicatessens (particularly Italian ones). But the quality does vary – so look for fish that is off-white or greyish in colour. Reject any that looks a dull yellow colour, as this is a sign that the fish has been left in the salt for too long.

The prime meat from the top side of the fish, often known as the shoulder, is the best. Unlike fish preserved by smoking or pickling, salt cod when re-hydrated can be cooked as if it were fresh cod.

Salted anchovies and herring The vast majority of anchovies and herring are preserved in a heavy salt brine. Salted anchovy fillets are sold in cans or jars, in oil, and can be drained and used immediately. Salted herrings, however, need roughly 24 hours soaking in cold water before they can be filleted and served.

TO RE-HYDRATE DRIED SALTED FISH

Before any dried, salted fish can be used, it must first be soaked in cold water to re-hydrate the flesh and remove excess salt. If large, cut the fish into pieces and put into a very large bowl or stainless steel saucepan, and cover well with cold water. Leave the fish to soak for 24–48 hours, depending on the size and thickness of the fish, changing the water at least two or three times. When it is re-hydrated and ready for cooking, the dried fish will have roughly doubled in size.

NUTRITIONAL INFORMATION

Salt cod is more calorific than fresh cod and its liver, which is particularly rich in vitamins A and D, is used for cod liver oil.

COOKING SALTED FISH

Rinse the soaked fish thoroughly under cold running water, then put into a large pan. Cover with cold water and bring just to the boil. Then reduce the heat and skim off any scum from the surface. Adjust the heat so that the water just ripples, then partially cover the pan with a lid and simmer for 10–20 minutes, or until the flesh flakes easily when tested with a knife. When it is fully cooked, drain the fish and flake the flesh, discarding the skin and bones.

DESALTING ANCHOVIES

Canned varieties are saltier than bottled ones. Soaking in cold milk for 20 minutes will make them softer and milder. Drain off the oil first and after soaking, drain the milk and then rinse under cold running water.

exotic and preserved fish

SMOKED FISH

As well as giving the fish a smoky flavour, the heat of hot smoking also cooks the flesh, which means that most smoked fish can be eaten cold. Some, such as kippers, which tend to dry out more, are heated through before serving. Although cold smoking colours the fish, the flesh retains its raw, translucent appearance. Some cold-smoked fish such as cod, haddock and Finnan haddock need to be cooked before serving, whereas those with more delicate flesh, like salmon, sturgeon, halibut and cod's roe, can be eaten uncooked. All smoked fish should be a good, rich-looking colour. Their flesh should be plump, and their skin shiny. Any that look dried out, curled or wrinkled, and have bones that are separating from the flesh, should be rejected. Much smoked fish is vacuum packed to keep it fresh.

Smoked salmon

In a long, slow process, the fish is first cured for at least several hours, either with a dry rub of salt or in a brine. It is then smoked, at a temperature of 32°C (90°F) or less. Flavour and texture vary with the variety of salmon, the cure, the duration and temperature of the smoking process and the wood used.

Dyed or undyed

When fish were smoked for longer and in a more traditional manner, they became richer and darker in colour. Today, some fish – such as haddock – are dyed to give them the appearance of having been smoked for longer. However, although the dyes used are natural, the practice of dying is being used less, as demand for undyed, naturally coloured smoked fish is growing.

SERVING SMOKED FISH

Unless sold as boneless fillets, most smoked fish need only minimal preparation. Remove heads (if necessary), skin and bones. Serve with lemon wedges and brown bread or toast and butter.

SMOKED SALMON KNIFE

This long, narrow, flexible-bladed knife is ideal for slicing smoked salmon very thin. The cutting edge is straight but the blade can be smooth or fluted and is usually rounded at the tip.

Type	Smoking method	Cooking methods
White fish		
Arbroath smokie	Cold-smoked	Grill or poach
Cod	Cold-smoked	Bake, grill, poach, steam
Large haddock (fillet)	Cold-smoked	Bake, grill, poach, steam
Finnan haddock	Cold-smoked	Poach
Halibut	Cold-smoked	Ready to eat
Oily fish		
Bloaters	Cold-smoked	Grill or fry
Buckling	Hot-smoked	Ready to eat
Eels	Hot-smoked	Ready to eat
Kippers	Hot-smoked	Poach, grill or fry
Mackerel	Hot-smoked	Ready to eat
Salmon	Cold or hot-smoked	Ready to eat
Freshwater fish		
Sturgeon	Cold-smoked	Ready to eat
Trout	Hot-smoked	Ready to eat
Other		
Cod's roe	Cold-smoked	Ready to eat

squid

Regarded as a great delicacy in Mediterranean countries, and popular in Asian-style dishes, squid (or calamari) is generally sold cleaned and ready prepared in frozen form. However, it is sometimes sold fresh and the following preparation steps will help you to cope with squid, octopus or cuttlefish.

POUCHES MADE FOR STUFFING

When left whole, the pouch is perfect for filling with a wide variety of stuffings. Use a piping bag or spoon to add the filling but don't over-fill; always leave room for the stuffing to expand. Secure the stuffing by sewing the pouches up with a trussing needle and some fine string.

COOKING TIMES

• Small, or baby squid require little more than blanching (see page 22) when being used for salads and hors d'oeuvre. If used in soups and stews, add them at the end and cook for just a few minutes.
• Small to medium-size squid can be cut into rings, coated with flour or batter and deep-fried.
• Medium to large squid require long, slow braising (to tenderise the flesh, which can be tough and chewy). Cook for anything between 1–4 hours, depending on the size.

What to do with the ink

Squid ink can be used, as in Italy, to colour and flavour pasta or risotto. Add to the liquid when cooking squid, so that it cooks in its own ink. You can also add it to paella to flavour the rice. If the squid has been frozen whole and unprepared, the ink will have turned into granules (coagulated). Restore these by removing from the sac and dissolving in a little hot water.

PREPARING SQUID

The pouch, tentacles, fins and ink are all edible.
• Holding the body firmly with one hand, gently pull away the head and all that is attached to it. If using, locate the ink sac, pierce, drain out the ink and reserve. Inside the pouch is a long, thin and transparent bony support, known as the 'pen'. Locate the top, pull it out and discard.
• Peel off and discard all of the transparent, purple membrane that covers the body and fins. With a knife, cut off the fins, taking care not to cut into the pouch.
• Place the head and the attached viscera on a board and separate the tentacles from the head by cutting just above the eyes. Discard the rest of the head and viscera. To remove the beak-like mouth, open out the tentacles and push the mouth up with your fingers. Then cut off and discard.
• Under a cold running tap, rinse the pouch (ensuring that no internal material remains), fins and tentacles. Dry with kitchen roll.
• Leave the pouch whole for stuffing, or cut into rings. Cut the fins into strips or chop. Leave tentacles whole for a garnish or chop (they must be cooked).

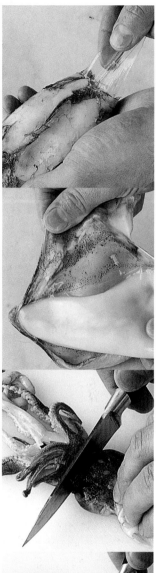

shrimps and prawns

These belong to the same family as the lobster. Shrimps are very much smaller than prawns and are always sold cooked. There are two types, brown shrimp and pink shrimp.

Many of the prawns we eat today are farmed, particularly tiger prawns, and almost all will have been frozen. The flavour of prawns varies depending on where they were caught or how they were farmed. Many farmed prawns can be watery and bland, but those that have their diet supplemented by feed are more flavourful and meatier in texture. Prawns from the cold waters of the North Atlantic are said to taste best.

The natural colour of raw prawns varies from greenish-brown, bluey-grey, brownish-pink, to pale orange, pink or red. When cooked, all prawns turn to varying shades of red.

Choosing

All prawns should look and smell fresh, and have shiny shells. If they look dry and shrivelled, they are not fresh or have not been stored properly. Except for black tiger prawns, never buy prawns with black spots on their shells as this is a sign that they are going off. Also avoid any with yellow or gritty shells, as these may have been bleached to remove black spots, or with white, dry spots as this can be an indication of freezer burn.

It is best to buy prawns frozen and defrost them yourself. It also is preferable to buy shell-on prawns (but remember that 25 per cent of the weight will be lost when shelled); peeled ones will have lost some of their flavour. Always feel packets of frozen prawns to make sure they are frozen solid.

Crevettes These are warm water prawns and are sold cooked (left), shelled and unshelled.

Tiger prawns These are warm water prawns. They vary in size, and are sold uncooked (below left) or cooked (below), whole or without their heads (as tails). They are also sold cooked and shelled.

Large freshwater prawns These look very similar to tiger prawns, but are larger and fatter, and are also without stripes. They are generally sold uncooked, and headless.

Shrimps Cooked shrimps are sold with their shell on. Small pink or brown shrimps can be eaten whole – as in France. Nip or bite off the head and discard it. Then eat the body whole (including the shell), with fresh bread and butter.

Common prawns They come mainly from cold seas and vary from 2.5 to 10 cm (1–4 in) in length, and are sold cooked, shelled and unshelled – fresh or frozen.

Take care

Never leave frozen or defrosted prawns lying around in a warm atmosphere as the natural bacteria in them can breed very quickly, causing them to spoil, and possibly cause food poisoning.

STORING

Unless they are being used immediately, frozen prawns should be put into the freezer as soon you get home. Defrosted prawns must always be kept, covered, in the fridge until ready to use and be used on the same day as thawed. Follow any information on the label and use by the date given.

YIELD

500 G (1¼ LB) PRAWNS

36–45 small

25–40 medium

21–30 large

16–20 extra large

---

10 jumbo

NUTRITIONAL INFORMATION

Prawns are a good, low-fat source of protein and contain omega-3 fatty acids. They are high in potassium, and are a useful source of zinc – but are also quite high in cholesterol.

PEELING AND DE-VEINING PRAWNS

A prawn's black vein is its intestinal tract. This can impart a bitter taste and is unpleasant to eat, so should be removed from raw prawns before cooking. It also can be removed from large cooked prawns in the same way; it is harder to remove the vein from small, cooked prawns.

Carefully snip large prawns along their underside with a small pair of kitchen scissors. Then gently peel away the shell, taking care to keep the prawn intact. The tail may be left on if wished. With a small, sharp knife, make a shallow cut along the back of the prawn, to expose the dark intestinal vein (note: in some prawns this vein may not be black and is a little more difficult to find).

Remove the vein with the tip of a knife then rinse the prawn under a cold, running tap and pat dry with kitchen roll.

BUTTERFLYING A LARGE PRAWN

If necessary, remove and discard the head. Gently pull off the legs, then with some small kitchen scissors cut all along the centre of the undershell, right up to the tail. With a sharp knife, cut through the flesh, right along and down to, but not through, the shell.

Carefully remove the black vein. Open out the prawn, and place on a board with its shell uppermost. Gently but firmly press all along the centre of the shell to flatten and create a butterfly shape, pulling the two sides apart.

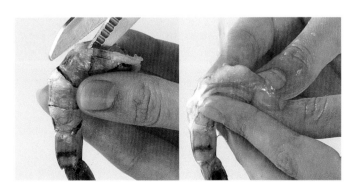

TESTING FOR DONENESS

Whether they are boiled, grilled or stir-fried, all raw prawns (with or without shells) are cooked as soon as they turn pink, within 3–5 minutes. However, very large, shell-on prawns may need 1–2 more minutes to cook all the way through. Test by gently squeezing the shell, the prawn will feel firm, and not squidgy. Alternatively, cut one open to see if the flesh is opaque all the way through.

Recipes

Chilli prawns and asparagus with dill and mustard sauce
A spicy dish of tiger prawns, dipped in a sweet chilli sauce and sesame seeds, served with tender asparagus spears and a sauce of whisked mustard, vinegar and soft brown sugar.

Prawn cocktail
Freshly cooked shelled prawns served over a bed of shredded lettuce in a spicy tomato sauce.

Prawns fried in garlic
A simple but delicious dish flavoured with brandy and served with lemon wedges.

shrimps and prawns

lobster

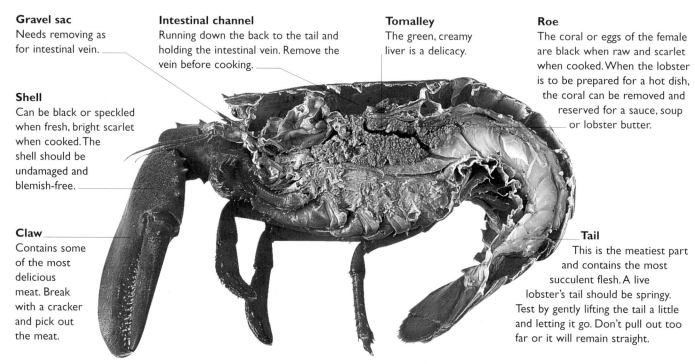

For ultimate flavour, a lobster should be bought live and be cooked at home to ensure that it hasn't been overcooked or kept on ice. Overcooking toughens the sweet and meaty flesh – and keeping on ice does nothing to improve the flavour.

Since most lobsters are sold ready-cooked, you will need to order a live one in advance. Native lobsters are in season from April through to November, and are at their best during the summer months.

The European lobster, found in the North Atlantic and Mediterranean, has large, almost over-sized claws, and is regarded as having the finest flavour of all crustaceans.

The Spiny or Rock lobster is harvested off Florida, southern California and South America. It has no claws, and is often sold frozen, as lobster tail.

Choosing

The best lobsters are those freshly caught, and bought at the coast – ideally straight from the lobster pot in which they were caught. The next best supplier is a reputable fishmonger, and it is wise to know what to look for when buying. Always buy a live lobster on the day you intend to cook it. Select an active lobster, and one that feels heavy in weight in proportion to its size.

Underweight and sluggish lobsters have been kept in a holding tank for many days and without food. Being underweight can also suggest that the lobster may have recently moulted its old shell and has not yet grown enough flesh to fill its new one. Reject lobsters that are damaged, and those with what looks like a hard, white spider's web over the shell; this suggests an old lobster. Avoid buying frozen lobsters, as they are watery and tasteless.

A CLOSER LOOK AT A LOBSTER

Gravel sac
Needs removing as for intestinal vein.

Intestinal channel
Running down the back to the tail and holding the intestinal vein. Remove the vein before cooking.

Tomalley
The green, creamy liver is a delicacy.

Roe
The coral or eggs of the female are black when raw and scarlet when cooked. When the lobster is to be prepared for a hot dish, the coral can be removed and reserved for a sauce, soup or lobster butter.

Shell
Can be black or speckled when fresh, bright scarlet when cooked. The shell should be undamaged and blemish-free.

Claw
Contains some of the most delicious meat. Break with a cracker and pick out the meat.

Tail
This is the meatiest part and contains the most succulent flesh. A live lobster's tail should be springy. Test by gently lifting the tail a little and letting it go. Don't pull out too far or it will remain straight.

HUMANE KILLING

There are many theories as to the most humane way of killing a lobster. The RSPCA recommends placing the lobster in a polythene bag in the freezer for at least two hours before cooking – this will stun the lobster and render it unconscious before it is to be immersed in boiling water or killed with a knife.

To kill a lobster with a knife, place it on a board, with its back facing up. Locate the centre of the cross-shaped mark at the back of the head. Then pierce right through the head, to the board, with the point of a heavy chef's knife. The lobster is killed instantly, although there may be some twitching from the severed nerves.

Cut the lobster in half along its entire length. Then remove the white gravel sac near the head, the thread-like intestinal vein, the grey-green tomalley underneath the canal, and, if it is a female lobster, the greeny-black coral. Then twist off the claws and cut into pieces as desired.

Dealing with a live lobster

For some hot dishes, like Lobster Newburg, a lobster is best cooked gently and not boiled. During boiling, some of the lobster's flavoursome juices are drawn out and lost into the water. Therefore, the lobster must be killed with a knife (see left) before it is cooked. With this method, death is virtually instantaneous, as the knife severs the spinal cord.

REMOVING MEAT

• Twist off the claws and legs. Carefully crack them open and pick out the meat. Twist the head from the tail to remove and set aside.
• Cut down each side of the thin shell on the underside of the body to expose the meat. Carefully pull the tail meat away in one piece.
• Make an incision along the outer curve of the tail to expose the dark intestinal vein. Remove and discard.
• Remove and discard the transparent stomach sac and gills. Carefully spoon out the green tomalley and any red coral. Lift out the rigid portion from the head shell and break into pieces and pick out the meat.

Recipes

Lobster butter Used for enriching soups and sauces, it is made with softened butter blended with the coral and a little lemon juice. It can be made with or without a little tomato purée.

Lobster Newburg A favourite American dish, made with lobster pieces, cooked, and served in a cream-enriched Madeira or sherry-flavoured velouté sauce.

Lobster Thermidor Cooked lobsters are sliced in half, lengthways. The meat is then removed from the shell, cut into large pieces and reassembled in the shell with a rich Parmesan and mustard sauce. It's finally sprinkled with Parmesan and browned under a grill or glazed in the oven.

Grilled lobster Pieces of lobster are sprinkled with salt and pepper and brushed with butter, then grilled and served with lemon slices and parsley.

crab

Crabs are usually sold ready-cooked, and very often already dressed by the fishmonger. Although live crabs can be boiled similarly to lobster, it really is a job that's best left to the experts, who know how to kill a crab humanely. Leg, claw or flaked meat is also available.

Our most widely available crabs are the native edible brown crabs and spider crabs. Edible brown crabs have large front claws, and are very meaty. Spider crabs – which have long spindly legs – are not so meaty. Although crabs can be obtained all year round, edible brown crabs are mainly available April–December, and spider crabs April–October. Both are at their best from May to August.

Other types of crabs can be bought locally around the coast and in specialist fishmongers. These include soft-shell crabs (which have shed their shells and are in the process of growing new ones) and Cromer crabs, a smaller variety of crab, favoured for its tender, sweet succulent flesh.

Choosing

Buy crabs that you can be certain are very fresh (never frozen) – and only from a reputable fishmonger. Always eat on the same day as buying, particularly in warm weather. Select medium to large crabs, as the meat in very large ones can be coarse in texture. Small crabs contain very little meat. Male crabs contain more (and some say better quality) meat than females. You can identify them by turning them over and looking at the tail, or apron flap. Males have a very small, pointed tail flap. Females have a larger, wider one. Crabs should have two claws and be heavy; a 1 kg (2¼ lb) crab will serve two.

A CLOSER LOOK AT A CRAB

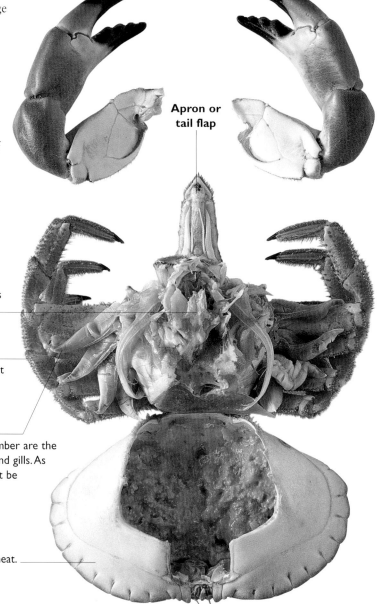

Claws
Use a crab cracker to break claw and remove the succulent white meat inside.

Apron or tail flap

Stomach sac
Located between the eyes, this should be discarded.

Legs
Use a pick to remove the meat from the legs, which is flakier than the claw meat.

Dead man's fingers
Located around the body chamber are the crab's feathery looking lungs and gills. As these are not edible, they must be removed and discarded.

Shell
Contains the creamy brown meat.

PREPARING A COOKED CRAB

The edible parts are the white, flaky meat and soft creamy, stronger flavoured meat. Colour varies from crab to crab, depending upon where it has been feeding. After flaking, cover the meat and chill until ready to use.

▲ Place the crab upside-down and first remove the large front claws. To remove the legs, grasp each one firmly, close to the body, and twist it sharply in the opposite direction to which the pincers face.

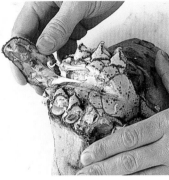

▲ Lift the apron, loosening it with the point of a small knife if necessary, and bend it back until it snaps off. With the apron end up, and the top shell towards you, stand the crab on the edge of its shell.

▲ Holding the crab very firmly with both hands, position your thumbs in the centre of the body (where the apron was snapped off) and push the body chamber out and away from the main top shell.

▲ Remove and discard the 'dead man's fingers', the stomach sac and any other attachments. Check the shell to see if any of these have fallen in, and remove. Scoop out and reserve the creamy brown meat.

▲ Place the body shell on a chopping board and cut it into quarters, with a large, heavy cook's knife. Then carefully pick out the white meat from the small cavities in the shell (use a small pointed knife or a skewer) and put it all into a bowl.

▲ Carefully crack each claw open with a heavy weight or nutcracker – trying not to damage the flesh beneath. Remove the shell and pull away the meat and flesh concealed within the pincers. Repeat with each of the legs. Flake and add it to the reserved body meat.

CRAB AT ITS BEST

The best way to enjoy fresh crab is in its shell – the perfect container for serving in. Holding the empty crab shell with its underside up, carefully break away the thin part of the shell, following the natural, curved line. Wash and dry the shell, then rub lightly with oil to bring out its colour. Fill with the seasoned crab meat, spooning the white meat into the sides and brown meat down the centre. Garnish with two lines of finely chopped parsley, along each side of the brown meat.

Accompany with lemon, brown bread and butter.

molluscs

Oysters are mostly eaten raw because they are grown in special oyster beds, under very strict conditions. But mussels, cockles and clams should never be eaten raw as any that have been gathered in polluted waters can be very dangerous.

Shellfish can cause allergic reaction in some people. Raw shellfish deteriorate very quickly when dead, and it is for this reason that most mussels, cockles and clams are sold alive. To test if dead or alive, tap the shell gently to see if it closes up. If the shell remains open, the shellfish is dead.

Choosing

To be absolutely sure of its freshness, all shellfish should be bought from a reputable fishmonger, or a supermarket with a fast turnover. Farmed mussels are meatier, tastier and less gritty than wild ones. Always enquire as to whether or not the shellfish were previously frozen and if they were delivered fresh that day. Choose those with undamaged shells, and only those that have a fresh, briny smell. Reject any that feel heavy as they may be full of sand. Any that feel light, or are loose in the shell, are probably dead.

STORING

Frozen, raw or cooked shellfish should be taken home as quickly as possible, preferably in a cool-bag, and put straight into the freezer unless cooking the same day. Always use frozen shellfish on the same day it is thawed, and be sure to thaw out slowly in the refrigerator. Keep refrigerated until ready to use and use as quickly as possible – preferably, immediately after defrosting.

CLEANING SHELLFISH

Because they live in shallow waters, most shellfish can be very gritty, and sometimes even muddy. Some, like mussels, can be encrusted with white barnacles.

▼ **Mussels** Pull away the hair-like strands (the beard) that are attached to the hinge of the shell. Rinse in several changes of water or under a cold running tap, and scrub with a small, hard-bristled brush.

▲ **After cleaning** Place mussels, clams and cockles in a bowl of lightly salted cold water for 2–3 hours. Change the water if it muddies. Add a handful of oatmeal to the water to help them disgorge any grit.

Shellfish	Season	Cooking methods	Substitute
Clams	All year	Steam or add to soups and stews	Mussels
Cockles	May to December	As above	Small clams
Mussels	September to March	As above	Medium-size clams
Oysters	September to April	Eat raw, steam or bake	None
Scallops	September to March	Poach, sauté or add to soups and stews	None
Whelks	February to August	Bought ready cooked	Cooked clams
Winkles	September to April	Bought ready cooked	None

OPENING CLAMS AND MUSSELS

These can be steamed open (see page 31) or prised open once cleaned.

◀ **To prise open** Holding firmly, insert a knife between the two shells and twist. Cut through the hinge muscle. Loosen the muscle in the bottom shell or, if serving the clams without their shell, tip the meat and juices into a bowl.

PREPARING SCALLOPS

Place scallop, rounded shell down, on a cloth-covered worktop. Hold firmly with cloth, inserting the tip of a knife into the opening between shells. Move the blade across the underside of the flat top shell to sever the internal muscle.

Pull the two shells apart. Insert the knife tip under the 'frilly' grey apron that surrounds the white flesh and orange coral – and work it all the way around to free the scallop. With your fingers, carefully pull away and discard the dark organs attached to the muscle flesh and the coral.

Rinse well under a cold running tap. Gently pull away the hard, crescent-shaped, muscle attached to the side of the flesh.

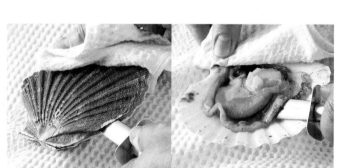

OPENING OYSTERS

Always work on a firm, steady surface and protect your hands with a cloth, lest the knife should slip. Place the oyster, with its flat, top shell uppermost, on a cloth-covered board or work top. Holding the oyster firmly with the cloth, insert the tip of an oyster knife, a little below the hinge, between the two shells on the straighter side of the oyster.

When you have managed to insert the knife between the two shells, twist the knife firmly to prise the shells apart. Slide the knife closely along the upper shell to sever the muscle. Discard the flat, top shell. Run the knife under the oyster in its rounded, bottom shell to loosen it; take care not to spill any of its flavoursome juices.

Place the opened oyster on a bed of crushed ice to keep cold and steady while preparing other oysters.

Recipes

Moules marinière Mussels steamed in a flavoured white wine broth; both the mussels and broth are eaten.

Coquilles St. Jacques Poached scallops are replaced in their shells in a mornay sauce, with a border of mashed potato and sprinkled with a little grated cheese, then baked in the oven.

Fettuccine alle vongole Small clams in a garlic and white wine flavoured sauce, tossed with pasta.

OYSTER KNIFE

For absolute safety it is essential to open oysters with a proper oyster knife, and one that has a safety shield attached. The shield protects your hand from the razor-sharp edges of the oyster shell and, of course, from the blade of the knife itself.

molluscs

79

garnishes for fish and shellfish

There are a number of classic decorations for fish, many made from lemons, which can be squeezed over the fish for fresh juice. For a formal occasion, wrap lemon wedges in muslin so the seeds don't scatter on the fish. Some garnishes, like parsley sprigs, can be used to hide an open eye. Other herbs that work well are chervil, chives, lemon balm and watercress. You also can use garnishes to add interest and colour to the presentation. To make decorations adhere to a whole fish, dip their tips in aspic or mayonnaise.

Barbecued citrus fruits Slice oranges, lemons and limes thinly, remove seeds and grill for 2–5 minutes on each side.

Caper flowers Drain capers, and with your fingertips, gently pull back some of the outer layers to make 'petals'.

Citrus curls With a canelle knife, cut a 15 cm (6 in) strip of orange peel. Curl the peel around a skewer until it holds the shape.

Courgette scales Blanch a courgette, cut into slices, then quarters. Lay the quarters over the fish so that they overlap like scales.

Anchovy loops Drain canned anchovy fillets and pat dry, cut into strips. Wrap each anchovy strip around a caper.

Double lemon twists Slice a lemon into thin rounds. Make a slit from the edge to the centre of each slice, and twist into a curl.

Lime butterflies Cut thin slices of lime, then cut into quarters. Place the two quarters next to each other and top with a star of blanched red pepper.

Winged lemon Cut long strips of peel using a zester. Cut around 180° leaving one end attached; turn lemon and repeat. Turn one cut point over another.

meat

beef

Choosing

When buying beef, a traditional butcher will prepare the meat to a much higher standard than is possible with packaged supermarket meat, and may also be willing to give advice, particularly if you need something specific for a particular recipe. If you want high-quality meat, wherever you buy it, you must be prepared to pay for it. Beef that is organically reared or from fine breeds, such as Aberdeen Angus, will always be more expensive.

- Although the colour of the fat and flesh is mainly determined by how the animal was fed and reared, generally speaking, the best beef is that with creamy-white fat and a deep, rich burgundy or plum-coloured flesh. Cattle grazed on grass will have quite yellow-looking fat. Most supermarket beef has white-looking fat. Bright red meat has not been allowed to hang sufficiently long and will not, therefore, be as tender nor as flavourful.
- Flesh that is marbled with fat will be richer and moister when cooked: the fat nourishes the meat as it melts during cooking. Lean meat, with little fat, can mean dry meat.
- Boned, rolled and tied joints should be neatly prepared and of an even thickness so they will cook evenly.
- The bones of joints sold on the bone should be neatly sawn, not chopped or hacked.
- Fresh meat will smell fresh and look moist. If it has a very sweet or unpleasant smell, or looks very wet and slimy, it is going off. If it looks dried out, it has not been stored properly.
- A layer of gristle between the muscle and the outer covering of fat is an indication that the meat may have come from an older animal.

STORING

After buying fresh meat, take it home as quickly as possible, unwrap and store in the refrigerator at 0–5°C (32–41°F) until ready to use.

Joints should be placed on a small rack or up-turned saucer, placed on a larger plate, and covered with a large bowl to prevent the meat from drying out. Use within three days. Placing the meat on a rack prevents it from sitting in any juices which may seep out and in which bacteria can multiply and contaminate the meat.

Sliced, cubed and minced beef should be put onto a clean plate and be covered with an up-turned bowl or foil. Use on the same day as buying or within 24 hours.

PRE-PACKED BEEF

- Always make sure the packaging isn't damaged in any way; if it is, don't buy. If the normally taut covers on sealed-top polystyrene trays and controlled atmosphere packs seem less firm than they should be, reject the pack, as even the tiniest pin-prick can release the gases within and cause the meat to deteriorate.
- Having bought pre-packed meat, it is vitally important that you note the label information, particularly the use-by date. Generally, meat on polystyrene trays, over-wrapped with film, can be removed and then stored as for fresh meat above. Sealed tops and controlled atmosphere packs should not be opened until you are ready to use the meat.

Know your beef cuts

Cuts of beef are generally known by the names given in the chart opposite, but they do vary from one part of the country to another – particularly when buying from a traditional family butcher. Although supermarkets label larger cuts such as sirloin and topside by name, others, such as shin, leg and flank, are simply described (in many supermarkets) as being suitable for casseroling, stewing or braising.

Cut	Description	Cooking methods
Blade and chuck	These are similar cuts. Both are fairly lean. Blade may contain a seam of gelatinous tissue, but this is left on as it melts and becomes tender when braised or stewed. Both can be minced. When sold sliced, are known as blade steak and chuck steak. Both are sold diced	Both are good for braising and for stewing, but require long, slow cooking to tenderise
Brisket	Sold on the bone or boned and rolled. Can be very fatty, so choose a joint that has a good proportion of meat to fat and bone. It can also be sold salted	Best braised. Can be poached, boiled or pot-roasted
Clod or sticking	This is neck meat and has a high proportion of gristle, but this can be trimmed off	Use for stews and casseroles
Leg/shin	Leg meat comes from the hind leg. Sold boned, cut into thick slices or cubed. Shin comes from the fore leg and is quite gristly. Sold on or off the bone, sliced or diced	Ideal for stock. Stewed or braised if well trimmed
Minced beef	Made from various parts of the animal, such as clod and trimmings. Is sold with varying percentages of fat	In burgers, sauces, meat loaves, pies, pasties and meatballs
Rib joints	All rib joints and fore rib should have a good, outer layer of fat	Best roasted on the loin
Rib	Rib steaks, and top and back have less bone than fore rib, and finer-grained meat	Single ribs on bone can be grilled
Wing rib	From between the ribs and the sirloin. Should have a good eye-muscle of meat and a good, outer layer of fat. All rib joints can be sold on the bone, or boned and rolled	If boned and rolled, rib joints can be pot-roasted, or braised
Top rump (thick flank)	A large joint from the upper hind leg. Sold boned and rolled, or sliced into steaks. Also sold as boneless steaks, or cubed for casseroles and stews	Joints – slow roasted or braised Steaks – braised or fried
Topside	From the inside of the hind leg. Is lean and fine-grained. Sold boneless, and with a good layer of barding fat tied around it	Slow roast, pot-roast or braise
Sirloin	A large, prime roasting joint with very tender meat. Sold on or off the bone, also contains the fillet	Quick roast. Steaks can be grilled or pan-fried
Silverside	Comes from the top end of the hind leg. Has a coarser grain than topside and top rump, but has a good flavour	Slow roast, braise, salt or spice and poach or boil
Steaks		All can be grilled or pan-fried
• **Châteaubriand**	Is very tender and cut from the centre of the fillet. Only large enough to serve two	
• **Entrecôte**	The eye muscle from the sirloin	
• **Fillet**	Attached to the underside of the sirloin. Those from the thin end are known as filet mignon, or tournedos	
• **Porterhouse**	Cut from the chump end of the sirloin	
• **Rump**	Should have a good layer of fat along one side	
• **T-bone**	Cut on the bone, comes from between the chump end and wing rib	

beef

83

Beef is an important source of high-quality protein, vitamins and minerals (especially iron and zinc). It contains all the B vitamins, except folic acid. Its lean meat is relatively low in calories, and an average 75 g (3 oz) serving will supply us with roughly 50 per cent of our RDI (recommended daily intake) for protein.

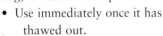

Bring to room temperature

All cuts of meat for roasting, grilling and pan-frying must always be brought to room temperature before cooking. But be sure not to leave them out in a warm atmosphere any longer than is necessary.

FREEZING BEEF

Although beef freezes well, it will, however, still lose some of its flavoursome juices as it thaws.

- Always prepare and freeze meat on the day it is bought.
- Pack in strong polythene freezer bags or rigid plastic containers, extracting as much air as possible.
- Interleave steaks, meatballs and burgers with freezer clingfilm or greaseproof paper for easy separation.
- Over-wrap large joints with foil to protect them.
- Set freezer to lowest setting, or fast-freeze first.
- For the best results, thaw all meat slowly in the refrigerator; loosen the wrappings on large joints. Always place the frozen meat on a large plate while thawing, to catch the drips.
  - Use immediately once it has thawed out.
  - Ideally, meat should be frozen in the form that it will eventually be used, such as ready-cubed for stews and casseroles, strips for stir-frying or minced.

HEALTHY EATING

- By buying beef that carries the Soil Association's Organic symbol, you will be assured that it has been reared without the use of inappropriate drugs and artificial foodstuffs, and have been cared for with rigorous animal welfare standards. Look for meat that is labelled as organically reared. Organically reared animals are fed a diet of organically grown food of plant origin. They will not have been fed any animal protein, nor genetically engineered products.
- Although meat does contain fat, over half of it is unsaturated, so there's really no need to be too hasty in removing all the visible fat before cooking. In fact, it plays an important part during cooking, and adds to the ultimate succulence and flavour of the meat. In addition, today's animals are bred to be leaner and have less fat. Fat can also be trimmed off, or removed after cooking.
- Bear in mind that fat nourishes meat and keeps it moist as it cooks, so don't be over-zealous with the amount you remove, particularly from larger joints, such as rib of beef. It is also desirable to leave a certain amount of fat on stewing and braising cuts, like the chuck shown below. During cooking, the fat will melt and help to keep the meat moist; it also will rise to the surface and can easily be skimmed off.
- The excess fat from joints, when cooked on a rack, will drip below and can be skimmed off from the pan juices before they are used to make a sauce or gravy.
- When making stews and casseroles, the fat rises to the surface and can easily be skimmed off before serving. If made the day before, cooled and refrigerated overnight, the fat will solidify on the surface, enabling it to be easily lifted off before reheating (also with the added advantage that stews and casseroles always taste better if they are made the day before!).

TRIMMING BEEF FILLETS

When buying fillet ready-cut into steaks it will have been well trimmed but, when buying a whole fillet (for stuffing or making filet de boeuf en croûte), the sinewy membrane may not have been removed. To cut this away, carefully insert the

tip of the knife under the membrane at the top end of the fillet. Then, keeping the knife as close to the membrane as possible, start to cut it free. Once you have separated a piece large enough to grip, hold the membrane taut and away from the meat as you cut.

Recipes

Mustard and peppered beef Stroganoff This is a traditional Russian dish in which strips of fried beef flavoured with black pepper and mustard seeds are cooked with mushrooms, brandy and a little anchovy essence.

Fillet of beef Wellington (Filet de boeuf en croûte) This classic French dish was renamed Beef Wellington in honour of the Duke after the Battle of Waterloo. Today, it is made with a whole fillet of beef, topped with sautéed mushrooms, wrapped and cooked in puff pastry.

Boeuf bourguignon Any lean and tender cut of beef cooked very slowly in red burgundy wine and a bouquet garni for two or three hours until tender.

Beef carpaccio An Italian starter consisting of thinly sliced beef strips seasoned with black pepper and served with a mustard, chive and red onion dressing.

CUTTING INTO CUBES

Long, slow cooking methods like stewing and braising – when tough muscle softens and gelatinous tissues melt into the sauce – are best for cuts like blade and chuck steak. To ensure even cooking, it should be cut into even-size cubes. For braising, cut into larger pieces; for stewing, cut into large, medium or small cubes as required.

▼ Cut the meat across the grain into thick slices, 3–4 cm (1¼–1½ inches) wide.

▲ Turn each slice on its side and cut in half lengthways, or into three if the meat is quite thick. Cutting across each strip, cut the meat into large pieces or cubes.

MAKING YOUR OWN MINCE

Mincing your own meat ensures that it is free of all fat, gristle and sinew. While tough cuts such as the neck or flank are best machine minced, small amounts and prime cuts such as fillet or rump can be minced with two large heavy knives, of roughly equal size and weight. Chuck steak and skirt can also be minced in the same way.

Cut well-trimmed meat into small cubes, then, holding the two knives loosely and parallel to each other, chop the cubes by alternately lifting and dropping the knives, with a rhythmic action – like beating a drum.

As you chop, lift and turn the meat occasionally to ensure that it is evenly chopped. Chop until the required texture is reached – coarse, medium or fine.

veal

The very best veal comes from young milk-fed calves, and is highly valued for its delicate flavour. Veal from older calves that have been fed with grain or have eaten grass will have darker, redder flesh and a slightly stronger flavour but will still be of good eating quality.

British veal is expensive, due to the high cost of rearing quality milk-fed calves. Also reflected in the price of veal is the extra care required in its preparation, as most is cut in the French style, where the meat is meticulously trimmed and the muscles are carefully divided along their natural seams.

Although veal is naturally very tender, it still requires careful cooking if its tenderness is to be preserved. Tougher cuts benefit from moist cooking such as stewing and braising. Lean ones can be cooked more quickly, yet gently, by grilling and pan-frying. When roasting, cook in a moderate oven and baste often.

Choosing

Most of the rules for choosing and storing beef (see page 82) also apply to veal. It should have smooth, fine-grained flesh that is pale to creamy pink in colour, with a light grey tinge. Any outer fat should be firm and white.

STORING

Because veal is a very moist meat, it will perish more quickly than beef and will keep for no more than two days, even in the refrigerator.

Animal welfare

Among those who eat veal, there is a growing demand for home-reared veal, bred to British standards (see Healthy eating, page 84) which have more concern for animal welfare. Check the label for the country of origin, and to see that it had been reared naturally. Check your guests' feelings about veal before serving it, too.

Veal cuts	Description	Cooking methods
Best end neck	Sold on the bone or boned. Also as cutlets	Roast, grill or pan-fry cutlets
Breast	On the bone, and boned	Pot-roast, stew, roast, braise (boned, stuffed and rolled)
Escalopes	Cut from the hind leg and fillet	Coat with flour or breadcrumbs and pan-fry
Fillet	Comes from the top of the hind leg, sold cut into steaks or whole	Grill or pan-fry steaks in one piece, whole fillet can be roasted
Knuckle	From lower part of the fore or hind leg	Braise (osso bucco) or stew
Leg	Topside is sold whole (as cushion of veal) or sliced into escalopes. With knuckle removed, the whole leg can be roasted in one piece. After the topside is removed, the remaining part of the leg is cut into smaller joints for roasting	Roast, or fry when cut into escalopes
Loin	Sold whole or cut into chops	Roast (whole), pan-fry, grill, barbecue (chops)
Middle neck	On the bone, as cutlets. Boned, as pie veal	Braise, stew or casserole
Scrag	Mainly sold cut into pieces on the bone	Casserole
Shoulder	Sold on the bone, or boned	Roast or braise

PREPARING VEAL ESCALOPES

Traditionally, escalopes are dipped in egg then coated with breadcrumbs or seasoned flour and they can also be rolled around a filling to make paupiettes or saltimbocca. First, however, they must be pounded thin, which helps to break down the tough connective tissue.

◄ Pounding until thin
Place each escalope between two sheets of clingfilm and pound lightly with a rolling pin until it is about 3 mm (⅛ in) thick. If the escalope is very long, cut each in half across the grain.

► Coating with breadcrumbs Beat 1–2 eggs in a bowl. Dip the veal in the flour (turning to coat), the egg and then the breadcrumbs, shaking off the excess.

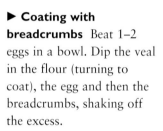

◄ Frying Cook the escalopes in hot olive oil, a few at a time, for 1 minute each side, or until brown. Drain them on kitchen roll before serving.

► Wrapping round a filling
To make saltimbocca place Parma ham and fresh sage leaves on each escalope, then roll the meat up to enclose the filling. Secure it with a wooden cocktail stick.

BONING A VEAL BREAST

Boneless joints are more versatile than bone-in ones: if used in casseroles they can be cut into pieces, and if roasted, they cook evenly and are easier to carve.

Draw the tip of a sharp boning knife down the sides of the rib bones and then cut away the meat beneath. Cut through the cartilage and around the breastbone. Remove the breastbone. Pull off the rib bones and then trim off any excess cartilage, sinew or fat.

STUFFING A BONELESS JOINT

Place meat fat-side down between two sheets of clingfilm and pound it into a rectangle, 30 x 25 cm (12 x 10 in). Place meat skin-side down and spread the stuffing evenly over the surface. Roll up joint from narrow end. Wrap kitchen string twice around length of roll and tie. Make a loop with string by wrapping it around one hand and slide this loop on to the meat at the far end. Repeat at 5 cm (2 in) intervals and secure.

CUTTING A POCKET IN A CHOP

Pat the chop dry first, then holding a knife parallel to the work surface, cut horizontally into the meat stopping short of the bone on the opposite side.

veal

87

lamb

Of all meats, lamb is the most valued for its tender, succulent, sweet flavour. It comes from sheep less than a year old; spring lamb is from animals aged 3–9 months. Sheep between one and two years old are called hoggets or yearlings, and those over two years are sold as mutton.

The colour, texture and flavour of lamb vary according to its age. Young, milk-fed lambs are usually under two months old and have a particularly mild flavour. Their flesh is soft, loose and paler. Three to four-month-old lambs also have a delicate flavour, but their flesh is rose-coloured, or a brownish-pink. As lambs get older they become fattier, their flesh darkens and their flavour becomes stronger.

Choosing

Meat from young lambs can be roasted or grilled, whereas meat from older lambs benefits more from moist cooking methods such as braising and stewing. If buying from a supermarket, look at the bones. In a young animal they have a pinkish-blue tinge. Older animals have white, less pliable bones and the colour of their flesh is darker. Good-quality home-produced lamb will have creamy white fat, that looks dry and waxy. Yellowing fat may be a sign of age. In general, all cuts should have an even layer of creamy white outer fat, and a light marbling of fat within the flesh. Breast and shoulder of lamb will have more visible fat. Bones should be cleanly cut, with no splinters and a reddish tinge at the ends.

PRE-PACKED LAMB

- Meat is sold in supermarkets either on polystyrene trays, overwrapped with film, or with a sealed, clear cover over the top of the tray only. It also comes in controlled atmosphere packs (rigid plastic containers with a sealed, clear cover) which contain special gases that help to keep the meat fresh for longer.
- Always check the packaging to make sure it has not been damaged in any way – if it has, don't buy. Even the tiniest pin-prick hole can release the gases within and cause the meat to deteriorate.
- Having bought pre-packed meat, it is vitally important that you follow the instructions on the label, particularly the use-by date. Those with sealed tops, and especially controlled atmosphere packs, should not be opened until you are ready to use the meat inside. If they are opened and the meat is not used straight away, the use-by date will no longer apply.
- Although lamb is generally well prepared before being sold, it may still require a little extra attention when you get it home, such as removing what is called the 'bark' – the thin, dry, parchment like tissue that covers the fat, or removing any excess fat.

STORING

Lamb joints will keep well in the refrigerator for up to four days, chops for two to three days. Minced lamb should be used on the day of purchase, or within 24 hours.

Always bring refrigerated lamb back to room temperature before cooking it.

Lamb freezes well when tightly wrapped in foil or heavy-duty polythene bags, and will keep for six to nine months. To defrost, place on a rack, on a plate to catch the drips and thaw slowly in the fridge; allow six hours per 450 g (1 lb). Once thawed, use immediately.

NUTRITIONAL INFORMATION

A 90 g (3½ oz) serving of cooked lamb will supply approximately 20 g (¾ oz) of protein – one-third of our RDI (recommended daily intake) – plus B vitamins and iron in the form of 'haem iron', which is easily absorbed by the body and also helps the absorption of iron from other foods. Although lamb is bred to be leaner than it used to be, it still contains a high proportion of fat within the meat itself.

YIELD

450 G UNCOOKED LAMB

=

boneless roasts –
three to four servings

=

bone-in roasts and chops –
two to three servings

=

riblets and shanks –
one to two servings

Cook's tip

A good butcher will prepare lamb in any way you want it, but elaborate, expensive roasting cuts, such as crown roast and guard of honour, do require a few days' notice as they take more time to prepare. But with just a little patience, and a good sharp boning knife, you can easily prepare them yourself, which is both satisfying and cheaper.

Whether roasted, barbecued, grilled or pan-fried, for the best flavour and texture lamb is best served still slightly pink. Should the bones of a crown of lamb or guard of honour start to darken too much during cooking, simply protect them with foil.

TO PREPARE A CROWN ROAST

A crown roast takes its name from the fact that, when prepared, the racks used for making it look like a crown. You will need two racks of lamb, chined (sawn through the ribs where they meet the backbone). If not already done by the butcher, start by stripping off the bark – the outer parchment-like membrane – from each rack. Place the racks fat side up on a chopping board. Free the bark at one corner with the tip of the knife, then, when there is enough to get hold of, grip it tightly and pull it away firmly – holding the rack steady with your free hand. If necessary, trim away excess fat. At one end of each rack, you may find a remaining piece of shoulder blade. If so, remove it by cutting it free with the tip of the knife.

About 5–7.5 cm (2–3 in) down from the tips of the rib bones, make a deep incision, in a long straight line, right through the fat and down to the bones. Insert the tip of the knife under the fat and flesh at one end, then – cutting close to the bones and working towards the tips of the bones – carefully cut away the fat and meat to expose the ends of the bones. With the tip of the knife, cut away the small pieces of fatty meat from between the bones. Clean the bones by scraping away any remaining pieces of fat and meat with the knife.

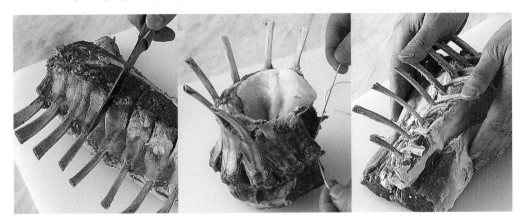

▲ **A crown roast** Carefully cut away the chine bone (backbone) from the thick end of the rack. Then make a small incision between each rib bone to enable the rack to curve. Place the two racks side by side on the worktop, with the bones facing upwards and the thick eye of the meat at the base. Curve them round, with the fat side inside, to make a neat crown shape.

▲ To secure, tie string around the middle of the bones. The centre may be left open or filled with your favourite stuffing. Or, roll up the strips of meat removed from the top of the bone and place in the centre (remove before serving).

▲ **A guard of honour** Prepare two racks of lamb as for the crown roast, but expose 7.5–10 cm (3–4 in) of the bones. Then join the two racks together with the bones interlocking – with their fat-sides to the outside. Next tie the racks together at intervals with clean, thin kitchen string. If wished, the cavity can be filled with a stuffing mixture or aromatic vegetables (such as garlic and onions) and herbs.

lamb

Cut	Description	Cooking methods
Scrag end and middle neck	Although fatty, both have a good rich flavour and are traditionally used for making Irish stew. They require long, slow cooking to make them tender. Both are sold whole, sliced or cut into pieces. Middle neck is also cut into chops	Stew or braise
Neck fillet	A boneless strip of meat cut from the scrag and middle neck. Good flavour	Marinate and use for kebabs, stew or braise
Best end of neck	An expensive, tender cut. Although known as best end of neck, this cut comes from the top, rib end of the loin	Roast
Neck cutlets	When cut into chops, they are known as best end of neck cutlets	Pan-fry or grill
Racks	This is the cut used for making guard of honour and crown roast, which are both made with a pair of racks. Each rack usually has seven cutlets	Roast
Noisettes	Round slices, about 2.5 cm (1 in) thick, cut from a boneless, rolled and tied best end	Grill or pan-fry
Loin cuts Saddle	A whole pair of loins, cut from the best end to the legs. It also includes the fillet, the most tender meat of a lamb. When cut without the chump end, it is known as a short saddle; with the chump, it is a long saddle. Perfect for a special occasion	Roast
Chops	Loin chops: with 'T' bone. Chump chops: with small round bone	Grill, pan-fry, braise, barbecue. Can also be casseroled
Butterfly chops	Double loin chops, left joined by the backbone	As above
Noisettes	Can also be cut from a rolled boneless loin, but are larger than those cut from a best end of neck	Grill or pan-fry
Breast	A long thin strip from the loin. Usually sold ready-boned. Two breasts, laid slightly overlapping, are preferable when stuffing and rolling into a roasting joint	Roast
Shoulder	Is sold whole or cut into two, to provide blade end, and knuckle end. Can be boned and stuffed	Roast, grill or braise
Leg	Sold whole, or cut into two smaller joints – the fillet end, and the shank end. When boned and cut into small cubes, can be used to make moussaka in the traditional way	Roast, braise or barbecue if boned. Can be spit-roasted
Gigot chops	Leg can also be cut into round steaks known as 'gigot chops'	Barbecue, grill, pan-fry or braise
Shank ends	Small joints cut from the end of the leg. Each is just sufficient to serve one person	Braise slowly for 3 hours

PREPARING LAMB FOR STUFFING

Apart from the scrag end and middle neck of lamb, all other cuts can be stuffed in one way or another. The stuffing can be inserted into a simple pocket cut in the eye of the meat, in chops; spread over and rolled up with a boneless best end or loin, and when making noisettes; or used to fill larger cavities in a boned shoulder, leg or saddle of lamb. When stuffing a whole saddle of lamb with the chump end attached, it is best if the chump bones are left in as this makes for a neater presentation.

▶ **Tunnel boning** Remove excess fat from the outside of the leg, and cut through the tendons at the base of the shank. Cut around the pelvic bone at the other end, and through the tendons. Remove the bone. Scrape flesh from shank bone, cut tendons at leg joint and remove shank bone.

▶ Next, with the tip of the knife, cut around the top of the leg bone to expose enough bone that you can get hold of it. Holding the bone tightly with one hand, work the knife carefully all the way round and down the bone until it can be twisted and pulled free.

▶ **Stuffing** Spoon chosen stuffing into the cavity in the leg, and pack it in neatly with your fingers (not too tightly, though, as it will expand during cooking). Tie the joint neatly with string and roast or braise.

NOISETTES

From a best end of neck of lamb you will get about six noisettes. Cut away the chine bone, then carefully remove each rib bone by cutting along each side, then underneath with the tip of the knife. The closer you cut to the bone, the more meat will be left. Roll up the boned joint, with the fat side outside, and tie securely with separate pieces of string, spaced evenly at 2.5 cm (1 in) intervals. Slice between the string into neat rounds about 2.5–5 cm (1–2 in) thick.

Recipes

Garlic and rosemary scented roast leg of lamb A variation on the classic roast in which the lamb is flavoured with sprigs of rosemary, slivers of garlic and red wine gravy.

Irish stew Onions and potatoes layered in a flavourful broth, with pearl barley.

Lancashire hotpot Lamb pieces cooked with leeks, carrots and potatoes and flavoured with Worcester sauce.

Moussaka Common in Greece and Turkey, this is made from layers of aubergine and lamb cooked in a cheese sauce.

BUTTERFLIED LEG OF LAMB

Butterflying lamb flattens it out for more even cooking. Using a sharp boning knife, cut through the meat, fat-side down, to expose the bone. Carefully cut along and round the bone until you come to the knee joint.

Holding the freed part of the bone, work around the knee joint with the tip of the knife until it becomes free. Then continue until the whole leg bone is free. To open it out more evenly, cut down but not quite the whole way through the centre of the larger muscle, and open out like a book. Trim away excess fat.

pork

As pigs are now bred to be leaner, modern-day pork needs to be treated very carefully if it is to remain juicy and succulent – as the old rule of cooking pork until well-done, to make it safe to eat, would now render it dry and tough. Due to the virtual eradication of trichinosis, it is now perfectly safe to eat pork slightly pink – at an internal temperature of 77°C (170°F) for large joints, such as leg of pork; 67°C (153°F) for smaller cuts. This means pork does not have to be cooked for so long, particularly when roasting and grilling. But care must still be taken to ensure that pork is properly cooked to the temperatures given above to make absolutely sure there is no chance of food poisoning from undercooked meat.

STORING

The rules for storing pork are the same as those for beef, see page 82.

Although pork can be frozen, it is not considered worthwhile as the meat does not really benefit from freezing: the meat tends to harden. However, cooked dishes made with pork – such as stews and casseroles – do freeze well.

Pork cut	Description	Cooking methods
Neck end	The upper part of the shoulder rib (not to be confused with spare ribs). Should have an even distribution of fat, and a larger ratio of lean meat. Spare rib is also cut into chops	Both can be roasted. The blade can be roasted on the bone or be boned, stuffed and rolled before roasting. Spare rib can be roasted, braised or stewed
Fore loin	A prime cut sold cut into chops or whole as a roasting joint. Can be made into a crown roast, or guard of honour – as for lamb (see page 89)	Roast whole. Pan-fry, grill, barbecue, roast or braise chops
Middle loin	Sold whole, or boned and rolled. Also cut into chops	Roast or braise. Ideal for stuffing. Grill, pan-fry, barbecue
Fillet (tenderloin)	Lies beneath the middle loin and the chump end	Roast whole, with or without stuffing. Can be sliced or cubed for pan-frying, braising or stir-frying
Chump end	Sold whole or cut into chops	Roast or braise whole. Grill, pan-fry, roast or braise chops
Leg	Sold whole, or cut into fillet end, knuckle end and trotters	Roast or braise whole or as separate joints. Smaller joints may be pot-roasted. Poach trotters
Belly	Sold rolled or cut into two – the thick end and thin end. Cut into thin slices Spare ribs are cut from the thick end of the belly	Roast or pot-roast. Grill, barbecue, stew slices Roast, glazed with rich sauce
Shoulder	When sold whole is known as hand and spring Can also be sold boned and rolled, or cut into cubes	Roast or braise Stew or casserole

Choosing

If possible, buy organically raised pork as these pigs are reared less intensively and are allowed to range freely outside in natural conditions. They are also moved regularly to new ground – so that they are less susceptible to infestation – and are fed on a diet of organically grown food of plant origin. Because they are reared outdoors, organically raised pigs are a different breed to those raised in factory-like conditions. And, because they are outdoors and have to adapt to different weather conditions, they build up more fat. But although organically raised pork is more likely to have a larger proportion of fat, its flavour will be better.

Overall, pork has only a small percentage of fat to meat. The fat is smoother than that of beef and lamb – and should look opaque and be white in colour.

The skin (rind) should be hairless, smooth and pliable. The flesh should be firm, smooth and moist, but not wet – and be pale pink in colour. The bones should be tinged with red and cleanly cut with no splinters. If the flesh is coarse-textured, and the bones are white and hard – it is an indication that the meat has come from an older animal.

All cuts should be neatly trimmed. Those that are rolled and tied should be of an approximately even thickness, so that they will cook evenly.

TO STUFF A BONED LOIN

A butcher will bone a loin of pork for you, but it is very easy to do yourself if you follow the technique for preparing a crown roast of lamb on page 89.

Open the boned loin out flat, flesh-side up, and cut two lengthwise slits in the meat, while taking care not to cut right through.

Insert your chosen stuffing in the slits and season the meat well with salt and pepper (shown here, sage leaves with apricots soaked in white wine). Then season the meat, roll up and tie securely with string.

TO STUFF PORK CHOPS

With a sharp knife, cut away most of the fat from the chop. Then, insert the tip of the knife through the fat-side into the centre of the meat. Next, keeping the knife horizontal to the bone, cut a pocket in the meat.

Spoon your chosen stuffing into the pocket and press the edges firmly together. If wished, the opening can be secured by tying the chop with clean, thin kitchen string.

PREPARING PORK FILLET

Lean, tender and quick to cook, boneless pork fillet (also known as tenderloin) is a favourite for stir-frying and Chinese dishes. It can also be cut into medallions for pan-frying, into cubes for kebabs or be grilled, roasted or braised whole, with or without a stuffing. The fat, membrane and tendon must always be removed before preparing and cooking a pork fillet.

Trimming off excess fat

When fat is removed from pork cuts, it does mean that there is little left to baste and nourish the meat as it cooks. To compensate, pork can be marinated, or brushed with healthier fat such as olive oil, which is high in polyunsaturates, that actually help to reduce cholesterol. Alternatively, fill it with a stuffing which will not only flavour the meat, but also help to keep it moist from the inside.

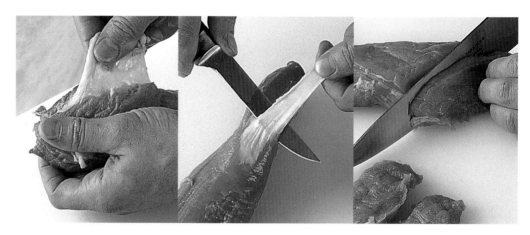

▲ **To prepare a fillet**
Carefully pull away any fat and membrane from the fillet and discard. Insert the tip of the knife just beneath the end of the tough white tendon and sinew and free a piece large enough to hold.

▲ Holding the tendon taut with one hand, carefully cut it away from the fillet, while keeping the blade of the knife as close to the tendon as possible.

▲ **Cutting noisettes**
Cutting diagonally, cut the tenderloin into slices, roughly 1–2 cm (½–¾ in) thick. Toss them lightly in seasoned flour, and shake off the excess, before pan-frying in butter and oil.

STRIPS FOR STIR-FRYING

Cut thin slices of pork fillet as above, then cut each one into thin strips and put into a bowl. Add your chosen marinade and leave to marinate at room temperature for 1–2 hours or overnight in the refrigerator. To stir-fry, drain pork well and fry in batches in a wok or large frying pan – in hot groundnut oil – until it is lightly browned. Don't fry too many strips at one time as this may cause the pork to steam, rather than fry.

Recipes

Normandy pork Pork fillet cooked with white wine, apple and mushrooms and served in a Calvados and cream sauce.

Barbecued spare ribs Baby back ribs coated with a thick barbecue glaze and roasted in the oven.

Sweet and sour pork Balls of minced pork fried until golden and served with a pineapple, vinegar and sugar sauce.

Pork steaks with gorgonzola Seasoned pork steaks fried with white wine, shallots, garlic, cream and Gorgonzola.

Roast pork with fennel, garlic and apple Loin of pork, smeared with a fennel and garlic paste and roasted with an onion and apple mixture.

Chunky pâté with port and peppercorns Made with belly of pork and chicken, duck, bacon and peppercorns with a port and gelatine glaze.

CRISPY CRACKLING

For perfect, crisp crackling, dry the skin with kitchen roll and, if necessary, remove any remaining hairs (by singing, or with an unused, disposable razor). Score through the skin at regular intervals to the fat below using a very sharp knife. Rub the skin with a little olive oil and generously with fine salt. Roast on a rack in a roasting tin, but do not baste.

TESTING FOR DONENESS

To check that pork chops and other small cuts are cooked through, insert the tip of a small, sharp knife into the centre to allow some of the juices to flow out. If they run clear, the meat is cooked. If there are any traces of pink, continue cooking until it is done.

Larger joints should be roasted with a meat thermometer inserted into the thickest part, but be sure to avoid any bones as this would affect the reading. Check temperature frequently and remove the roast from the oven when it reaches 2°C (35.5°F) below the desired doneness. Loosely cover with foil and allow to stand for 10–15 minutes, during which the meat will continue to cook within its own heat.

IMPRESSIVE PRESENTATIONS

Twin racks of fore loin of pork can be made into a crown roast or a guard of honour (using the same techniques as those shown for best end of neck of lamb – see page 89). Both are perfect dishes for a dinner party or special celebration, particularly when roasted filled with a delicious stuffing and elegantly presented surrounded with carefully prepared vegetables such as sautéed cherry tomatoes and courgettes, as shown here.

NUTRITIONAL INFORMATION

Pork is rich in protein, minerals and B vitamins – particularly thiamin (vitamin B_1), which is essential for the release of energy from carbohydrate foods.

ham and bacon

Although all these meats come from the pig, each has its own totally different characteristics. Ham is the hind leg of a pig, removed from a side of pork and preserved separately, either by drying, salting or smoking – or by a combination of these. Hams can be bought in different forms. Whole and raw, ready for cooking, ready cooked or cured and air-dried, to be eaten raw (such as Parma, Bayonne and Westphalian ham). The very best British hams are those still preserved by the old traditional methods – York, Suffolk and Wiltshire hams, for instance. Cooked and air-dried hams can be bought, cut to order, from the delicatessen counter in most supermarkets. They are also available pre-packed and ready sliced.

Gammon also comes from the hind leg of the pig – but it is cured in brine while still attached to a side of pork. After brining, the leg is removed and may be processed further (if it is to be sold as smoked gammon) by drying and smoking.

Bacon comes from the main body of the pig. The flavour varies according to the curing ingredients and the wood used during the smoking process. When cured in brine and matured, it is known as 'green' or unsmoked bacon. It is lighter in colour than smoked bacon, has a more delicate flavour and has a white rind. Smoked bacon is, after being cured in brine, processed further by drying and smoking – which gives it its distinctive dark colour, flavour and a pale brown rind. Streaky bacon and Pancetta are fatty cuts taken from the belly of the pig, and are ideal for wrapping or covering meat or fish prior to roasting. Stretch fatty bacon before use to reduce shrinkage.

Choosing

The flesh on all bacon and gammon cuts should be firm and moist, but not wet. The fat should be white to pale brown, with no yellow or green tinges.

COOKING TO PERFECTION

When larger joints of bacon, gammon and hams are cooked in water, they are often referred to as being boiled. However, if a joint of bacon, gammon or ham is to remain sweet, tender and succulent, the water must never be allowed to boil. Simply immerse in cold water and heat until the water just starts to ripple. Then, immediately reduce the heat and allow to simmer for 15 minutes per 450 g (1 lb). When the time is up, remove the pan from the heat and allow the joint to cool in the water.

Large hams and gammon

Unless you have an extremely large cooking pot, cooking a whole ham or gammon can be a problem. However, they both cook extremely well in the oven, wrapped in foil to keep the meat moist. Even better, you can wrap and seal the meat in a plain flour and water dough – an old traditional method which preserves all the flavour and moisture. Cooked by this method, a 6.3 kg (14 lb) ham will take approximately 3 hours in a moderate oven.

STORING

Originally, pork was cured to enable it to be kept for long periods without refrigeration. But today, the curing processes only allow bacon and gammon to be kept for a maximum of two weeks, but preferably should be used within seven days. Store, covered, in the refrigerator. Pre-packed rashers and joints should be stored as instructed on the label. Once opened, they should be used quickly.

Large whole pieces of cooked ham will keep for up to ten days, but always follow instructions on the label if bought vacuum-packed. To prevent drying out, wrap closely with clingfilm, or put on a plate and cover with an up-turned bowl.

Sliced ham, bought from the delicatessen counter, should be used within 1–2 days. Pre-packed ham should be eaten as soon as possible after opening – or as instructed on the label.

Bacon or ham cut	Description	Cooking methods
End collar, middle collar, prime collar	These come from the frontal part of the pig	All can be poached or roasted. Collar joints, although slightly fattier, have a good flavour. End and middle collar are both good for soups especially when added to dried, green pea soup
Fore hock, fore slipper, butt, small hock	From the front leg	Baking and poaching
Bacon rashers	From the back (the top of the loin) and from the flank (the belly)	Grill or fry
Top back rashers	From the back	
Middle cut	Also known as through cut, and include some streaky. Also sold whole as a small joint	
Short back rashers	From the back	
Oyster cut rashers	Also sold as a small joint	
Long back rashers	From the back	
Streaky rashers	From the belly. Can be bought as a piece, or in rashers	Green and smoked streaky bacon are very good for larding and barding. Thick strips cut from a piece of streaky make especially good lardons
Gammon cuts	Can be bought whole or as small joints: corner gammon, middle gammon or hock	Poach or bake wrapped in foil
Gammon rashers	From the hind leg	Grill or pan-fry

MAKING LARDONS

Used in cooking as a flavouring ingredient, small pieces of bacon impart a strong, often salty, taste to meat dishes. Cut thick rashers lengthwise into strips. Stack the strips and cut crosswise into dice.

FINISHING TOUCHES

Before serving, all joints of bacon, gammon and ham, be they hot or cold, must have their skin removed – or they would be difficult to carve. As the fat below the skin is less than attractive, it can be enhanced by simply sprinkling with browned breadcrumbs, finely chopped parsley or other herbs. Alternatively, give it an attractive glaze.

▲ **Scoring the fat** with the tip of a sharp knife in a diamond pattern allows the glaze to penetrate and flavour the meat.

▲ **Spread the glaze** evenly over the scored fat using a palette knife. Let the glaze seep into the meat before cooking.

ham and bacon

offal

A collective name for the edible parts of an animal remaining after the carcass has been cut into joints, offal is mainly internal organs such as the heart, kidneys, liver and tongue, but also includes external parts such as the feet and head.

Choosing

While supermarkets sell only a limited selection, a good butcher should be able to supply all types. As offal perishes more quickly than any other meat, it is best cooked and eaten on the day it is bought – particularly sweetbreads.

All offal should look and smell absolutely fresh. Do not buy any that smells strong and unpleasant, or has a greenish colour and slimy surface. Liver, kidneys and hearts should have a bright, glossy shine and no dry patches. Sweetbreads should have a pearly sheen, and be pinkish-white in colour.

NUTRITIONAL INFORMATION

Liver and kidneys are a very rich source of protein and minerals and, unlike the carcass meat, are also rich in vitamin A and folic acid. However, both do contain high levels of cholesterol. Both ox and calf's liver are extremely rich in iron.

STORING

Once purchased, offal must be taken home quickly and be put straight into the refrigerator. Pre-packed offal should be left in the packaging, and the use-by date be stringently adhered to. All offal bought loose should be unwrapped, put onto a clean plate and be covered with an upturned bowl or clingfilm.

PREPARING LIVER

Carefully insert the tip of a small, sharp knife under one corner of the fine membrane that covers the liver, freeing enough to get hold of. Carefully peel away and discard the membrane. Whether cooking whole or sliced, remove any large tubes from the liver. This is much easier when the liver is sliced. If slicing, cut about 5 mm (¼ in) thick.

Type	Description and cooking methods
Liver	
Calf's	Light brown, delicately flavoured. Roast whole, or slice and pan-fry or grill
Chicken's	Delicate and mild in flavour. Sauté in butter, or use for pâtés
Pig's	Soft in texture, yet stronger in flavour than calf's and lamb's. Pan-fry or grill
Lamb's	Light brown liver comes from young lambs. Any that is dark in colour will have come from an older animal, and will have a stronger flavour
Tongue	
Ox	Requires long, gentle boiling to make tender. Skin and bone before pressing or serving
Lamb's	Soak in lightly salted water before cooking in boiling water or braising
Heart	
Ox, calf's, lamb's or pig's	All, even the smaller lambs' hearts, require long slow cooking to make them tender
Sweetbreads	
Calf's or lamb's	Elongated, connected glands that form the thymus gland, found in the throat. Calf's sweetbreads are the most delicate. Both can be sautéed, deep-fried, or lightly braised
Kidney	
Ox	Strongest flavour. Best cooked with stewing or braising steak in pies and stews
Calf's or pig's	Fry or grill. Its strong flavour makes it good for pâtés and terrines
Lamb's	The best for pan-frying and grilling

STORING

As they contain preservatives, pre-packed sausages from a supermarket keep longer than home-made sausages or those made by a butcher (which should preferably be used on the day they are bought or made).

Store pre-packed sausages wrapped, in the coldest part of the refrigerator, and use by the date specified on the packet.

Sausage casings

Most sausages are made by forcing the sausage meat mixture into casings, which can be natural (the cleaned intestines of a pig, lamb or ox) or manufactured. However, casings are not entirely essential as the sausage meat can be shaped and lightly floured before cooking, or be hand-wrapped in pig's caul. Sausages made by this method are known as crepinettes after the French word for caul – crepine.

The majority of sausages are made with pork, but an ever-increasing variety of other meats are now being used. As well as traditional pork and beef sausages, you can also buy sausages made from lamb, veal, venison, wild boar, chicken and turkey as well as combinations of these. Soya-based vegetarian sausages, and black pudding – a sausage made with pig's blood – are also available.

Whether bought or home-made, sausages consist of coarsely or finely ground meat mixed with fat and seasonings, ranging in flavour from mild to hot and spicy. Herbs are also used to flavour sausages, particularly sage, as are other slightly more exotic ingredients such as wild mushrooms, red peppers, spinach, onion and apple.

COOKING BOUGHT SAUSAGES

Most sausages, particularly English ones, can be fried or grilled, but there are others that are specifically made for poaching, such as German Frankfurters, Bockwurst and Knackwurst, French andouille, cervelat and boudin blanc, and Scotland's famous haggis (although not sausage-shaped, haggis is regarded as a type of sausage).

When frying or grilling Cumberland sausage, secure the coil with bamboo or metal skewers to stop it uncoiling during cooking.

▲ **Poaching** Two-thirds fill a wide shallow saucepan or frying pan with water and bring to the boil. Then add the sausages and cook for 35 minutes, depending on their size. Frankfurters, as shown here, only require 1–2 minutes.

▲ **Frying and grilling** As there is a risk of splitting if they are cooked at too high a temperature, sausages should be pierced and then cooked over a moderate heat if frying and not too near the grill if grilling. Most sausages take about 10 minutes to fry or grill.

offal and sausages

cured meats

Curing is a process that uses salt to retard the growth of bacteria. It was originally used to preserve pork, but is now more to enhance the flavour and texture of meat. Traditional methods include dry-curing, where salt and spices are rubbed into the meat, and soaking the meat in a brine and spice solution. Quicker modern methods include injecting a brine solution into meat, but meats cured this way are not of the same quality – hence the high cost of traditionally cured meats. After being cured with salt, the meat is dried or smoked or both, to give it both colour and flavour.

These delicious meats and sausages range in flavour from those that are mildly flavoured, such as Italian Parma ham and mortadella, to those that are either garlicky or hot and spicy or both, like chorizo (from Spain), which owes its deep red colour and fiery taste to hot paprika.

Most cured meats and sausages are made from pork but some, such as Italian bresaola, are made from beef, or a mixture of pork and beef, as is keilbasa (from Poland). Their textures also range from fine and smooth, like mortadella, to those that are more coarse, like German Bierwurst.

Meat	Description
From Italy Bresaola	Lean and tender beef, salted and air-dried. Expensive, as its curing process is long
Mortadella	Also known as Bologna in Italy. One of the largest, and most famous Italian sausages. Contains large chunks of fat and black peppercorns, and sometimes pistachio nuts. The best is made with pure pork
Pastrami	Brisket of beef, dry-cured with a mixture of sugar, spices and garlic, then smoked
Pepperoni	Has a deep red colour, due to being flavoured with red pepper, as well as fennel. A popular topping for pizza
Salami	Numerous types made from coarsely minced pork and pork fat. Some have beef and veal included. Flavoured with spices, garlic, paprika and peppercorns
Prosciutto (Parma ham)	True Parma ham comes from the area around the town of Parma, in the region of Emilia-Romagna. San Daniele hams come from the region of Friuli
Pancetta	Salted raw belly of pork
From Germany Bierschinken	Made with pork and ham and contains pistachio nuts and peppercorns
Bierwurst	Is made with pork and beef. Highly seasoned with cardamom and juniper berries
Landjager	Made with beef and pork, and flavoured with caraway seeds and garlic, this sausage is air-dried or smoked
From Spain Chorizo	Pork, brilliant red paprika, garlic, spices, herbs and other seasonings
From Poland Kabanos	A long, thin, spicy smoked sausage

Choosing

When buying, always make sure that the meats or sausages look fresh. If they appear dry, and are curling up at the edges, don't buy. If bought ready sliced and in sealed packaging, store unopened until ready to use – and use them by the date given on the packet.

STORING

Salami, kabanos, chorizo, saucisson and Parma ham will all keep longer if bought whole, or in large pieces, and kept refrigerated and sliced as and when needed. However, when bought ready sliced they will deteriorate quite quickly and should be used within two days. Keep them wrapped in clingfilm, in the refrigerator.

poultry and game

chicken

Chicken is an excellent, cheap source of protein, and contains most of the B vitamins. It is also low in fat, particularly saturated fat. Today we have a wider choice of chicken than ever before, though for traditional quality and flavour, the more expensive organically reared chicken is the best. We can choose not only from fresh or frozen whole birds and portions but also between standard, free-range and organically reared chicken. How chicken is reared and fed ultimately determines how it tastes. So, before buying, take a little time to consider the options.

Standard chickens are reared in purpose-built chicken houses, on a floor covered with deep litter wood shavings or straw, where they are free to move around and have constant access to food and water. Free-range chickens fall into three different categories: free-range, traditional free-range and free-range total freedom. The main differences between them are the amount of space allocated to the birds when indoors and outdoors. Those with total freedom have access to the outside without being fenced into a restricted space.

Organically reared chickens will have been fed on a diet of organically grown food of plant origin, and most will have had total freedom.

Choosing

Select birds that are plump and neat in shape, with meaty breasts. The skin should be clean and look moist, but not wet; this is a sign that the bird may have been frozen. Also, the skin should not be bruised or blemished in any way. Occasionally, when unwrapped, a fresh chicken may have quite a strong chickeny odour but this should disappear quite quickly once it comes into contact with the air. However, should it not go away, return the bird to the shop where it was bought. Make sure that all packaging on fresh or frozen birds is fully intact.

Roasting chicken Small sizes are 1.3–1.8 kg (3–4 lb), and will serve four people. Larger sizes are 1.8–2.75 kg (4–6 lb), and serve six people.

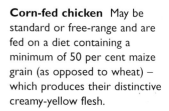

Corn-fed chicken May be standard or free-range and are fed on a diet containing a minimum of 50 per cent maize grain (as opposed to wheat) – which produces their distinctive creamy-yellow flesh.

Poussin Four to six week old baby chickens. They weigh up to 450 g (1 lb) each and will serve one person.

STORING

Once bought, take your chicken home as quickly as possible after buying and store in the fridge, or in the freezer if frozen. Use by the date given on the label, or, if bought unpacked from a butcher, use within one to two days.

Unwrap and place a whole chicken on a rack or upturned saucer, on a plate to catch any juices which seep out. Cover with a large, upturned bowl. Chickens and chicken portions, minced, cubed and stir-fry strips in sealed, controlled atmosphere packs should not be removed from the pack until you are ready to use them.

Giblets should be stored, covered, in a separate bowl. Use within 24 hours.

Store in the coldest part of the refrigerator, usually towards the bottom or directly under the freezer compartment.

Before cooking, rinse the cavity well under a cold running tap and pat dry with kitchen roll.

Cooked chicken can be kept, covered, in the refrigerator for two to three days.

Thawing chicken

The safest way to thaw frozen chicken (and all other poultry) is slowly in the refrigerator, as the cold slows down the growth of bacteria. Leave chicken in its original wrappings, but puncture in one or two places to allow any liquid to flow out. Place on a rack, or upturned saucer, on a large plate to catch any drips. Thaw for about 12 hours per kg (2¼ lb) for whole birds, overnight for pieces and portions.

MASTERING THE SIMPLE ART OF JOINTING

Make a deep incision down the centre of the breast, right through to the bone. Keeping as close to the bone as possible, carefully cut away the flesh from one side of the breast bone, cutting it free around the wing where it is joined to the main carcass. Repeat on the other side of the bird.

Cut the leg, the thigh and the wing free from the main carcass. If you wish, you can also separate the thigh bone from the drumstick by cutting through the joint connecting them.

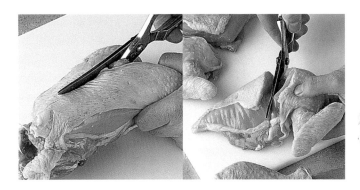

Wing **Breast**

Drumstick **Thigh**

HOME-FREEZING

• If pre-packed, remove wrappings and re-wrap tightly in fresh clingfilm and foil or put into a strong polythene bag, extract the air and seal. Set freezer to coldest setting or fast freeze.
• Chicken cuts and portions packed in sealed, controlled atmosphere packs can be frozen in the pack.
• Any giblets should be removed, washed and dried, and frozen separately.

FOOD SAFETY

Chicken can carry salmonella bacteria, therefore it is necessary to take extra care when handling it and cooking with it.
• Always wash hands before and after dealing with raw chicken, and especially before handling other food.
• Scrub boards, clean worksurfaces and wash all utensils after preparing raw chicken.
• Never cut cooked meats or prepare salads on a board after preparing raw chicken.
• In the refrigerator, store raw chicken below all other foods that are to be eaten uncooked or cold.
• Allow cooked chicken and chicken dishes to cool completely before covering and refrigerating or freezing.
• Do not reheat chicken more than once.

POULTRY SHEARS

The strong serrated blades and spring-loaded mechanism of poultry shears makes light work of jointing a chicken. After using shears, wash them well in hot soapy water, dry well and close with the loop that holds the blades together.

chicken

PREPARING THIGH MEAT

The darker meat of chicken thighs is more flavoursome than the white breast meat. Thighs are economical to buy and are perfect for stews and casseroles. They can also be boned out and used for making kebabs

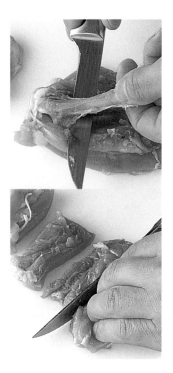

◄ Remove the skin. Place the thigh, skinned-side down, on a chopping board and expose one end of the thigh bone by cutting around it with the tip of a knife. Lift the bone and scrape away the flesh.

◄ Cut the meat into large cubes, removing any pieces of sinew. For kebabs, marinate for 1–2 hours or overnight. When ready to cook, thread the marinated chicken onto skewers, alternating with vegetables, such as pieces of red pepper and small mushrooms.

Cook's tip

If keeping leg and thigh portions whole, to ensure that they maintain a neat shape during cooking, pull the skin back a little to expose the flesh at the knee joint. Make a cut about 1 cm (½ in) deep, between the two bones. Re-cover the flesh with the skin and tuck the portion into a neat 'U' shape; the cut will prevent the flesh expanding as it cooks.

CHICKEN SUPREMES

These are skinless, boneless chicken breasts. Remove the skin from a chicken breast simply by pulling it away from the meat with your fingers. Discard the skin and the membrane that comes away with it. If using a bought chicken breast on the bone, cut the flesh away with a sharp boning knife. Remove the tendons and place the breast on a chopping board, skinned-side up, and trim any fat from the edges. If necessary, also trim any ragged edges.

REMOVING TENDONS FROM A CHICKEN BREAST

There are two tendons in a chicken breast, one in the small fillet and one in the main breast. Although it is not essential to remove these tendons, it does make the breast more pleasant to eat. Also, they can cause the meat to curl up as they contract during cooking. Gently pull the small fillet away from underneath the breast. Insert the tip of a sharp knife under the end of the tendon and free enough to hold. Then gently scrape the knife along the tendon until it is free. Remove the larger tendon in the same way, using a knife or cleaver.

PREPARING ESCALOPES

Escalopes can be plain, or coated with breadcrumbs. Pan-fry them in butter and oil or marinate and chargrill them in a ridged frying pan. For anyone who does not eat veal, chicken escalopes are the perfect alternative for making schnitzels.

► Remove the skin and tendons from the breast. Leave small breasts whole. Cut larger breasts in half horizontally to make two escalopes. Place between two sheets of baking parchment or clingfilm and pound evenly until flattened to about 1 cm (½ in).

► **For schnitzels** Coat the escalopes with flour, beaten egg and breadcrumbs. Mark a criss-cross pattern in the coating with the back of a knife, then shallow fry in butter and olive oil over a moderate heat for 2–3 minutes each side.

Recipes

Coq au vin Whole or jointed chicken flamed with brandy and then cooked in a rich red wine sauce with mushrooms and onions.

Chicken Kiev Chicken breast fillets stuffed with garlic-infused butter, rolled in breadcrumbs and fried. The butter melts during cooking and flows out when the breast is cut.

Chicken korma Chicken breast fillets cooked in ghee with onion, garlic, spices and a creamy yogurt sauce.

Southern fried chicken with corn fritters Chicken drumsticks rolled in spices and flour and deep-fried until crisp and brown. Served with corn fritters and tomato salsa.

Chicken puff pie Leftover or freshly cooked chicken, gammon or ham mixed with vegetables in a cream cheese sauce, topped with flaky puff pastry and baked.

STUFFING CHICKEN

Whole chicken, breasts and fillets can be transformed into something quite sensational simply by filling the cavity with a stuffing or adding the stuffing to a pocket made in breasts or fillets (see page 24).

MAKING SATAY

Satay are small kebabs made with long strips of chicken breast, marinated and threaded onto soaked bamboo skewers and grilled. Traditionally served with peanut sauce.

▶ Cut chicken breasts into long, thin slices, working diagonally across the grain. Marinate for 1–2 hours, or preferably overnight. Soak bamboo skewers in water for 30 minutes.

▶ Thread the marinated chicken strips onto the skewers, twisting them into a spiral pattern. Cook under a very hot grill for no more than 4–5 minutes, turning and basting them frequently with the remaining marinade. If overcooked, the chicken will become dry.

MAKING GOOD USE OF THE DRUMSTICKS

Because they have have a higher fat content than the breast meat, which bastes them from the inside and keeps the meat moist and tender, chicken drumsticks (and thighs) are especially suited to barbecuing. An oil-based marinade will not only flavour and crisp the skin, it will also prevent the drumsticks from sticking to the rack.

Place the drumsticks on a large plate. Prepare a marinade of your choice and brush it all over the drumsticks until they are evenly coated (slashing through the skin and into the meat will help the marinade penetrate deeper). Cover and leave to marinate at room temperature for 1 hour (if it is very hot, then marinate in the refrigerator).

Cook the drumsticks on a rack, in a grill pan, 6 cm (2½ in) below a hot grill or on a rack 15 cm (6 in) above white-hot coals on the barbecue for 15–20 minutes. Turn and baste them frequently with any remaining marinade.

turkey

Once only available at Christmas, turkey can now be bought all year round, both fresh and frozen, whole, cut into joints, boned, minced, diced and cut into stir-fry strips. Whole birds range in weight from 2.75 kg (6 lb) to a massive 18 kg (40 lb). The most popular size is 4.5–6 kg (10–13.5 lb).

Choosing

Whole birds should be plump with well rounded breasts and legs. The skin should be white with a slight creamy-yellow tinge, moist but not wet, and be unblemished.

For quality, well-flavoured birds, choose free-range turkeys and organically reared, free-range turkeys (which are not treated with antibiotics). Look out for Norfolk Black and Cambridge Bronze as these are the juiciest and have the most flavour. These birds are also hung and dry-plucked in the traditional way.

STORING

Store fresh and frozen turkeys – whole birds, joints and prepacked pieces – as instructed for chicken on page 102. Thaw frozen birds at room temperature for 4–6 hours per kg (2¼ lb), or slowly in the refrigerator for 10–12 hours per kg (2¼ lb). Also, see Food Safety on page 103.

Cook's tip

Before cooking a turkey, it is important to rinse the cavity under a cold running tap to flush out any blood and moisture which could contain bacteria. After rinsing, pat the turkey dry with kitchen paper and remove any remaining feather ends with a pair of tweezers.

TRUSSING

To keep turkeys in a neat shape during cooking, the legs and wings should be trussed (tied) into position before cooking. This can be done simply by inserting metal skewers or with a large trussing needle and clean kitchen string.

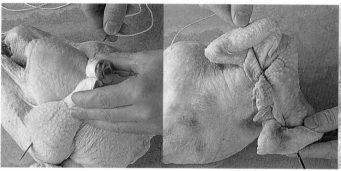
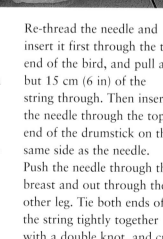
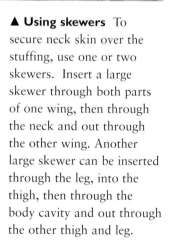

▲ **Using a needle and thread** Insert the needle through the thickest part of the drumstick. Push through the body and out the other leg, pulling through all but 15 cm (6 in) of the string. Fold the wing tips under the body and cover with the flap of skin from the neck. Thread the string through the wings and flap of skin. Both ends are now on the same side; tie them tightly and cut off the excess.

Re-thread the needle and insert it first through the tail end of the bird, and pull all but 15 cm (6 in) of the string through. Then insert the needle through the top end of the drumstick on the same side as the needle. Push the needle through the breast and out through the other leg. Tie both ends of the string tightly together with a double knot, and cut off any excess.

▲ **Using skewers** To secure neck skin over the stuffing, use one or two skewers. Insert a large skewer through both parts of one wing, then through the neck and out through the other wing. Another large skewer can be inserted through the leg, into the thigh, then through the body cavity and out through the other thigh and leg.

Boning a Turkey Breast

▶ Hold the knife almost flat against the bone and rib-cage, then gently cut and scrape meat away, pulling it off in one piece. Discard the bones. Remove the skin gently cutting away the white tendon.

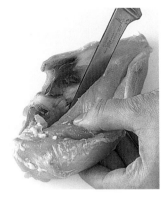

Giblets

Any giblets sold with the bird should be removed as soon as you get the turkey home, then rinsed under a cold running tap and dried. Store in a covered bowl in the refrigerator for up to 24 hours. Use the giblets, except the liver, to make stock for the gravy. Roughly chop the liver, sauté in butter and add to stuffing.

Stuffing a Turkey

Stuffing the cavity of larger birds is not recommended as it can prevent the heat from penetrating right through to the centre. Alternatively, to help keep the meat moist, and also to add flavour, aromatic flavourings, such as a peeled and quartered onion, a halved lemon, apple or orange, and herbs such as rosemary, thyme and parsley can be inserted into the body cavity before cooking.

▶ Stuffings can be put into the neck end of the bird, or inserted under the skin and spread over the breast. Slices of plain or flavoured butters can also be inserted under the skin to help keep the breast meat moist.

    Stuffings must be used cold, and should only be put into the turkey just before cooking.

Roasting to Perfection

There are many theories as to which is the best way to roast a turkey – on its breast, draped in muslin soaked in butter, or wrapped completely in foil, to name but a few. Generally speaking though, the old traditional methods of either quick or slow roasting on a rack, in a roasting tin, are still the best. However, the ultimate succulence and flavour of a turkey when it has been cooked is also largely determined by the quality of the bird itself.

▶ To help keep the bird moist during cooking, stuff the neck end and put some aromatic ingredients and herbs in the cavity (see below left). Weigh the bird, complete with stuffing, to allow you to calculate the cooking time (see page 37).

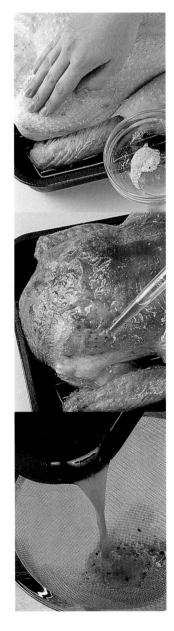

▶ Place the turkey on a rack in a roasting tin and smear the breast thickly with butter, or bard with rashers of streaky bacon. Baste frequently during cooking, and cover loosely with foil if over-browning.

▶ Once the turkey is cooked, carefully remove it from the roasting tin and put it onto a serving plate, loosely covered with foil. Leave to stand while making gravy (see page 35) with sieved drippings from the roasting pan. Standing allows the flesh to re-absorb its juices and makes carving the bird easier.

turkey

107

duck

There are several types of duck bred for the table, but most of the ones sold in the UK are a hybrid Lincolnshire duck, based on the white-feathered Peking duck. Other varieties include Nantes and Barbary duck imported from France. Nantes is a smaller duck, between 1.3–1.8 kg (3–4 lb), and has fine, delicately flavoured flesh. Barbary ducks have a stronger, more gamey flavour, and can be rather tough. English Aylesbury duck, in its original form, is no longer available, but hybrids descended from it are. The term 'duck' applies only to birds that are more than two months old; anything younger is 'duckling'. But it's not until a duck reaches its full grown size that its rich flavour can be fully appreciated, especially when roasted.

Choosing

Ducks and duckling are available all year round, fresh and frozen, sold whole, or pre-packed in halves, quarters or as breast meat only. Barbary duck breasts are usually sold vacuum packed. Ducks and duckling should have supple, waxy looking skin, with a dry appearance, and have a long body with tender, meaty breasts. If the feet are left on, they should be soft and supple. Duckling range from 1.6 to 1.8 kg (3½–4 lb) in weight and will serve two people; ducks range from 1.8 to 2.7 kg (4–6 lb) and will serve from two to four people.

STORING

Store fresh and frozen ducks as instructed for chicken on page 102. Thaw frozen birds as instructed for chicken, see page 103. Also, follow food safety information on page 103.

QUARTERING A DUCK

Because of its elongated shape, a duck does not cut into quite the same neat portions as chicken, and is therefore best cut into four pieces only. The joints can be roasted, braised or casseroled. Alternatively, you can use the joints to make duck confit.

- Cut off the wing tips (as shown for chicken on page 103) and remove the wish bone.
- Using poultry shears, cut through the centre of the breast bone, cutting from the tail to the neck.
- Open out the duck and, using poultry shears, cut along each side of the backbone to separate it into two halves.
- Cutting diagonally, divide each piece of duck in half.

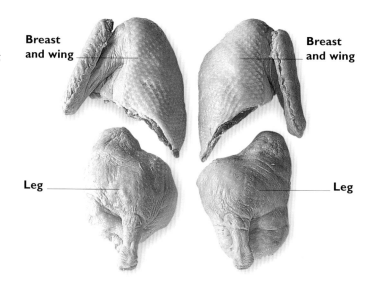

Breast and wing

Breast and wing

Leg

Leg

DUCK BREASTS

Duck breasts can be bought ready-cut, particularly Barbary duck breast. But it is more economical to prepare them yourself, which has the added advantage that you will also have the legs and thighs to use another day. You can roast or braise leg portions, or bone and skin them for stir-frying or making kebabs.

▲ Remove breasts from duck as instructed for chicken on page 103, leaving the skin on.

▲ If necessary, trim away any rough edges of skin from the breast, then remove the tendon with a boning knife, or a small, sharp pointed knife.

▲ Turn the breast over and score a diamond pattern in the skin, to help release the fat during cooking. Roast or pan-fry. Leave to rest, covered, then slice into thin, diagonal slices to serve.

Recipes

Duck and mango salad Duck breasts pan-fried with honey and spices, served with salad and a warm nutty, soy and rice wine sauce.

Roast duck with orange sauce Duckling stuffed with orange zest and thyme, served with a sweet orange sauce.

Duck with beetroot and red onion relish Roasted breast with an orange, ginger, wine, port and beetroot sauce.

Traditional roast duckling Served with an apple sauce and stuffing balls.

PREPARING DUCK FOR ROASTING

As duck is a fatty bird, some of its fat can be removed before cooking. Roasting on a rack will allow the excess fat to drip below as it cooks. Goose should also be prepared in the same way.

First, rinse the cavity of the bird well under cold running water and pat dry with kitchen paper. Then, place the duck breast-side up on a board and cut or pull away excess fat from the tail-end of the cavity.

Season the inside of the duck with salt and pepper, and some spice such as nutmeg or mace. Then place one or two bay leaves and some wedges of orange into the cavity.

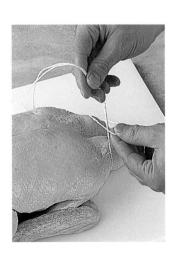

◄ Tie the tail and legs together with kitchen string. Place the bird with its breast-side up on rack in a medium-sized roasting tin.

► With a skewer, prick the skin in several places to allow the fat to drain during the cooking process.

PEKING DUCK

Crisply roasted duck – the skin removed and cut into small squares, the flesh shredded – is traditionally served accompanied with small, thin pancakes, sticks of cucumber, long, thin strips of spring onion and hoisin sauce. To eat, each diner takes a pancake and spoons on a little hoisin sauce, and then adds some duck skin and meat, cucumber and spring onion. Finally, the pancake is rolled up and eaten with chopsticks or with fingers.

CHAUDFROID DUCK

Chaudfroid is a cooked aspic covering that is left to set and chill on cooked meat. Pieces of fruit and vegetables are then placed on the aspic, to garnish.

► Whisk in 250 ml (8 fl oz) seasoned liquid aspic to 500 ml (17 fl oz) simmering, reduced stock until well blended. Leave to cool then ladle over cooked duck breast slices on a rack. Chill until set and repeat 3–4 times.

► Decorate cooled slices of duck with thin strips of blanched orange zest and pipings of pâté.

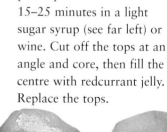

SALMIS OF DUCK

A salmis is traditionally a ragout or stew made from game but it can also be made with roast duck. A whole duck is roasted and then cut into serving portions, reheated in a rich sauce made with pan juices or with sautéed mushrooms. The duck is traditionally served garnished with croûtes of fried bread which are shaped into hearts or triangles.

DUCK GARNISHES

The rich flavour of duck is complemented by the tartness of sweetened apples, oranges and other fruit. Chaudfroid, a cooked aspic covering left to chill over the duck, can be further decorated (see above).

▼ **Caramelised orange** Cook orange slices briefly in a light sugar syrup – about 250 g (9 oz) sugar to 500 ml (17 fl oz) water until golden brown. Add parsley sprig to each centre.

▼ **Glazed apples** Unpeeled golden apple slices are sprinkled with caster sugar and grilled for 2–3 minutes until golden and bubbling.

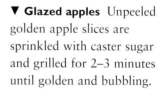

▼ **Poached pears** Peel and poach pears whole for 15–25 minutes in a light sugar syrup (see far left) or wine. Cut off the tops at an angle and core, then fill the centre with redcurrant jelly. Replace the tops.

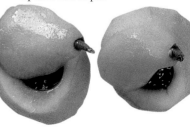

poultry and game

110

goose

The richest of all birds, goose was once traditionally eaten in Britain starting on Michaelmas Day (29 September), the time of year when geese are at their best, until the end of December. At Michaelmas, geese tend to weigh around 4.5–6.3 kg (10–14 lb), but will continue to grow until December when they will average around 8.2 kg (18 lb) – hence the old nursery rhyme, 'Christmas is coming, the goose is getting fat.'

Choosing

Goose is a fatty bird, with a large proportion of bone to its dark flesh. This means that even a fairly large bird will serve only six to eight people, and not very generously at that. Although fatty, the fat on a goose lies under the skin and not within the meat itself. As with duck, the fat melts during cooking and helps to flavour the flesh and keep it moist.

Not all supermarkets sell geese, and those that do sell mainly frozen birds. A good butcher is the best place to go as you will be able to examine the birds and choose the best – ideally a young bird. Distinguishing between young and old birds is easy. Young birds have soft yellow feet, and legs which still have a little down left on them. Older birds have drier, stiff webs.

A goose should also have a plump breast with a flexible backbone, a light-coloured waxy skin, and yellow fat in the body cavity. Although fresh geese are readily available over Christmas, it is best to order them in advance. Frozen geese can usually be bought fairly easily at other times of the year. The quality is generally good, as geese freeze well.

COOKING GOOSE

• Prepare for roasting as for duck on page 109.
• Cut into smaller pieces for braising, cooking en daube, or for confit – as shown for chicken on page 103.
• Some recipes advocate scalding a goose in boiling water before roasting to tighten the skin, in order that it will help to squeeze out the fat during cooking.
• Goose can be cooked in any way suitable for chicken, but more especially by any method used for turkey.
• Choose younger birds for roasting but older birds can be braised, used for cooking en daube or for confit.

Recipes

Roast goose with apples and prunes Seasoned goose roasted with a goose liver and port stuffing. Served with apple, prunes and wine.

Roast goose with sour cherry sauce Oven-ready goose stuffed with onion quarters, sliced carrot and celery and flavoured with bay leaves and thyme. Served with a smooth, glossy cherry sauce and topped with fresh cherries.

FOIE GRAS

One of the world's most luxurious foods, foie gras is the enlarged liver of a specially fattened goose or duck. Pâté de foie gras (right), a rich velvety smooth paste, was known to the Romans, who used various methods of fattening ducks and geese, 2000 years ago. The finest foie gras comes from geese raised in Alsace and south-western France. Fresh, raw foie gras can be bought vacuum-packed, but only from very specialist stores. The colour and texture of a fresh foie gras is an indication of its quality – ideally, it should be creamy-white, tinged with pink and very firm. Cooked foie gras can be bought in cans (with and without black truffle) but is not of the same quality as fresh foie gras. Care should be taken when handling foie gras as it is very fragile, especially when separating the two lobes with your hands.

duck and goose

111

game birds

The term 'game' applies to all wild animals hunted for sport and eating. The season for hunting, known as the game season, is restricted to the autumn and winter months – starting with grouse shooting in August and ending in March. The rest of the time, when hunting is forbidden, is known as the close season. Pigeons, though, are not protected by this law and can be hunted all year round. The game law not only applies to hunting, but also to the selling of game, as it must not be sold more than ten days after the close of the season – unless frozen. Quail and guinea fowl (originally game birds) are now farmed, making them available all year round.

Game can be bought only from licensed dealers, butchers and supermarkets, and traditionally from some licensed fishmongers. However, out of season it is possible to buy some frozen birds. A good dealer will be able to give advice on the age of a bird, and the cooking method most suited to it.

Choosing

When buying birds choose those that are plump and firm, with supple skin. If still feathered, the feathers should be smooth and firmly attached. Although game birds have quite a strong odour, they should never smell unpleasant or 'off'.

The flavour of game birds will vary not only according to how long they have been hung, but also upon what they've been feeding on. For instance, red-leg grouse generally feed on heather-clad moorlands, the black grouse in grassy woodland clearings, and English wood-pigeons on corn, beechnuts and acorns.

Game bird	Season
Duck (mallard, teal, wigeon)	Inland: 1 September–31 January. Foreshore: 1 September–20 February. Mallard are at their best from November to December. Teal and wigeon are at their best from October to November
Grouse (black Devon and Somerset)	20 August–10 December. New Forest: 1 September–10 December. Grouse are at their best from August to September
Grouse (red)	12 August–10 December. Red grouse are at their best from August to October
Guinea fowl (farmed)	All year
Partridge	1 September–1 February. At their best from October to November
Pheasant	1 October–1 February. At their best from October to January
Quail (farmed)	All year
Snipe	12 August–31 January. At their best from December to January
Woodcock	England & Wales: 1 October–31 January. Scotland: 1 September–31 January. Best from November to December
Wood pigeon	All year

Hanging game birds

Game is allowed to hang in a dry, cool and airy place for a few days to allow the enzymes within the flesh to undergo a chemical change that tenderises the meat, and gives it its characteristic 'gamey' flavour. The longer it is hung, the richer its flavour becomes. Most game birds are usually allowed to hang from the neck, fully feathered, from one to ten days.

A sign that it has been hung long enough, and is ready for cooking, is when the feathers just above the tail can be plucked out easily. However, if you prefer it well hung or 'high', with a more gamey flavour, it can be hung for a further one to two days. Should you be given any game birds that have not been hung, hang them in a cold, well ventilated room or out-building such as a garage or shed. They should not touch each other or any surface, such as a wall, as this would cause them to putrefy.

COOKING GAME BIRDS

- All game birds are very lean and should be cooked very carefully or they can end up tough and dry.
- When roasting young birds, it is important to bard their breasts with pork back fat, or with rashers of streaky bacon (see page 34), both of which will also add flavour to the meat. Wrapping small birds, such as partridges and quail, in vine leaves also helps to keep them moist.
- In general, young birds are best for roasting. Older, tougher birds are best braised, casseroled, or pot-roasted, as demonstrated with small grouse below. Marinating before cooking (see page 105) will also help to tenderise the flesh, as well as moisten and flavour it.

STORING

Properly hung, ready-plucked birds bought from a dealer are best used within 24 hours of buying, and should be stored in the refrigerator until ready to use.

VISIBLE SIGNS OF AGE

- **Partridges and grouse**
On younger birds, the two outermost large flight feathers should have pointed tips. Older birds have rounded ends. They should have supple breast-bones and flexible beaks. Young, grey partridges have yellowish legs – on older birds they are slate-grey.
- **Pheasants** Spurs on young birds are softly rounded at the ends, whereas old birds have long, sharp spurs.
- **Pigeons** Young birds have soft, rosy pink legs. The older they get, the redder they become.

POT-ROASTING GROUSE

Season the birds well with salt and pepper, then bard the breasts with pork back fat or streaky bacon, tying in place with kitchen string. Brown the birds in hot oil, in a large flameproof casserole, turning them frequently.

Add aromatic vegetables such as carrots and onions to the pan, and sweat the vegetables gently for 5 minutes, stirring them occasionally to coat them with the fat from the birds.

Pour enough red wine into the pan to half cover the birds. Cover and simmer gently until birds are tender and the wine is reduced to a rich sauce – about 30 minutes on the hob, or 1 hour in the oven at 180°C (350°F). Check seasoning and serve – garnished with croûtes of fried bread.

game birds

113

BONING AND STUFFING QUAIL

Quail can be fiddly to eat when roasted on the bone but by using the simple technique shown here, not only are they easier to eat, but they can also be transformed into a most impressive dish – especially when served with a port or wine sauce.

▶ With a small, sharp pointed knife, remove the wishbone from the quail. Pull the leg bones free of the main carcass, then cut off the wings (as shown for chicken on page 103). Starting at the neck end, insert the tip of the knife between the flesh and the rib-cage. Then carefully work the knife around the rib-cage to free the flesh.

▶ When the rib-cage is completely free, pull it out with your fingers. (The bones and wings can be browned with the onions when making the sauce.) Season the inside of the quails and fill them loosely with your chosen stuffing. Truss and roast (preferably in duck or goose fat) in the oven, at 200°C (400°F), for 15–20 minutes.

◀ Serve the roasted quail on a platter flooded with sauce, and garnished with sautéed wild mushrooms, rosemary and parsley.

CLASSIC ACCOMPANIMENTS FOR GAME BIRDS

As well as the accompaniments below, game birds also lend themselves to being cooked in or served with rich sauces made with cream, wine and spirits, such as Armagnac.

- **Grouse and partridge** Serve with fried bread hearts, bread sauce and straw potatoes (see page 165). Watercress, rowan or apple jelly, and cranberry sauce also make excellent accompaniments.
- **Pheasant** Bread sauce, clear gravy, fried breadcrumbs, game chips and watercress. Garnish with tail feathers.
- **Wild duck** Game chips or straw potatoes (see page 165), gravy (see page 35) or bigarade (orange) sauce.
- **Woodcock** are plucked but not drawn before roasting, and are served on the untoasted side of a slice of bread which has been toasted on one side only.

NUTRITIONAL INFORMATION

Game birds are low in fat (especially saturated fat) and calories compared to farm-raised birds. They also contain much less sodium than chicken, turkey, duck and goose. They are particularly high in protein, and also rich in B vitamins and iron.

furred game

The most common furred game meat is wild deer and rabbit. Both of these are hunted, although most of the rabbit sold in supermarkets is farmed.

Wild deer meat, or venison, can be obtained all year round because the seasons for hunting the different types of deer overlap. Farmed deer meat is also available all year. Venison can be bought from specialist butchers, and a limited range of cuts are available from some supermarkets.

Choosing

Venison should be dark red with a fine grain and have firm, white fat. The best meat comes from young male deer between 1½ and 2 years old. Venison is sold cut into joints. Joints from roe and fallow deer will be smaller than those from red deer. Venison is also available both fresh and frozen.

Rabbits are sold both whole and cut into joints – such as the saddle (the main body) and the legs.

Venison cut	Description	Cooking methods
Leg	A prime cut, known as the haunch. It can be cut short or long	Roast or braise
Saddle	A prime cut that includes the fillets. It can also be cut into chops	Roast whole. Grill, sauté or braise chops
Shoulder	Sold whole, cubed or minced	Braise whole. Casserole or stew cubed meat. Use minced meat for burgers
Neck	Cut into cubes or made into sausages	Stew cubed meat

COOKING VENISON

- Before cooking venison, remove and discard any fat as it has an unpleasant taste.
- Venison has little or no marbling of fat, so great care must be taken when cooking – otherwise the meat can end up dry and tough.
- To help keep the flesh moist during cooking, bard or lard (see page 34) joints before roasting with pork back fat, rashers of green (unsmoked) bacon, or wrap in caul.
- Marinating in red wine or olive oil before cooking will also help to tenderise the meat, and keep it moist and flavoursome. Baste frequently during cooking.
- Venison, like beef, is best served rare – cooked through yet still slightly pink and juicy in the middle.
- As with all meats, roasted venison should be loosely covered with kitchen foil and left to rest for 15–20 minutes before carving. This allows the flesh to re-absorb its juices, which makes it not only more flavoursome, but also a lot easier to carve.

Wild and farmed rabbit

Although wild and farmed rabbits belong to the same species, they differ quite considerably in flavour. Wild rabbit has darker flesh and a stronger gamey flavour; farmed rabbit has light pink flesh and a more delicate flavour, rather like chicken.

COOKING RABBIT

- When roasting whole, bard or lard with pork back fat, or wrap in caul to help keep the flesh moist and tender. Or bone the main body and fill with a stuffing. Baste the rabbit frequently during cooking.
- Marinate in wine or olive oil, with aromatic vegetables and seasonings, before cooking to help tenderise the meat.
- Poach or braise the young rabbits; stew or casserole the older ones.
- Use a rabbit to make a terrine (see right). Mince the rabbit meat with 2 shallots and mix in 2 eggs, 150 ml (¼ pint) double cream, 2 tbsp (30 ml) shelled pistachios, 1 tbsp (15 ml) dried cranberries, 2 tbsp (30 ml) chopped fresh parsley and seasonings. Place in a terrine lined with bacon rashers and bake in a bain marie at 180°C (350°F) for 2 hours. Add 300 ml (½ pint) liquid aspic after cooking. Allow to cool and refrigerate until set.

JOINTING A RABBIT

Although rabbit can be roasted whole (stuffed or unstuffed), it is most often cut into pieces and cooked slowly in a casserole or stew. Wild rabbit (sold whole – fresh or vacuum packed) will require jointing. Farmed rabbit, although available as saddle or legs, may still need to be cut into smaller pieces before cooking.

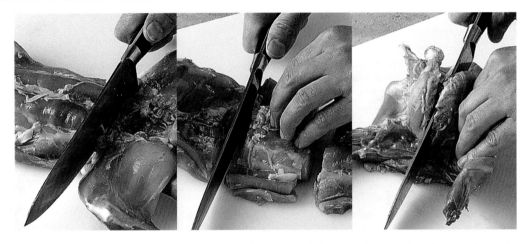

Lay the rabbit, on its back, on a chopping board and cut the legs away from the main carcass with a large chef's knife. (To cut right through the bone, it may be necessary to tap the back of the knife with a kitchen weight or mallet, protecting the back of the knife with a cloth.)

Cut down the centre of the legs to separate them. Then divide each leg in two, cutting through the knee joint. Cut the body into three or four pieces, making the last cut just below the ribcage.

Cutting lengthways through the centre of the breastbone, divide the ribcage section in half. If you wish to remove small bones from the flesh around the breastbone, use pliers or pull them with your fingers.

dairy products

milk

Although the majority of milk is consumed as a beverage, it is a major ingredient in many recipes, particularly desserts. It also is used to make sauces, as a soaking medium, and as a poaching liquid.

Choosing

Check the label when buying milk. It should always be stored in the fridge and will last three to four days. Milk will sour quickly if left at room temperature – within hours if the room is warm. It is not normally recommended to freeze milk, as it is only suitable for cooking after freezing. If you need milk as a standby, buy longlife or powdered milk.

Whole This is, as the name suggests, the whole milk from the cow, with nothing added or taken away. Unpasteurised milk is available but the vast majority of milk is pasteurised. The fat content is roughly 4 per cent in whole milk, but this varies according to the season and the food that the animal eats – in summer, the milk is creamy and pale yellow in colour.

Standardised Here a small proportion of the cream is taken away, and the fat content is 3.5 per cent. This milk is widely available in EC countries and is becoming increasingly available in the Britain in line with EC harmonisation.

Semi-skimmed and skimmed Skimmed milk is virtually fat-free (0.1 per cent fat) and semi-skimmed contains less than half the fat of whole milk (1.6 per cent). Since vitamin A is found only in the cream portion of milk, semi-skimmed milk contains less of this vitamin and it isn't present in skimmed milk at all. However with regard to the other vitamins and minerals, skimmed and semi-skimmed milk are the same as whole milk.

Guernsey/breakfast This is the creamiest of all milk and is pale yellow with a good rich flavour. It normally has a fat content of around 5 per cent and has a marked cream line. It is good for custards and rich sauces as well as on breakfast cereals.

Homogenised Homogenised milk has been mechanically treated to break up the fat globules. Instead of floating to the surface, the cream is suspended in the rest of the milk. The milk has a distinct 'creamy' flavour, which works well heated in coffee, but is not so agreeable served cold.

Longlife/UHT UHT stands for ultra-high temperature. The homogenised milk is heated to 132°C (270°F) for 1–2 seconds, quickly cooled and packed. Unopened, cartons of milk will keep for several months, but once opened keep in the fridge and treat as you would normal milk.

Buttermilk In the old days, this was the milky liquid left over from butter making – that is, milk with most of the fat and other milk solids removed. Unlike skimmed milk it is slightly sour. Today, buttermilk is mostly made from skimmed milk, soured with lactic acid. It is often used with bicarbonate of soda for making soda bread and scones.

Goat's Lactose, present in all mammals' milk, is more easily digestible in goat's milk making it a useful alternative to cow's milk particularly for people who have an intolerance to this. Nutritionally, goat's milk is similar to cow's milk. It has a distinctive musky aromatic flavour which is particularly liked by various cheesemakers who have exploited goat's milk to superb effect for centuries.

Soya Made from soya beans, this milk is a popular substitute for animal-derived milk for anyone wishing to avoid dairy products. Thicker than normal milk, it also has a mild nutty flavour and can be easily substituted in cooking for making sauces as well as for adding to tea and coffee.

Condensed This is whole milk to which sugar is added and from which more than half the water is removed. It usually contains 40–45 per cent sugar.

Evaporated Milk that has been heated to remove about 60 per cent of its water, then sealed in cans and heat-treated for sterilisation. To reconstitute evaporated milk mix equal quantities of water and evaporated milk.

Non-fat dry or powdered Pasteurised skimmed milk from which all the water is removed. This reconstitutes readily in warm water.

Type of milk	Energy per 100 g	Protein per 100 g	Fat per 100 g	Vitamin A	Thiamine (B$_1$)	Riboflavin (B$_2$)	Vitamin (B$_{12}$)	Calcium
Whole and homogenised	66 kcal (275 kJ)	3.2	3.9	***	***	****	****	****
Semi-skimmed	46 kcal (195 kJ)	3.3	1.6	**	***	****	****	****
Skimmed	33 kcal (140 kJ)	3.3	0.1	*	***	****	****	*

**** excellent source   * negligible source

SOURING MILK

If buttermilk is called for in a recipe but is not available, you can substitute the following. Place 15 ml (1 tbsp) fresh lemon juice or distilled white vinegar in a glass measuring jug, then pour in enough milk to equal 250 ml (8 fl oz) and stir. Allow the milk to stand for about 5 minutes to thicken before using.

SUCCESS WITH CUSTARDS

A stovetop custard requires close attention to prevent the mixture from curdling. Make sure the milk doesn't boil as it cooks. A baked custard is best cooked in a bain-marie.

- Keep the heat gentle and stir constantly around the sides and bottom of the pan to prevent the custard scorching.
- Heat the custard mixture gently and stir constantly with a wooden spoon until it thickens. Test the consistency by running your finger through the custard along the back of the spoon. It should leave a clear line. Place individual pots of custard in a baking dish and add sufficient water so it reaches halfway up the sides. Bake as directed.
- Cream always rises to the surface in milk, which is why you often get a skin on custards and sauces. You can help to prevent this from happening either by placing a layer of clingfilm or else buttered greaseproof paper over the top of the sauce.

MAKING A WHITE SAUCE

For a pouring sauce, use 15 g (½ oz) each butter and flour to 300 ml (½ pint) milk; for a coating sauce, use 25 g (1 oz) each butter and flour. Melt the butter in a small pan. Add the flour to the melted butter and stir with a wooden spoon over a low heat for 1–2 minutes to create a white roux. Remove the pan from the heat. Slowly add the milk, beating to blend it with the roux. Bring to boil, stirring constantly. Reduce heat and simmer for 1–2 minutes. Season as required.

Recipes

Crème patissière
A custard thickened with both plain flour and cornflour and used as a base for soufflés and as a filling for cakes and tarts.

Crème anglaise
A rich custard sauce traditionally flavoured with vanilla.

Crèma catalana
A thicker pastry cream enriched with butter and used as a filling for sponge cakes and a base for desserts.

INFUSING MILK

A classic béchamel sauce is simply a white sauce made with milk that has been infused with flavourings. To be absolutely correct, the flavourings should be onion, cloves, bay leaves, freshly grated nutmeg and salt and pepper. There are, however, many variations.

Heat the milk and flavourings, stirring occasionally. Remove from the heat. Cover with a plate and let stand for 10 minutes. Strain the infused milk through a sieve. Discard the flavourings. Add hot infused milk to the roux as for a white sauce.

milk

cream and yogurt

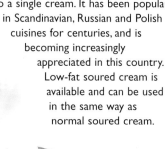

CREAM

The concentrated fatty part of milk has a velvety texture and adds a delicious richness to all sorts of savoury and sweet dishes. Unfortunately, by definition it contains lots of fat and too much is considered a 'bad thing'. The consistency and flavour of cream is determined by various factors, among which is the fat content, the cream-making process and even the breed of cow and the season.

Single cream Does not contain sufficient butterfat to enable it to be whipped, but can be used for pouring or adding to sauces and soups. Extra thick single cream contains the same amount of butterfat as single cream but it has been homogenised to a thick spoonable consistency.

Double cream This is a thick and rich cream used for whipping and decorating sponges, and for filling cakes, éclairs and other desserts. Extra thick double cream is made using homogenised milk so is spoonable, but has the same fat content.

Whipping cream Contains less butterfat than double cream, but sufficient to make it suitable for whipping. Cream is best whipped using an electric or balloon whisk. It should double in volume, but take care not to over-whip. This cream is also useful for adding to sauces and gravies, as it will not separate when heated.

Soured cream This rich, thick-textured cream is made by adding lactic acid to a single cream. It has been popular in Scandinavian, Russian and Polish cuisines for centuries, and is becoming increasingly appreciated in this country. Low-fat soured cream is available and can be used in the same way as normal soured cream.

YOGURT

Yogurt is fermented milk, a process which accounts for yogurt's sour taste. It is normally made using low-fat milk, but any milk can be used. The consistency of yogurt varies too. Greek-style yogurt, which is made from semi-skimmed or whole milk, is thick and higher in fat. These yogurts can be added carefully to cooked dishes, but low-fat varieties are best for serving with fruit or desserts, or used for making low-fat dressings.

Smetana Russian smetana is a rich sour-cream made from sweet double cream and soured cream. A version available in the UK is made from skimmed milk and is similar to a thick buttermilk. Unlike authentic smetana, it will curdle if overheated. Treat like thick yogurt.

Crème fraîche Richer than soured cream, with a velvety texture. Its high fat content means that it will not curdle when cooked.

Clotted cream The traditional cream of Devon and Cornwall made by skimming the creamy top off heated milk. Serve with scones and strawberry jam for a traditional cream tea.

Cream	Fat content
Half cream	12 %
Single cream	18 %
Extra thick single cream	18 %
Soured cream	18 %
Whipping cream	34 %
Double cream	48 %
Crème fraîche	48 %
Extra thick cream	48 %
Clotted cream	55 %

EQUIPMENT

ELECTRIC WHISK

Hand held mixers are inexpensive, but make sure that the model you choose has a choice of speeds.

BALLOON WHISK

Made of loops of stainless steel wire bound around a handle, this is simple yet very effective. You can judge more accurately the consistency of the cream and there is less danger of over-whipping – but hand whipping cream is tiring.

MAKING CREAMS

Soured cream If you don't have or can't get soured cream, add a little lemon juice or drop of vinegar to fresh single cream. Stir 15 ml (1 tbsp) fresh lemon juice into 250 ml (8 fl oz) single cream in a glass bowl. Let the mixture stand at room temperature for 10–30 minutes or until it has thickened. Cover the bowl and refrigerate until ready to use.

Crème fraîche This partially soured, tangy cream is made by mixing buttermilk, soured cream and double cream, heating it, then letting it stand. You can buy it ready-made.

Mix 500 ml (17 fl oz) buttermilk, 250 ml (8 fl oz) double cream and 250 ml (8 fl oz) sour cream. Put bowl over a pan of hot water and heat to 30°C (86°F). Pour the warm mixture into a glass bowl; partially cover and leave to stand at room temperature for 6–8 hours.

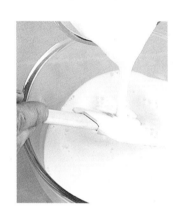

DECORATING WITH CREAM

For a dramatic presentation of a brightly coloured cream soup, spoon or swirl cream in the centre, or use it to make an attractive pattern. The key to success is to make sure the consistency of the cream is similar to that of the soup. In most cases, the cream should be lightly whipped first. Make the pattern just before serving.

Catherine wheel Stir pesto into lightly whipped cream. Place 15 ml (1 tbsp) in the centre of each serving. Draw the tip of a knife away from the centre to make a swirl.

▶ **Romantic rim** Drip cream on to the soup in a circle. Draw the tip of a knife through each drop to form connecting hearts.

WHIPPING CREAM

Cream is best whipped at about 5°C (40°F), and will not give such a good volume if whipped straight from the fridge. On hot days, add a spoonful of cold milk to each 150 ml (¼ pint) cream, to prevent it turning to butter. Use a large bowl, as it will double in volume.

▼ **Soft peaks** Using an electric mixer, start slowly, gradually increasing the speed. Stop when the cream forms into gentle folds.

▲ **Stiff peaks** When the cream keeps its shape when the beaters are lifted, stop. Stiffly beaten cream is used for topping pies, icing cakes or as a filling.

cream and yogurt

121

butter and other fats

As well as being used on its own in sandwiches and as a topping, butter adds flavour and richness to a variety of cooked foods. It is the base of several important sauces, a cooking medium, an ingredient and can also be used as a garnish.

Unsalted butter This is the choice butter for sweet pastries and cakes. It has a mild sweet flavour and is excellent served at the table, for spreading onto bread or toast. Some people, though, who are used to more distinct salted butter, find it rather bland.

Ghee Clarified butter obtained by boiling butter and straining off the sediment that separates from the butterfat. It gives a rich, buttery taste to foods and is used for many Indian recipes. Because of its purity, ghee can be kept without refrigeration for many months.

Lard Lard is an animal fat, being purified pork fat. Before concern about saturated fats gave animal fats (and lard in particular) a bad name, lard was the fat mostly used for frying and particularly for making chips. Nevertheless, lard is popular among some pastry cooks, since if used half and half with butter, it produces an excellent, light pastry.

Shortening This is a blend of vegetable and animal fats. It is pure white in colour, without aroma or flavour. It is, however, very popular for making pastry and hence its name, since it means in pastry-making terms that it is capable of producing a 'short' crust. Shortening has a soft texture making it more easy to rub in. Use it for savoury pastries – for pasties, raised pies or for shortcrust pastries for meat or chicken.

Salted butter Since salt acts as a preservative, it has always been added to butter. Some blends of butter are only slightly salted, others are horribly over-salted; however, it is largely a matter of taste – there are no rules, except it is normally recommended to avoid salty butter for making delicate sweet sauces.

Margarine A non-dairy fat alternative to butter, it is as versatile as butter, used at the table and for cooking and baking. Mostly made from vegetable fat, but some brands add milk or other animal fats, so check label carefully if you wish to avoid dairy products. Low-fat margarines are unsuitable for cooking or baking, owing to their high water content. Soft margarine is not recommended for frying as it burns easily. Hard margarines make good pastry.

Suet Suet is the white fat that surrounds the kidneys of lamb and ox. It can be bought fresh from butchers (in which case it needs shredding), or ready-shredded in packets. Suet is used to make suet puddings, steak and kidney pudding, jam roly-poly and other favourites. It is often added to Christmas pudding, so vegetarians should check the label carefully.

Vegetable fat These are vegetable-derived fats which, like animal fats, can be used for frying, baking or pastry-making. They can be made from any vegetable oils, and some manufacturers make vegetable fats high in polyunsaturates from sunflower or safflower.

Unsalted butter

Salted butter

Ghee

Margarine

Lard

Suet

Shortening

Vegetable fat

BUTTER SAUCES

Many of the classic French sauces rely on an emulsion of egg yolk and butter. Others, like white butter sauce, use cream.

▶ **Hollandaise sauce** can be made by hand but using a food processor is simplest and substantially reduces the risk of curdling. Put the egg yolks and water in a warmed, dry food processor bowl and process for a few seconds to blend. With the machine running, pour in the warm clarified butter in a thin stream. Finally add lemon juice and seasoning.

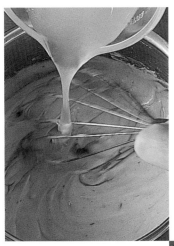

◀ **Béarnaise** Béarnaise has a more biting flavour than hollandaise. Boil crushed peppercorns, finely chopped shallot and tarragon with vinegar until reduced. When cooled, whisk in beaten egg yolks and water over a very low heat until the egg has thickened. Slowly add clarified butter, whisking hard after each addition.

▶ **Beurre blanc** Wine, vinegar, herbs and shallots are reduced to a thick glaze, and softened butter is then whisked in. Boil the ingredients as for Béarnaise, add crème fraîche or double cream, remove from the heat and whisk in small pieces of butter, one at a time, making sure each one has completely dissolved before adding the next.

CLARIFYING BUTTER

Also known as drawn butter, or ghee in Indian cooking, clarified butter is unsalted butter with its milk solids removed. The result is a very pure fat. It is used in many dishes.

Melt the butter slowly over a very low heat without stirring. Remove the pan from the heat and skim the foam off the surface. Spoon the butter into a small bowl, being careful to leave the milky sediment behind in the pan.

BEURRE MANIÉ

A paste made from blending equal quantities of butter and flour, it is used for thickening casseroles, sauces and other liquids. Soften the butter with a fork to mix in the flour.

WHAT WENT WRONG

Making hollandaise or béarnaise sauce is one of the more tricky things to do in the kitchen. Flavours and seasonings should be added carefully, but the most common problem is if the sauce curdles. This will happen if:
- the butter has been added too quickly or the cooking temperature was too high.

To put this right:
- place a spoonful of boiling water in a clean pan and gradually whisk in the curdled sauce OR
- place an egg yolk in a clean pan and whisk lightly over a very gentle heat. Remove from the heat and add the curdled mixture.

butter and other fats

123

cheese

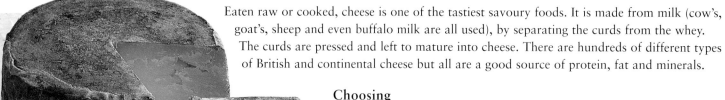

Eaten raw or cooked, cheese is one of the tastiest savoury foods. It is made from milk (cow's, goat's, sheep and even buffalo milk are all used), by separating the curds from the whey. The curds are pressed and left to mature into cheese. There are hundreds of different types of British and continental cheese but all are a good source of protein, fat and minerals.

Choosing

Soft cheese rind should be evenly coloured and slightly moist with a 'bloomy' look. Hard cheese rind should not be too dry or cracked, nor look moist or 'sweaty'. When matured in cheesecloth, it should cling to the paste. Hard cheese should have a clean, firm or crumbly texture with no discoloration. Fresh cheese should be moist and white, with no sign of mould. Hard blue cheese should have even veining throughout and a creamy-yellow paste. Some soft cheese has a 'washed' orange rind. This should be evenly coloured with no cracks.

Fresh cheeses These are unripened, rindless cheeses which range in consistency from the creamy and smooth – fromage frais, cream cheese and mascarpone – to thicker curd mixtures – ricotta, pot cheese and cottage cheese. The fat content varies, with many low-fat skimmed-milk versions available. It is very important to use fresh cheese within the use-by date on the packaging.

Soft cheeses Containing a high percentage of fat and moisture, these have been briefly ripened, have a creamy texture and are easy to spread. When fully ripe, some soft cheeses, such as Brie and Camembert, ooze gently. These have a characteristic 'bloomy' rind, while others, such as Pont L'Evêque and Livarot have a 'washed' rind and a sharper, richer taste. Soft cheese should be springy to the touch, and smell nutty, sweet and aromatic. Avoid any with a chalky white centre or a strong smell of ammonia.

Semi-hard cheeses such as Reblochon and Port Salut are matured longer and, because they contain less moisture, are slightly firmer and hold their shape when cut.

Hard cheeses Often high in fat, though low in moisture, these long-matured cheeses have flavours ranging from mild to sharp and textures from 'flexible' to crumbly. Some cheeses in this category, such as Emmenthal, have characteristic holes, caused by the gas-producing bacteria introduced within the ripening cheese.

Hard-grating cheeses such as Italian Parmesan and Pecorino are the driest of the hard cheeses. Aged until they have a dry, granular texture, they will keep for months in the refrigerator, if wrapped tightly. Taste the cheese before buying if you can and reject any that taste over-salty or bitter. The rind should be hard and yellow and the paste yellowish white.

Blue cheeses These have had a bacteria culture introduced which creates their characteristic blue-green veining. Immature blue cheeses have little veining near the rind. Look for a firm, crusty rind with no signs of discoloration underneath. Blue cheeses may smell strong but should not smell of ammonia. Sample before purchase if possible, and avoid cheeses that taste over-salty or chalky.

Goat's and sheep cheeses Curds made from goat's milk are lightly packed into small moulds to produce cheese in a variety of shapes and sizes. They can be sold at any stage of the maturing process, the age determining the character of the cheese. Initially soft and mild, they mature to become firm with a tangy, strong flavour. Buy goat's cheese from a shop with a rapid turnover to ensure freshness. When fresh, goat's cheeses should be moist with a slightly sharp, but not sour, flavour. Of a medium fat content, most ewe's milk cheeses are milder in taste than those of cow's milk. Famous exceptions include Roquefort, Pecorino and ewe's milk feta.

Cheddar A versatile, popular cheese that can be used cooked or uncooked. It is ideal for grating – use it in sauces, on toast, in omelettes and in quiches, pies and pastries.

Neufchâtel A soft French cheese from Normandy that has a dry, velvety rind and a firm but creamy texture. It is delicious sliced and grilled on crusty bread or cut into small pieces and tossed with mixed salad leaves and French dressing.

Emmenthal A good melting cheese similar to Gruyère (they are both from Switzerland) – used in fondues and quiches. Good in toasted sandwiches and bakes.

Mozzarella Delicious raw in salads but most famous as a topping for pizzas and in traditional Italian dishes.

Gorgonzola This soft blue-veined Italian cheese makes a tasty addition to creamy pasta sauces or combine with apples or pears in pastry to make tartlets.

Ricotta Used in sweet and savoury dishes such as moussaka and cheesecakes, this creamy but grainy Italian cheese can be used cooked or uncooked.

Parmesan Sprinkle on pasta dishes or add to sauces and pasta bakes for an authentic Italian flavour. Avoid dried Parmesan – it has an unpleasant odour and tastes nothing like the fresh variety.

cheese

125

TESTING A CHEESE FOR RIPENESS

When a soft cheese develops its characteristic texture, flavour and aroma, it is deemed ripe. Eat soft cheeses at their peak because they deteriorate very quickly, especially once the rind has been cut.

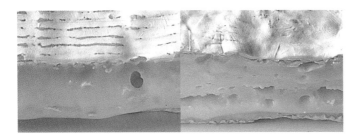

Brie that is just ripe should feel spongy in the centre and be creamy throughout.

Over-ripe brie has thin, patchy rind, a bitter flavour, smells of ammonia and 'oozes' excessively.

MELTING

Always melt grated cheese slowly over a low heat in a heavy-based pan. This will help prevent the melted cheese becoming stringy or grainy, or separating. Not all cheeses melt well; each has a different fat and moisture level, which react differently to heat.

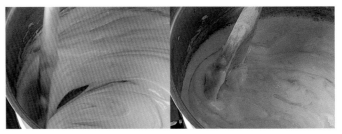

Correct Cheese that is melted gently over a low heat is smooth and glossy.

Incorrect Cheese that is melted too quickly over a high heat will separate into oily lumps.

MAKING A GRATIN TOPPING

Dishes that are to be finished by browning under the grill or in the oven are often topped with grated cheese. The cheese melts quickly and forms a crisp, golden crust, making a delicious gratin topping.

GOOD MELTING CHEESES

Several cheeses are prized for their ability to achieve a specific consistency when heated. Soft cheeses such as mozzarella, for instance, melt easily when simply sliced. A hard cheese like Gruyère is best grated.

- Mozzarella is the traditional topping for pizza. It melts evenly to produce gooey 'strings' of cheese.
- Fontina is a well-tempered, nutty flavoured cheese that withstands high temperatures. It can even be coated in breadcrumbs and deep-fried.
- Gruyère, France's favourite cheese for gratins, is best grated for even melting. Use well-aged Gruyère for fondue.
- Goat's cheese holds its shape well when warm and colours to an appetizing golden brown. It is good on croûtes.
- Cheddar melts and browns well. It is excellent for grilling.

ROTARY GRATER

Equipped with a selection of drums, this time-saving tool (also called a mouli grater) grates hard cheese easily into shreds of various sizes.

Recipes

Welsh rarebit One of the most popular cheese snacks. Use a good melting cheese like Cheddar, Lancashire or the traditional Welsh Caerphilly.

Caesar salad Parmesan cheese is an essential part of this delicious salad. To savour the taste of the cheese fully, use a vegetable peeler to make wafer-thin shavings (see right). The dressing is made from olive oil, egg, garlic, anchovy fillets, mustard and balsamic vinegar.

Tricolore salad Mozzarella, tomato, avocado and basil, with a simple dressing of lemon vinaigrette spooned over it and sprinkled with chopped parsley. This is one of Italy's most famous and popular salads.

Croque monsieur This is France's answer to the British toasted sandwich. At its simplest, it is made with cheese and ham. Cheddar or any English cheese can be used, but the French would always use Gruyère or Emmenthal.

Cheese fondue In Switzerland fondue is made with Gruyère and Emmenthal cheese. The French use their version of Gruyère, Beaufort. Either way the effect is the same – a superb dish consisting of melted cheese and wine, served with warm crusty bread for dipping.

PREPARING CHEESE

Different types of graters can be used to prepare cheese according to the variety of cheese you are grating and the size of shreds required.

◀ **Grating fine shreds** Use cheese straight from the refrigerator for best results. A rotary grater makes light work of fine grating. Simply put the cheese in the hopper and turn the handle.

▶ **Coarse shreds** An upright grater creates thick shreds that hold up in a salad or melt evenly.

◀ **Cheese shavings** Use a vegetable peeler to pare off pieces from a block of hard cheese such as Parmesan.

▶ **Parmesan** Use a special small Parmesan grater to grate this very hard cheese into tiny shreds.

eggs

One of our most versatile and nutritious foods, eggs are used for a wide variety of purposes in the kitchen. They can be cooked in numerous ways on their own, the whites create meringues, help add volume to many dishes and clarify stock; yolks help to emulsify sauces. Whole eggs help to bind food to other ingredients and vice versa, they also help other ingredients adhere, they are vital to glazes, and to thicken sauces and mixtures.

Choosing

Its important to buy eggs as fresh as possible. Check the best before dates on the carton lid. If there is no date, test the freshness by immersing the egg in water (see right). As the egg gets older it loses water through the shell, making the air pocket larger – so the older the egg, the lighter it will be. A cloudy white is a sign of freshness, not age, it is due to the high carbon dioxide content when the egg is laid.

STORING

Put the eggs in the fridge as soon as possible after buying them. Eggs age more in one day at room temperature than in one week in the refrigerator. If kept in the fridge, eggs will keep for four to five weeks beyond their 'sell-by' date. An egg shell has thousands of tiny pores over its surface through which they can absorb flavours and odours. Therefore store in their cartons and away from strong-smelling foods. Store the eggs pointed-end down to keep the yolks centred.

Separated whites and yolks or shelled whole eggs should be stored in the fridge in airtight containers. Whites will keep for one week, yolks and whole eggs for up to two days.

Use food containing raw eggs within two days.

A CLOSER LOOK AT AN EGG

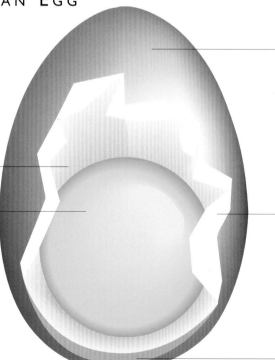

White
This is also called the albumen. Half the protein of an egg is contained in the white. When fresh, the white is thicker immediately around the yolk. The strands that anchor the yolk to the white are called chalazae; they are best strained out if making custard or a sauce. The white contains about 17 calories.

Yolk
The yolk contains the remaining protein. It is also one of the few foods to contain vitamin D and is an excellent source of vitamin A. It contains 5 g of fat, all the egg's cholesterol and about 59 calories. The yolk colour depends on the diet of the hen. Feed containing corn produces a fairly yellow yolk, while those of wheat and barley are paler.

Shell
This makes up 12 per cent of the total weight of an egg. It is composed mostly of calcium. Being porous, it can absorb flavours and odours. The colour of the shell is determined by the breed of the hen; it does not affect nutrition, quality, flavour or appearance.

Membrane

Air pocket
Located at the rounded end of the egg, the membrane pulls away from the shell creating a space that is filled with air. As the egg ages, air passes through the porous shell, and the space fills with more air and is consequently lighter.

Hen's eggs Almost all the eggs we eat come from hens. Most come from cross-bred birds but there are smaller breeds, like the Bantam and Silkies, that produce much smaller eggs. These have the same flavour as normal eggs, but are good if you just want small helpings (for children, for instance), however you will need to use double the quantity for baking. Eggs are now sold as small (was size 4 or 5), medium (was size 3) and large (was size 1 or 2).

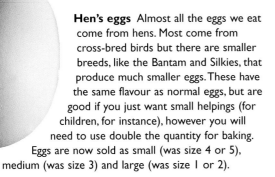

Quail's eggs These are about one-third of the size of hen's eggs and are the smallest eggs you can buy. They look attractive as a garnish and are good in starters or canapes, or for adding whole to pilafs and salads but take care not to overcook.

TESTING FOR FRESHNESS

If you're not sure how fresh your eggs are, there's a simple test you can use to check.

A fresh egg is heavy due to its high water content. It will settle horizontally on the bottom of the glass (top).

With a less fresh egg, the air pockets will expand, water is lost through the shell and the egg will float vertically, tip down.

An old egg contains more air than a fresh egg, so it is lighter and will float to the surface (below). Do not use an egg if it floats.

SEPARATING THE YOLK FROM THE WHITE

It is easiest to separate eggs when they are cold – the yolk is firm and there is less chance that it will run into the white. Whites will not whisk properly if there is any yolk in them.

▶ **Hand method** Crack the egg into a bowl, then lift it up and cup it in your hand; the white will run through your fingers.

▶ **Shell method** Crack the egg shell in half. Pass the yolk backwards and forwards between the halves until all the white has fallen into the bowl.

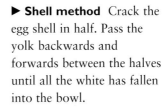

Preventing salmonella poisoning

Eggs contain a bacterium, salmonella, that in rare cases can cause food poisoning. It can be prevented by thorough cooking. Most cases of salmonella poisoning result from undercooked or raw eggs. People most at risk are the elderly, pregnant women, infants and anyone with a compromised immune system. To ensure safety, cook eggs to 60°C and keep at that temperature for 3½ minutes or cook to 70°C. If you don't want to use raw eggs in recipes calling for uncooked whites, use meringue powder or powdered egg whites, which are pasteurised substitutes.

eggs

WHISKING EGG WHITES

To achieve greater volume and stability, break the whites into a bowl, cover loosely and allow to stand for one hour. Whether whisking by hand or by machine, make sure all utensils are free of grease and that the bowl is deep enough to hold the volume of whisked whites.

By hand Put whites in a stainless steel or glass bowl. Whisk from the bottom upwards in a circular motion. For greater volume, use a large balloon whisk.

By machine Use the whisk attachment of the electric mixer and start slowly, to break up the whites, increasing the speed as they thicken. A little salt relaxes the albumen and makes whisking easier.

Stiff peaks Properly beaten egg whites form stiff but not dry peaks. When the whisk or beaters are lifted from the bowl, the peaks stand upright and don't fall over.

Soft peaks Soft peaks should be just stiff enough to hold their own shape. As the whisk is lifted from the bowl, the peaks should just flop over at the top.

> **Cook's tip**
>
> *Even tiny amounts of egg yolk will prevent whites whisking properly. Remove flecks of yolk with a piece of shell; any other implement, such as a teaspoon, will have you chasing it round forever. Over-whisked whites can be saved by stirring an additional unbeaten white in a small bowl, add some of the over-whisked whites and add this mixture to the rest of the damaged whites. Whisk 30 seconds more.*

FOLDING IN EGG WHITES

The delicate texture of whisked egg whites, often used to add lightness to heavier ingredients, can be destroyed if they are added too roughly. To lose less whisked-in air, fold whites into the heavier mixture using a rubber spatula and a scooping and cutting action. Turn the bowl a little after each stroke.

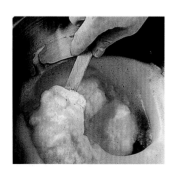

Recipes

Omelette Arnold Bennett This omelette of smoked haddock and cream was created at the Savoy Hotel for the well-known writer and critic who used to dine there after an evening at the theatre.

Cheese soufflé An egg and cheese dish from France but popular everywhere. A base roux made of egg and flour is created and lightened with beaten egg whites. Cheese and mushrooms are probably the most popular additions to soufflés, but crab, smoked fish and ham are also excellent. Sweet soufflés make an interesting dessert.

Eggs Benedict A rich but delicious snack, comprising toasted muffin or bread, ham and poached egg topped with hollandaise sauce.

Scotch eggs Still a favourite picnic food, hard-boiled eggs are coated in sausage meat and breadcrumbs and then deep-fried.

Crème caramel No one country can claim authorship of this all-time favourite. Greece, Spain, Morocco, as well as Britain and France, all have their own versions of this delicious creamy pudding.

Spanish tortilla A thick omelette made from gently fried potatoes and onions – one of Spain's most famous tapas.

Zabaglione Egg yolks, sugar and Marsala are whisked and heated to make this favourite Italian dessert.

EQUIPMENT

When it comes to egg cookery, there are all sorts of gadgets that are useful, and some equipment is essential.

EGG TIMER

Quite useful if you enjoy boiled eggs. The classic hourglass-shaped timer takes 3 minutes, which is about right for a soft-boiled egg, but it depends on size, temperature, altitude and, of course, how you like your eggs. Better to buy the more versatile timer that runs off batteries.

EGG PIERCER

This creates a tiny hole at one end of the shell which prevents the egg from cracking during cooking.

WOODEN SPOON

Have several of different sizes, for making batters, sauces, scrambled eggs etc.

OMELETTE PAN

Very useful, but do not use it for anything else. It should have gently curving sides, have a 18 cm (7 in) heavy base and be made of aluminium, steel or cast-iron (see below).

SOUFFLÉ SUCCESS

The pièce de résistance of every cook is a perfectly presented soufflé. Here are some tips to ensure it reaches the table properly puffed up.

- Add an extra egg white to the mixture to give the soufflé more lightness and volume.
- Use a straight-sided soufflé dish or casserole of medium depth for a tall and impressive looking soufflé. Fill the dish three-quarters full to ensure that the soufflé puffs up well above the rim during baking.
- Prepare the mixture and let it stand in its dish at room temperature for up to 30 minutes before baking.
- During baking, don't open the oven door to check the soufflé or else the cold draught could cause the delicate mixture to collapse.
- Serve the soufflé as soon as you remove it from the oven.

BATTER

Combined with flour, salt and milk or a mixture of water and milk, eggs are one of the key ingredients in batter. Batter is used all over the world to make pancakes that are served in numerous different ways – from the simple traditional Shrove Tuesday pancake served with lemon and sugar, French crêpes or galettes to Chinese pancake rolls and Russian blinis.

Batter can also be used to make Scotch pancakes (right), waffles and popovers. Batter benefits from standing for 30 minutes before cooking. Stir thoroughly before using.

MAKING EGG WASH

A mixture of egg yolk and water is brushed over bread or pastry before baking to give a rich, golden colour and a glossy glaze. Mix 1 egg yolk with 15 ml (1 tbsp) water and a pinch of salt. Whisk together with a fork until combined. Brush the egg wash over bread or pastry with a pastry brush just before baking.

TYPES OF MERINGUE

• **French** The simplest meringue with a light texture: use for piping and shaping, poaching as in oeufs à la neige (floating islands), or baking as in vacherin cases and nests. Use 115 g (4 oz) sugar to 2 egg whites. Ground nuts such as hazelnuts also can be added.

• **Italian** A firm-textured but velvety meringue, made with a hot sugar syrup that 'cooks' the egg whites; use in uncooked desserts, such as cold mousses, soufflés and sorbets. It holds its shape well, so is also ideal for piping. To make 400 g (14 oz) Italian meringue make a sugar syrup with 250 g (9 oz) sugar and 60 ml (2¼ fl oz) water, boil to the soft-ball stage (118°C/245°F) and whisk into 5 stiffly whisked egg whites.

• **Swiss** Gives a much firmer result than French. Use for piping and other decorative effects. Allow 125 g (4½ oz) sugar to 2 egg whites.

MAKING MERINGUE

Make sure all utensils are scrupulously clean and free of grease. To ensure maximum volume, allow the egg whites to stand in a covered container at room temperature for one hour before use. There are three ways to make meringue, depending on your recipe and its application.

French Whisk the egg whites using a balloon whisk until stiff peaks form. Gradually whisk in half the sugar, then fold in the remainder.

Italian With a tabletop mixer on low speed, whisk hot sugar syrup into whisked egg whites, down the side of the bowl in a steady stream.

Swiss Whisk egg whites and sugar in a bowl set over a pan of simmering water. Keep turning the bowl to prevent pockets of egg white cooking.

SERVING MERINGUES

You can fill meringues or sandwich them together with flavoured cream, or try one of the following ideas.

• Sandwich shells with chocolate ganache, sprinkle with chocolate curls, then dust with icing sugar and cocoa powder.

• Toss a selection of seasonal fruits in a little Cointreau. Pile high in nests.

• Layer discs with chocolate or fruit mousse to make a gateau (see right).

pulses and grains

pulses

LENTILS AND DHAL

Lentils are cultivated all over the world. They are extremely nutritious and have been part of our diet for thousands of years. They need to be cooked before they can be eaten, but they do not require soaking.

Dhal or dal is the Hindi word for any split lentil or pea (gram). The word also applies to any dish that includes lentils or dried peas and beans.

There is a bewildering variety of lentils in India. A few of the most popular dhals are available in some large supermarkets, but you'll find a much wider selection in Indian grocery stores.

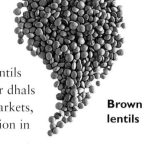

Brown lentils

Lentil type	Description	Cooking time	Use for
Red split	These small bright orange discs are the best known of all the lentils. Red lentils disintegrate to a thick purée during cooking	20 minutes	Dhals, thickening soups or casseroles
Green and brown	These disc-shaped pulses, sometimes known as Continental lentils, keep their shape when cooked. They have a distinct, slightly musty taste and go well with herbs and spices	40–45 minutes	Salads, purées, thick soups, casseroles
Puy	Of all the lentils, these are considered to be the best. A dark blue-green in colour, they retain their bead-shape during cooking. They have a delicious and distinct, peppery flavour	25–30 minutes	Purées, soups, casseroles, hors d'oeuvre

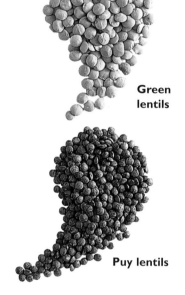

Green lentils

Puy lentils

▼ **Masoor** This is similar to the Egyptian split red lentil and is regarded in India as the most humble of the dhals. It is nevertheless a versatile and very popular pulse.

▲ **Chana dhal** This looks similar to a yellow split pea, but is smaller, coarser and paler in colour. It has a slightly sweet flavour.

▼ **Mung** The split mung bean, this is a favourite dhal in India. It is very digestible and needs relatively little time cooking.

▲ **Urid dhal** This is a small lentil, commonly ground and used for making poppadoms.

▼ **Toovar dhal** This is a dull-orange coloured lentil. It has a distinctive, earthy flavour.

pulses and grains

134

SOYA AND TOFU

Soya beans are used in a mind-boggling number of different non-edible products: soap, plastics, paint and fuel to name but a few. They are also used to provide bulk in numerous processed foods, as an emulsifier, and to make vegetarian alternatives such as vegetarian sausages and artificial 'chicken'. Soya beans are also used for making miso, soy sauce, soya oil and tofu.

The fresh and dried beans are eaten as a vegetable, and they can be used to make a drink which has become a worldwide substitute for milk. Liquified with water, it is jelled to make tofu.

Tofu, also known as beancurd, is extremely versatile. In Japan and China there are numerous different forms. The most commonly available tofus in the UK are as follows.

NUTRITIONAL INFORMATION

Beans and pulses are extremely good for you. The soya bean is virtually a complete food, which is why it is sometimes known as the 'meat of the soil'. Beans are also low in fat and sodium, and high in fibre. Since they contain complex carbohydrates, a serving of haricot or kidney beans will keep you feeling satisfied for far longer than a richer meal of meat, eggs or cheese. All beans are a good source of protein, particularly soya beans with 35 per cent protein. They are a good source of iron, magnesium, calcium, potassium, zinc and copper and contain many B complex vitamins, especially B_6 and B_3. Beans are also one of the best sources of folate, which the body uses to manufacture new blood cells and boost immunity. They are high in soluble fibre and most are low to very low in fat.

Soya beans

▶ **Silken tofu** Softer than firm tofu, this has a silky smooth texture and is useful for sauces, dips and in soups.

▼ **Firm tofu** Sold in blocks. Slice or dice and use in stir-fries, soups, salads or kebabs. It has a bland, non-assuming flavour and benefits from being marinated since its porous texture absorbs other flavours.

▶ **TVP** Textured vegetable protein is available in most supermarkets and is useful for anyone avoiding meat. It can be bought in chunks or as mince and, like tofu, readily absorbs other flavours. Some needs to be

▼ **Beancurd skins** Like firm tofu, these have no noticeable flavour but readily absorb the flavour of other ingredients. Soak first for 1–2 hours then

Type	Other names	Description	Soaking time	Cooking time	Cooking tip
Haricot beans	White bean, French bean, navy bean and Boston bean	Numerous varieties but all tend to be small, white and oval-shaped. The navy bean (so called because it was used by the American navy), is the popular choice for Boston baked beans. These are the beans used by Heinz for their ever-popular baked beans	3–4 hours	1–1½ hours	Versatile beans that go well with well-flavoured ingredients. Use in cassoulets and other bean stews
Soissons		Large white haricot beans with an excellent flavour	3–4 hours	1–1½ hours	Considered by some the finest white bean and popular in France. The choice bean for cassoulet
Flageolets		These are an immature haricot bean, picked when young. They are kidney-shaped and pale green in colour. In France you can buy them semi-dried and they are delicious in a variety of classic dishes. In Britain they are only available dried but still have a good, fresh flavour	3–4 hours	1–1½ hours	Use in French legume recipes, like gigot d'agneau. Also good in salads
Cannellini beans	White kidney bean, fazola bean	A large white bean, very popular in Italy, particularly Tuscany. They are probably native to Argentina. They have a nutty flavour	8–12 hours or overnight	1 hour	The classic bean for minestrone. Also use for other Italian dishes which call for white beans such as pasta e fagioli
Red kidney bean	Mexican bean, chilli bean	The best known of all the beans, and most famously used in Mexican chile con carne	8–12 hours or overnight	1–1½ hours	Boil hard for 10 minutes. Use with well-flavoured ingredients like garlic and hot spices. Used to make the popular Mexican refried beans: frijoles refritos
Black beans	Turtle bean, Mexican black bean, Spanish black bean, frijole negro	Large kidney shaped bean with glistening black skins	8–12 hours or overnight	1 hour	Use as for red kidney beans. An essential ingredient in Brazil's national dish, feijoada. Also popular in the United States in soups
Black-eyed beans	Black-eyed peas, cowpea	A cream-coloured bean with a distinctive black spot. They have a smooth texture and a subtle flavour	8–12 hours or overnight	1–1½ hours	Good in soups and casseroles. A staple in Creole cooking and also used in the traditional American South dish of 'Hoppin' John', a mixture of black-eyed beans, rice and bacon, that is served on New Year's day

pulses and grains

Type	Other names	Description	Soaking time	Cooking time	Cooking tip
Borlotti beans	Cranberry bean	A pink bean with beige streaks. Very popular in Italy	8–12 hours or overnight	1–1½ hours	Use in Italian dishes like the soup pasta e fagioli and risottos
Pinto beans		A beige bean with brown streaks, similar to the borlotti bean	3–4 hours	1–1½ hours	Popular in Spanish bean dishes. Pinto is the Spanish word for 'painted'
Broad bean	Fava bean, Windsor bean, horse bean	Large, orange-brown coloured bean with a strong flavour	8–12 hours or overnight	1½ hours	Popular in Spain, where they are used in a hearty dish of beans, cured meats, sausage and garlic. Soak and remove skins before cooking
Butter bean	Lima bean, Madagascar bean	A large white flattened bean. Popular in US	8–12 hours or overnight	1–1½ hours	Butter beans become soft and mealy when they are cooked and are best used for purées and soups
Adzuki beans	Asuki bean, aduki bean	Considered one of the most delicious of the beans, the adzuki is a small, reddish brown bean with a sweet flavour. The bean is native to China and Japan and is widely used in sweet and savoury dishes	4–8 hours or overnight	30–45 minutes	In Japan the bean is crushed and used in desserts and cakes and for a traditional and extremely popular dish called red rice
Chickpeas	Channa, Egyptian bean, garbanzo beans	A small, hard, hazelnut shaped pea. It is indigenous to the Levant and has been important for centuries in the Near, Middle and Far East for dhals and vegetable dishes. It is also ground to a flour, in which case it is called gram, and is used for making fritters and flat breads	8–12 hours or overnight	1½–2½ hours	Use in salads, for Middle Eastern and Indian vegetable dishes. Chickpeas are used in such classics as hummus, falafels and for the soup eaten by Muslims during Ramadan, Harira. Soak well before cooking. For smooth pâtés and purées, remove the outer skins after cooking
Ful medames	Egyptian brown bean, field bean	A small brown bean	4–6 hours or overnight	1½–2 hours	The basic ingredient for the Egyptian dish of the same name, Ful medames
Soya beans	Soybeans	A hard round bean that comes in many colours. Extremely nutritious, the bean has been used in numerous ways for thousands of years in China	12 hours or overnight	2 hours	They go well with well-flavoured ingredients like garlic, herbs and spices as they do not have any intrinsic flavour in themselves. They make a healthy addition to soups, casseroles, bakes and salads

DRIED PEAS AND SPLIT PEAS

Dried peas are a separate species from the fresh garden pea. They can be whole or split but either way will disintegrate when cooked, making them popular for purées, soups and dhals. Split peas are either yellow or green and are mostly used for making soups. Marrow fat peas are used for the traditional British 'mushy peas'. Unlike split peas, these do require soaking.

Yellow split peas

Green split peas

STORING

Buy pulses in small quantities from stores with a good turnover. They should be stored in a dry, airtight container away from the light, and use within six to nine months. It's a mistake to think that pulses and lentils can be stored indefinitely. If kept for too long, beans and peas will toughen and lentils will acquire a musty flavour.

Marrow fat peas

Chickpeas

SOAKING AND COOKING

Dried beans and peas need to be soaked to soften them before cooking. There are basically two methods. A long soak, for 6–12 hours or overnight, and the quick soak method, whereby the beans are boiled rapidly for 2 minutes, then allowed to soak for 2 hours. Whichever method you use, cook the beans until tender after soaking.

▶ **Soaking** Put the beans in a large bowl. Add cold water to cover. Soak for 6–12 hours or overnight. Drain the beans and then rinse thoroughly under cold running water. The beans can now be cooked according to the recommended time.

Cook's tip

Beans contain three sugars which the body cannot break down. The answer is to soak well in plenty of cold water, which helps remove some of the indigestible sugars. Most beans and pulses need soaking before they can be cooked. The exceptions are black-eyed beans, mung beans, green and yellow split peas and all lentils. For best results use nine cups of water for every one cup of beans. Always discard the soaking water. Changing the water during soaking will also help to remove excess sugars. Soaking times vary, but the easiest and most convenient way is to soak them overnight. When it comes to cooking, once again use plenty of fresh water without any salt, which will toughen the skin. To help reduce the possibility of flatulence, change the water during cooking or add a pinch of aniseed, caraway or fennel seeds to the water.

pulses and grains

Grains are the edible seeds of grasses and include the familiar wheat, oats, barley, corn, rice, cous cous and polenta. Grains can be used whole, for example, rice in risottos or they can be flaked, for example, oats in porridge and they can be ground to make the most common grain product – flour. Grains can also be puffed up or flaked and flavoured to make breakfast cereal.

A CLOSER LOOK AT WHEAT

Wheat germ
This is the embryo plant and is rich in proteins, fats, minerals and vitamins B_1, B_2, B_6 and E. It is present in wholemeal flour, but is removed partly or entirely in brown and white flour respectively. It can be bought separately.

Wheat kernel or endosperm
This is the starchy inner part of the wheat grain. It contains starches and proteins. The type of proteins determine whether the flour is suitable for bread-making or not.

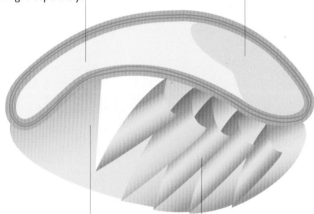

The wheat grain
A wheat grain is golden in colour when ripe and about 5 mm (¼ in) long. It is cleaned before milling, but for wholemeal flour, nothing else is removed.

Bran
The papery skin that covers the wheat grain. It has no flavour and cannot be digested but provides important fibre in our diet. Wholemeal flour contains all the bran, and brown flour contains a proportion of it. It is completely removed for white flour.

NUTRITIONAL INFORMATION

Wheat is a complex carbohydrate containing protein, vitamins B_1, B_2, B_6 and vitamin E and the minerals iron, selenium and zinc. The whole wheat grain (and thus wholewheat flour) is most nutritious, containing a greater proportion of vitamins and minerals and dietary fibre. Corn contains vitamin A and some B vitamins. It is also a source of iron.

Oats are extremely nutritious, being a source of protein, vitamin E, iron, zinc and niacin. They are also rich in vitamin B_1. They contain water soluble fibre, which may help control blood cholesterol levels.

Rye contains protein, iron, phosphorus, potassium and calcium. It is also a good source of folate and is high in fibre. Barley contains niacin, B_6, folate, together with zinc, copper and iron and calcium. The whole grain is more nutritious. Millet is a good source of iron, and vitamins B_1, B_2 and B_3. Buckwheat is very nutritious, containing all eight essential amino acids. It is also rich in iron and some B vitamins.

pulses and grains

Type	Description	Name	Description
Wheat berries	Wheat is usually ground into flour, but the whole grain, called the wheat berry, is available from health food shops. Soak and boil before adding to breads, soups or salads for a sweet, nutty flavour. It is also sometimes boiled in milk with cinnamon and sugar to make a pudding called frumenty	**Hominy**	Whole, hulled kernel of maize, made by soaking and boiling it until the outer skin can be rubbed off. It is still used as a starchy food, but more often it is dried and ground into coarse or hominy grits
Wheat flakes	Made by softening and rolling wheat berries. Use for muesli or add to bread, biscuits or cakes	**Cornflour**	Mostly used as a thickening agent for sauces, but can also be used for cakes and biscuits
Cracked wheat	Similar to bulgar. It is made from crushing whole wheat berries and therefore contains all the nutrients of the wholegrain. Use in salads or pilafs	**Popcorn**	Made using a particular strain of corn. When heated, the starchy interior of the kernel swells until the hard outer casing bursts and turns inside out
Bulgar wheat	Unlike cracked wheat, the wheat grain is cooked then dried, cracked and sieved to remove the bran. Bulgar wheat should be soaked for 20 minutes	**Oats**	Oats, like most grains apart from wheat, do not contain gluten so are unsuitable for bread-making, but if rolled they can be used for making porridge, or ground for oatcakes and pancakes. Use rolled oats for porridge, muesli, flapjacks and biscuits, medium oats for cakes and breads, and fine oatmeal for pancakes. Oatbran can be sprinkled over cereal
Wheat germ	The tiny seed of the wheat grain with a pleasant nutty flavour. Add to white flour for bread or scones or add to muesli. Wheat germ has a short shelf life. Keep in the fridge and check use-by dates	**Rye**	A popular grain used for bread-making in northern and eastern Europe. The meal makes a dark, dense loaf with a distinct flavour which goes well with the sour-dough method of leavening. It is available as grains, flakes and flour
Bran	The papery skin around the wheat grain which cannot be digested, but is very important in the diet, providing valuable fibre. Use sparingly when making bread or sprinkle over cereal	**Barley**	One of the oldest cultivated grains. A mild, slightly nutty flavour that is used in soups and stews or can be mixed with wheat flour for breads, biscuits and scones. Available in various forms: pot barley is the whole grain, pearl barley has the bran removed. Barley flakes and barley flour are also available
Cous cous	Made from durum wheat. A type of flour-coated semolina with a pleasant grainy texture. Mild flavour, with the wonderful ability to absorb other flavours, which no doubt accounts for its popularity, making it an excellent accompaniment to stews, or as a base for salads	**Millet**	Nutritious, with a pleasant crunchy texture and a nutty flavour. The whole grain can be used to accompany casseroles and curries while the flour is sometimes used for baking, although it should be mixed with wheat flour for making leavened breads
Semolina	Coarse, medium or fine ground. Best known in Britain for the milk pudding, semolina is surprisingly versatile. It can be added to cakes, biscuits and breads, is used in Italy for making gnocchi, and in the Middle East and India for breads, cakes and sweets	**Buckwheat**	Nutty, earthy flavour. In Eastern and Central Europe, the processed grain is used for making puddings, when it is known as kasha. Buckwheat flour can be added to leaves or used with wheat flour to make blinis in Russia, and buckwheat pancakes in Brittany. In Japan, the flour is used for making soba noodles
Cornmeal/ polenta	Made by grinding corn. Although corn does not contain gluten and cannot be used for risen loaves, cornmeal is used extensively for making flatbreads. Polenta is essentially the Italian word for cornmeal. It comes in several grades, from coarse to fine and is normally cooked in boiling salted water	**Quinoa**	First cultivated by the Incas. Use it as you would rice, as a side dish or add to soups. It has a slightly bitter flavour and firm texture

Preparing Bulgar Wheat

These are grains of wheat that are boiled until cracked, then dried. To reconstitute, place the bulgar in a bowl with enough cold water to completely cover the grains. Leave to stand for 15 minutes. Tip bulgar into a fine sieve set over a bowl. Squeeze out as much of the excess water as possible after soaking.

Preparing Polenta

Polenta is a coarse cornmeal. It can be served moist, enriched with butter and grated Parmesan cheese, or in firm, crisp-crusted pieces that have been pan-fried or chargrilled and topped with chargrilled vegetables or fresh tomato sauce.

Bring 1.75 litres (3 pints) salted water to the boil. Reduce heat to very low and simmer. Slowly add 300 g (11 oz) polenta, stirring constantly. Cook, stirring, until it pulls away from the pan for about 20 minutes. Serve the polenta with butter and Parmesan. For fried or char-grilled polenta, omit the butter and Parmesan and spread polenta 2 cm (¾ in) thick on a worktop. Leave to cool, then cut into wedges. Separate the wedges, brush the tops with olive oil and pan-fry or char-grill. Halfway through cooking, turn and brush with a little more oil. Cook for about 6 minutes until golden.

Recipes

Cous cous with summer vegetables This is a variation on the famous cous cous aux sept legumes, the national dish of Morocco. Cous cous is also commonly served with meat, poultry and fish.

Tabbouleh A favourite Middle Eastern salad, originating in the Lebanon, tabbouleh is made using bulgar wheat, chopped parsley, mint, tomatoes, cucumber and onion, and can be dressed with mint sprigs, lemon juice and olive oil.

Blinis A thick yeast-leavened pancake from Russian cuisine, made traditionally entirely or partly with buckwheat flour. Blinis are wonderful served with soured cream and caviar or smoked fish.

Polenta Polenta is a popular grain in Italy, especially in the north of the country where maize is grown extensively. At its most simple it is cooked as porridge until thick and then cooled and cut into squares. It can be served with butter, Parmesan cheese or even with shavings of truffle.

Preparing Cous Cous

Most cous cous is pre-cooked, and only needs moistening and steaming according to packet instructions. Serve it with a Moroccan tagine, or cool and add vegetables, herbs and a dressing and serve as a salad. Put 250 g (9 oz) cous cous in a lightly buttered pan. Add 500 ml (17 fl oz) hot water; stir with a fork until well blended. Cook over a medium-high heat for 5–10 minutes. Lower the heat and stir in 50 g (2 oz) butter. Fluff up with a fork, and coat with melted butter.

Couscousière

In North Africa, the cous cous grain gives its name to a spicy dish of meat and vegetables cooked in a special bulbous pot. Called a couscousière, the pot comes in two parts. The stew cooks in the bottom part of the pot, while the grain steams in a perforated pot on top, gaining flavour from the heady aromas of the stew beneath. The stew and grain are then served together.

rice

American long-grain and easy-cook

Arborio rice

Japanese rice

Pudding rice

Wild rice

Brown basmati rice

White basmati rice

Thai (jasmine) rice

Among the world's most versatile staples, rice is the basis of many traditional dishes around the globe. In India, rice pilaf is prepared by browning rice in hot oil or butter before cooking it in stock, which helps to keep the grains separate. Japanese cooks prefer a starchier variety, while in northern Thailand, a stickier rice is eaten with the hands. In all, there are more than 40,000 varieties of rice.

WASHING AND SOAKING RICE

Most rice, including basmati, Thai and ordinary long-grain rice, is improved if rinsed and/or soaked before cooking. The exception is any rice that is to be fried, such as rice for a risotto or for special fried rice.

Soaking rice will speed up the cooking time by increasing the moisture content of the grains. Soaking is recommended for white and brown long-grain rices, particularly basmati. Place the rice in a large bowl and pour over double the volume of cold water. Set aside for 30 minutes or according to the recipe and then drain well through a sieve or colander.

▶ **Washing** Washing rice removes excess starch and is recommended for most rices, particularly basmati. Put the rice in a large bowl, cover with cold water and stir with your fingers. The water will become cloudy. Let the rice settle, then gently tip the bowl so the water drains away. Repeat two or three times until the water runs clear.

COOKING QUANTITIES

- **To serve with curry, casseroles etc** 50–75 g (2–3 oz) uncooked rice per person
- **Pilafs** 50 g (2 oz) uncooked rice per person
- **Salads** 25–40 g (1–1½ oz) uncooked rice per person
- **Rice pudding** 15–20 g (½–¾ oz) uncooked rice per person

THE DIFFERENT TYPES OF RICE

Rice	Types available	Description	Cooking methods
Long-grain or patna or American long-grain	White, brown, organic, mixed with wild rice	Most widely available rice. Most long-grain rice comes from America (rice grown in China and the Far East is mostly for home consumption). The grain is three to four times longer than wide and the individual grains are not sticky but separate when cooked	Hot water method, microwave
Basmati	White, brown, organic, mixed with wild rice	Long-grain rice from the Punjab region of northern India. Considered the prince of rice with a delicious aromatic flavour	Hot water method, absorption method, microwave
Thai fragrant or jasmine rice	White only, organic	Long-grain fragrant rice. Slightly more sticky than basmati; suitable for sweet and savoury dishes	Absorption, microwave
Pudding rice	White only	Short-grain rice, the grain being almost as broad as it is long. The grains are sticky when cooked	Check recipe. Most pudding rice is cooked slowly in the oven
Risotto rice	Arborio, Vialone Nano, Carnaroli	Short-grain rice that has been developed especially for the Italian dish of risotto. Arborio is the most easily available; Vialone Nano and Carnaroli are considered superior with a creamier consistency and more 'bite' once cooked	Absorption method, normally adding liquid gradually and stirring in
Sushi rice	White only; normally Japanese Rose, Kokuho Rose and Calrose	White short-grain rice. Although a sticky rice, it is not as starchy as Italian risotto rices and is the best choice for sushi	Absorption method; check packet for cooking instructions
Glutinous rice	Can be black or the more common white	Very sticky rice, used for dim sum in China but otherwise mostly used in Asia for desserts	Absorption method
Red or Camargue rice	Red only	Semi-wild rice that has been developed in the Camargue region of France. Bright red with a pleasant nutty flavour, a little similar to brown rice	Hot water method
Wild rice	American or Giant Canadian	This is not a true rice but an aquatic grass. It has a nutty flavour and firm texture	Hot water method
Easy-cook or parboiled rice	White long-grain, white basmati	The rice is treated in order to lock in the nutrients, a process that results in a very well defined and separated grain, which is rarely soggy or sticky	Hot water method, microwave

COOKING RICE

See chart on previous page for rice types suitable for each method.

- **Hot water method** Place rice in a pan and add plenty of boiling water. Cook for the recommended amount of time (see below), then drain through a colander. The rice can be rinsed to remove excess starch. This method is particularly suitable for salads or other dishes if the rice is to be served cold.
- **Absorption method** The rice cooks in a measured amount of water – usually 2 parts water to 1 part rice – which is completely absorbed when the rice is cooked. The rice is cooked in a tightly covered pan over a low heat so that it cooks in its own steam. Put the water, rice and salt in a pan; bring to the boil. Stir, lower the heat and cover. Simmer for 15 minutes then let stand for a further 15 minutes. Fluff up grains with a fork.
- **Microwave method** Put the rice and boiling water or stock into large bowl. Cover with cling film and cook at full power. Check the manufacturers' instructions for timings. Allow the rice to stand for 10 minutes after cooking.

STORING

Uncooked rice should be stored in a cool, dark place where it will keep for up to three years. It is essential to ensure rice is kept dry, as it will absorb water and eventually will turn mouldy if kept in a damp place. Conversely, the older the rice, the more water you are likely to need for cooking.

Cooked rice should be cooled, covered and then kept in the fridge for up to 24 hours. Do not store for longer than this. It is essential to reheat rice until piping hot once it has been allowed to cool.

Rice variety (200 g/½ lb)	Amount of liquid	Cooking time (hot water method)	Cooked yield
Brown	450–575 ml (15–19 fl oz)	45–50 mins	600–800 g (1 lb 6 oz–1¾ lb)
Long-grain	400–450 ml (14–15 fl oz)	18–20 mins	600 g (1 lb 6 oz)
Risotto	350–400 ml (12–14 fl oz)	8–20 mins	600 g (1 lb 6 oz)
Wild	450–575 ml (15–19 fl oz)	45–60 mins	450 g (1 lb)

Perfect rice

Other than risotto, never stir rice while it is cooking; you will break up the holes that allow the steam to escape. Test for doneness by squeezing rice grains between the fingers; the rice should be tender with no hard centre.

SUCCESSFUL RISOTTO

For perfect risotto, use a heavy pan with a thick base that heats evenly and maintain the rice at a steady, gentle simmer. The stock must be added gradually so the rice, although always kept moist, is not drowned in liquid. Stir constantly at first, then less frequently as the rice cooks. Serve risotto at once; it continues to absorb liquid as it stands.

Fry the rice for a minute or two in butter or oil to coat all the grains. Add the first amount of stock, making sure risotto bubbles gently. Wait until the stock is almost all absorbed before adding the next amount.

Repeat the process, adding more stock until the rice is almost tender, of a creamy consistency but still firm to the bite.

RICE EQUIPMENT

ELECTRIC RICE COOKER

If you cook a lot of rice, it might well be worth investing in an electric rice cooker, so that you can be assured of perfect rice every time. Any rice can be cooked in an electric cooker. It also keeps rice warm after cooking, without it becoming either dry or getting soggy.

RICE PADDLE

In Japan, this small, flat utensil, made out of wood or bamboo, is used to turn cooked sticky rice – a technique that fluffs it up and enhances its appearance. The paddle is also used to serve rice to guests. It is the custom for each person to get two paddlefuls from a wooden tub, regardless of the quantity of rice that has been cooked. When fluffing up rice, use a sideways cutting motion.

JAPANESE ROLLING MAT

If you intend to make sushi, you will need to invest in one of these simple but efficient mats. The mat acts as a guide for rolling up rice and/or the nori (seaweed).

Recipes

Sushi A popular dish of Japanese rice flavoured with rice wine and vinegar, topped or rolled with raw fish or vegetables. It is generally served with a hot wasabi paste and some sweet pickled ginger.

Biryani A superb all-in-one Indian dish of rice and yogurt, with chicken or beef, vegetables, nuts, herbs and spices.

Paella A colourful mix of saffron, rice and other ingredients. The original Valencian paella contained eels, snails and beans. Today, though, there are no strict rules, and all sorts of favourites can be combined to wonderful effect. Rice and saffron are essentials, but after that feel free to add what you will – fish, shellfish, squid, chicken, rabbit and chorizo sausage are just a few possibilities you could try, along with tomatoes, onions and almost any vegetable that you care to name.

Wild mushroom risotto Risotto is a famous dish from the Piedmont region of Italy. Stock is slowly and gradually stirred into a starchy short-grained rice so that the final dish is rich and creamy. As an alternative to mild or dried mushrooms, fish, shellfish, chicken, sausages and beans are among the many other ingredients that can be added to risotto. Parmesan cheese, however, is a must.

rice

flours

Used as the basis for breads, pasta, noodles, cakes and biscuits, different flours are produced from different parts of the grain. Although it has a few other uses in the kitchen – as a coating and for thickening sauces – flour is generally used to create doughs, and the type of flour employed will produce different effects.

White flour
White flour has had all of the bran and wheat germ extracted, leaving just the white starchy part of the wheat grain.

Brown flour This contains about 85 per cent of the original whole grain, with a proportion of the bran and wheat germ extracted. Brown flour gives a slightly lighter result than 100 per cent wholemeal, and is popular for pastry-making and for some sauces.

Granary flour Granary flour is the proprietary name for a blend of brown and rye flours, and malted wheat grain. Breads made using granary flour are slightly sweet and sticky due to the malted grain.

Wheat flour Wheat flour is a hugely important ingredient. We use it for making sauces, for pastry, for cakes and biscuits and not least of all, for bread-making. Unlike almost any other grains (the exception is rye), wheat contains gluten, without which loaves and cakes would not rise. Choose the flour you need to suit the recipe.

Wholemeal flour Wholemeal flour, or 100 per cent extraction flour, is made using the whole of the wheat grain, including the bran and wheat germ. Most flour today is milled between steel rollers. Stoneground flour is made in the traditional way, ground between two stones, which is a slower process and consequently the flour is considered to have a better flavour.

Plain wholemeal flour can be used for wholemeal pastry, either by itself, or mixed with a proportion of white flour for a lighter result.

Spelt This is a coarse type of wheat and is one of the oldest cultivated grains. Spelt has a nutty flavour and is popular among nutritionists as it contains more protein and B complex vitamins than other wheat. It is available in most health food shops.

Strong flour or bread flour Strong flour contains a higher proportion of a special kind of protein which, when mixed with water, forms gluten. Gluten gives dough its elasticity which, if kneaded and proved sufficiently, gives a well-risen and soft loaf. There are strong wholemeal, brown and white flours and are the best choice for bread-making.

American cake flour This has been finely milled to produce a very soft flour and is recommended for cakes. American all-purpose flour comes somewhere between British strong and plain flour.

WORKING WITH FLOUR

▼ Sifting Sifting flour aerates the dough and helps make finished pastry crisp and light. Use a sifter or it can be shaken through a fine sieve into a large bowl.

▼ Making a well Many doughs call for forming a well with flour before putting in wet ingredients. Place the flour on a clean worktop and push flour from the centre to the sides so that you have a large depression in the middle to add eggs or other liquids in.

▲ Rolling out Flouring both the worktop and your rolling pin will prevent the dough sticking to either.

▲ Coating Flour, usually seasoned with salt and pepper and occasionally chopped herbs, can be used to cover escalopes, fish and so on. Place some flour in a flat bowl, then add any seasonings. Place the meat in the flour making sure both sides are covered.

Bleached flour

Flour producers once routinely bleached their flour by treating it with chlorine. This is less common nowadays. Unbleached flour is light cream in colour. Check packets if you want to make sure you avoid buying bleached flour.

BREAD DOUGHS

Strong, steady kneading develops the gluten in dough which is responsible for even-textured loaves without holes or dense spots. Too much flour makes a dry, heavy loaf.

Using the heel of your hand, push the dough down and away with a rolling motion. Give it a quarter turn, fold, then push down again. Repeat for 5–10 minutes until the dough is smooth and tiny blisters appear.

STORING

Refined flour can be kept in an airtight container in a cool, dry, dark place and should be used within six months. If refrigerated, white flour will keep for up to a year.

Whole grain flours, because they contain oil-rich germ and bran, turn rancid much faster. They should be stored in an airtight container and used within three months. To avoid contamination, store refined and unrefined flours in separate containers.

breads and yeast

Bread is the basis for sandwiches, bread puddings and eggy bread, but it has much wider uses when transformed into crumbs, croutons and croûtes. Breadcrumbs provide a protective coating for fried and baked foods. They also thicken soups and help bind stuffings. Croutons add texture to soups and salads. Croûtes are used to accompany soups, absorb cooking juices from game or meat, or float on top of soups like French onion.

BREADCRUMBS

For dried crumbs, bake fresh crumbs at 190°C (375°F) for 3–5 minutes. For fried crumbs to serve with game, fry fresh crumbs in hot oil and butter for 3–5 minutes until golden.

To make fresh breadcrumbs, put torn pieces of crustless bread into a food processor and pulse until fine crumbs form. To give the breadcrumbs a fine, even texture and remove any lumps, work them through a fine metal sieve.

MELBA TOAST

These thin slices of curled toast triangles are the traditional English accompaniment for rich smooth pâtés and savoury mousses, as well as creamy soups and salads. The techniques work best if you use day-old thinly sliced white bread, lightly toasted on both sides.

Remove crusts and slice horizontally through the toast using a serrated knife. Place, untoasted side up, on a baking sheet. Bake at 190°C (375°F) for 5–10 minutes, until the toast is golden and the ends have curled up. Cool them on a wire rack.

CROUTONS AND CROÛTES

Croutons are small dice of white bread while croûtes are larger. Croûtes can be cut from thickly sliced brown or white bread, in any shape you like. For the crispiest croutons and croûtes, French chefs use day-old bread.

▶ **Frying croutons** Heat a 1 cm (½ in) layer of olive oil with a knob of butter until foaming. Add the bread cubes and toss over a high heat for about 2 minutes until crisp. Drain.

◀ **Toasting croûtes** Toast medium-thick slices of baguette under a hot grill for about 2 minutes until golden brown. Turn over and toast on the other side.

▶ **Shaped croûtes** Use a biscuit cutter to cut shapes or rounds. Grill, as above, or bake on a baking sheet at 190°C (375°F), turning once, for 10–15 minutes until golden. For added flavour, rub toasted croûtes with a cut garlic clove.

CROSTINI AND BRUSCHETTA

Crostini are thin slices of toasted bread topped with a savoury mixture. Bruschetta are thicker slices of grilled or toasted country bread. Either can be rubbed with a cut garlic clove and drizzled with fruity olive oil (see below) and then topped with a variety of ingredients.

Olive oil crostini Toast slices of bread. While they are still warm, brush one side of each slice with virgin olive oil.

Garlic bruschetta Rub both sides of slices of bread with the cut side of a peeled and halved garlic clove, then toast until golden.

BREAD-BASED PUDDINGS

For bread-and-butter type puddings, always use good-quality bread, such as a traditional loaf or brioche, for perfect results. When using bread to line a basin (as for summer pudding, right), make sure you position the bread neatly for an attractive finish. Start by lining the basin with a bread slice or slices cut to the right size to fit the base, then overlap slices evenly around the side. Stale bread works best because it holds its shape better against moist fruit.

RAISING AGENTS

Yeasts Fresh and dried yeast can be used interchangeably in recipes. As a guide, 15 g (½ oz) fresh yeast is equivalent to 15 ml (1 tbsp) dried yeast granules. Both will rise up to a maximum temperature of 30°C (86°F) – any hotter and the yeast will be killed.

Bicarbonate of soda Also known as baking soda in the US or sometimes simply as soda. Mixed with an acid ingredient and a liquid, it releases carbon dioxide which causes a batter, cake or bread to rise. Lemon juice, vinegar or sour milk can be used as the acid. For soda breads, buttermilk is the traditional ingredient, but cream of tartar, an acid that is made from fermented grapes, is often used.

Baking powder A mixture of bicarbonate of soda and a dry acid. Mixed with a liquid, such as a batter, the dry acid and baking soda react together to release carbon dioxide. Work quickly once you have added liquid to the dry ingredients, as carbon dioxide will quickly escape.

USING YEAST

▶ **Fresh yeast** Crumble the yeast into a bowl and add a little of the measured warm water from the recipe. Cover and leave to stand until bubbles appear on the surface.

▶ **Dried yeast** Sprinkle the granules over a little of the measured warm water from the recipe. Most recipes will also recommend that you use a little sugar to encourage the yeast to multiply. Cover and leave until frothy.

▶ **Easy-blend yeast** Add straight to dry ingredients and stir. Add the warm liquid and mix. Some brands need only one rising – check the packet for instructions. Also check use-by dates, as easy-blend and fast-action yeasts have a relatively short shelf life.

pasta and noodles

The majority of pastas from southern Italy are made with just flour and water, but in the north of the country, egg is often added to the dough (pasta all'uovo). At first, egg pasta could be made only at home, but gradually manufacturers found ways of producing egg pasta and it is now widely available. Egg pasta has a richer flavour than plain pasta and goes well with creamy sauces. Plain pasta suits the traditional ingredients of the south – tomatoes, garlic, onions and olive oil. Although some pastas, such as spaghetti, are typically always plain, you will need to check the packet to see whether pasta contains egg or not.

COOKING PASTA

Use a large pan so the pasta can move freely in the boiling water. As an approximate guide, allow 5 litres (8¾ pints) water and 15 ml (1 tbsp) salt for 450 g (1 lb) pasta. Add salt and 15 ml (1 tbsp) oil to help stop the pasta from sticking together during cooking. Cook uncovered at a rolling boil until the pasta is al dente (see opposite), stirring occasionally.

◄ **Short pasta** Bring a large pan of water to the boil. Add salt and 15 ml (1 tbsp) olive oil. Add the pasta all at once, bring the water back to the boil. Cook uncovered at a rolling boil until the pasta is al dente, stirring occasionally.

Drain the pasta thoroughly in a colander, shaking it vigorously to release all the water. Return it to the pan and reheat with a knob of butter or 15–30 ml (1–2 tbsp) olive oil or turn it into a warmed serving bowl and toss with a sauce.

◄ **Long pasta** The technique for long pasta, like spaghetti and long tagliatelle, is to ease it gently into the water. As it softens in the boiling water, you can push it further into the pan, allowing it to coil round in the pan without breaking. Calculate the cooking time from the moment the water returns to the boil after all the pasta is submerged. The special Italian pasta cooker is ideal for cooking long pasta. When cooked, drain the pasta thoroughly. Rinse out the pan, then return to the heat and add a knob of butter or else 15–30 ml (1–2 tbsp) olive oil. Return the cooked pasta to the pan and toss over a high heat until the pasta is glistening.

COOKING TIMES

Calculate cooking times of all pasta types from the moment the water returns to the boil after the pasta has been added and always test before draining. If the pasta is to be cooked further (lasagne, for example), reduce the initial cooking time slightly.

- **Fresh pasta** 1–3 minutes or according to instructions on packet
- **Fresh stuffed pasta** 3–7 minutes or according to instructions on packet
- **Dried pasta noodles** 8–10 minutes or according to instructions on packet
- **Dried pasta shapes** 10–20 minutes or according to instructions on packet

WHICH SHAPE FOR WHICH SAUCE

Before deciding which sauce to make, an Italian cook would see what type of pasta they had first. Thick and creamy sauces are best with chunky shapes such as penne or fusilli. Oil-based sauces are best served with fine pastas such as spaghetti or linguine, and chunky meat sauces are good cooked with sheets of pasta such as lasagne or cannelloni.

PASTA EQUIPMENT

PASTA COOKER

A worthwhile investment for cooking large quantities, especially as it can be used for other purposes too. Made of stainless steel, it consists of a perforated pan which fits inside a solid pan. When the pasta is cooked, simply lift the inner pan out of the water to drain the pasta.

PASTA MACHINE

To make your own pasta at home, you will need a pasta machine to roll the dough to the required thickness and to cut it to your chosen shape. Without a pasta machine you'll need to hand-roll the dough the equivalent of ten times!

PASTA TONGS

These allow spaghetti and tagliatelle – both notoriously messy to serve – to be transferred to plates with ease. The toothed tongs grab the pasta without cutting it. They are also useful for lifting out one or two strands when testing for doneness.

Recipes

Minestrone Stellette, macaroni or other dried soup pasta go into this famous Italian vegetable, pasta and bean soup. Meats such as unsmoked bacon may also add to the taste. This hearty soup is almost a meal in itself.

Spaghetti alla carbonara One of the best-known and loved spaghetti dishes with a creamy sauce made principally of eggs, bacon and cream.

Fettuccine Alfredo (or tagliatelle) A rich sauce made with double cream and Parmesan cheese. It was invented by and named after a Roman chef called Alfredo, and is very quick and simple to prepare.

Pasta primavera A fresh-tasting dish in which tagliatelle is cooked with mixed herbs and a large variety of summer vegetables, served hot and sprinkled with Parmesan shavings.

pasta and noodles

151

Name	Type	Description	Similar pastas
Spaghetti	Long pasta	The most familiar of all the pastas and still the most popular pasta in its hometown of Naples. Length and width vary from region to region and there are numerous different flavours and colours available, such as spinach, tomato, wholewheat and chilli	Linguine (very thin spaghetti with flattened edges); linguinette is even thinner. Fusilli (corkscrew-shaped spaghetti)
Tagliatelle	Long pasta	From Bologna in Northern Italy. It is normally sold in nests (dried) or loose loops (fresh). A ribbon-shaped pasta, it can be made either with or without egg. Numerous different flavours are available, spinach (verde) being the most popular apart from the plain noodle	Fettuccine (Roman version of tagliatelle – the noodles are slightly thinner). Tagliatelline, tagliarini (thinner versions of tagliatelle). Pappardelle – normally sold as a fresh pasta – the ribbons are wider than tagliatelle and traditional pappardelle have wavy edges
Vermicelli	Long pasta	A very fine form of spaghetti, which came originally from Naples. Available plain or made with egg	Capelli d'angelo (angel's hair)
Macaroni	Short pasta	Hollow short pasta shapes. There are many versions, varying in size and length. Plain and egg macaroni are both available	Penne (slender tubes cut diagonally). Rigatoni (ridged tubes). Tubetti (miniature macaroni used in soups). Ziti (a more slender version of maccheroni). Chifferini (small curved tubes, either plain or ridged)
Maccheroni	Long tubular	Tubular pasta popular in southern Italy	
Conchiglie (shells)	Short pasta	Shell-shaped pasta. Available in a variety of sizes, colours and flavours	Lumache (snail shells)
Farfalle (butterflies or bow-ties)	Short pasta	Pretty, bow-tie shaped pasta. They normally have crinkled edges and can be ridged or plain. Available in a variety of colours	
Fusilli	Short pasta	Thin pasta spirals. The spirals open out during cooking. Traditional fusilli is plain and uncoloured, although egg and spinach flavours are now available	Eliche (very similar to fusilli, although the spirals are more like the thread of a screw). Eliche does not open out during cooking
Lasagne	Flat pasta	The sheets may be plain, ridged, fluted at both or just one edge. Plain and egg lasagne are available and they most commonly come in three different flavours or colours: plain (yellow), spinach (green) and wholewheat (brown). Lasagne is normally pre-cooked and then baked in the oven (al forno) between layers of sauce	Cannelloni. Ready-made cannelloni is a large pasta tube. Like lasagne it is used for baking in the oven with a meat, vegetable and/or cheese sauce. Lasagnette (a cross between tagliatelle and lasagne, the edges can be fluted on both or just one side)
Pastina	Soup pasta	A generic name for an almost countless number of tiny pasta shapes used for broths and soups	Stellette (stars). Risoni (rice-shaped). Anellini (tiny thin rounds). Farfalline (little butterflies)
Ravioli	Stuffed pasta	Square envelopes stuffed with a filling. The pasta itself can be plain, wholewheat or egg, flavoured with spinach, tomato, squid or saffron. There is an almost endless variety of fillings	Rotondi (oval ravioli). Tortelloni (stuffed and folded circles of pasta pinched into rounds). Cappelletti (similar to tortelloni but made using squares of pasta)

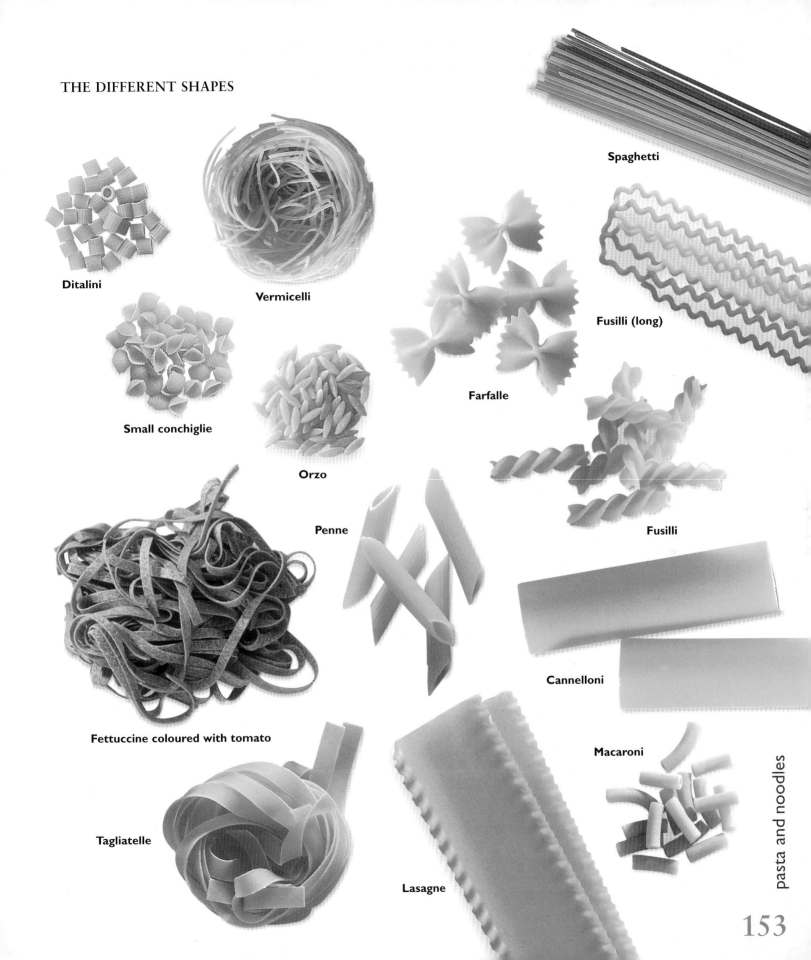

THE DIFFERENT SHAPES

Spaghetti

Ditalini

Vermicelli

Fusilli (long)

Small conchiglie

Farfalle

Orzo

Fusilli

Penne

Fettuccine coloured with tomato

Cannelloni

Macaroni

Tagliatelle

Lasagne

pasta and noodles

153

Rice noodles

Flat rice noodles

Mung bean noodles

Egg noodles

Buckwheat (above) and Udon noodles (below)

ASIAN NOODLES

The Chinese have been eating noodles since the first century BC and their popularity seems to have spread to other parts of Asia in the centuries that followed. As with Italian pasta, there are many varieties. The majority of Asian noodles are made of wheat, rice, buckwheat or mung bean, but corn and seaweed are among others that are available in some regions.

Rice noodles These are mostly popular in rice-growing regions of China and southeast Asia. Rice noodles are pale and brittle; they come in various thicknesses, mostly sold in loose coils or loops. Rice noodles have been pre-cooked so require only the minimum cooking. Check the packet for timings.

Mung bean noodles Also called cellophane noodles, glass noodles or bean thread vermicelli, these look like rice noodles, but unlike the rice variety, are surprisingly firm and resilient, and will not break. Cut mung bean noodles into short lengths as required by the recipe using scissors (they will not break like rice noodles). They go well in casseroles, soups and spring rolls, absorbing the flavours of other ingredients. Soak in hot water before using.

Egg noodles Common in China, and Japan where they are called Ramen noodles. They come in various thicknesses and are also available fresh or dried. All wheat noodles should be cooked either by themselves or as part of the recipe. Many benefit from pre-soaking, but it's best to check the instructions on the packet.

Buckwheat noodles Soba noodles are the best known of the buckwheat noodles. They are grey/brown in colour and have a stronger flavour than wheat noodles. Check the packet instructions as timings will depend on the thickness of the noodles.

Udon and somen noodles Japanese noodles. They can be fresh or dried. Check the packet instructions for cooking times. Dried noodles benefit from being pre-soaked.

COOKING NOODLES

Most Chinese and Japanese noodles need to be cooked before being stir-fried. Exceptions are cellophane and rice noodles, which only require soaking.

▼ Cook noodles in boiling salted water until just tender. Drain and rinse under cold water to prevent them cooking any further. Drain the noodles again, ensuring all excess water is removed.

▲ They are now ready for stir-frying. Heat a wok until hot but not smoking. Add 15–30 ml (1–2 tbsp) oil and heat until hot. Add the noodles and flavourings and stir-fry over a high heat for 2–3 minutes, tossing the noodles until they are glistening with oil and warmed right through.

vegetables

onions

The onion family is wide and varied; onions and garlic are generally round and have papery outer skins while spring onions and leeks are long and green with bulbous ends.

Choosing

Onions should have a good colour, with no visible blemishes or signs of sprouting. They should feel firm – onions that have been exposed to the frost feel slightly squashy, so take care if the weather has been quite cold.

YIELD

1 SMALL ONION

⅓ CUP

5 ml (1 tsp) onion powder

15 ml (1 tbsp) dried onion

STORING

Onions should be kept in a cool, dry place such as a larder or outhouse, where they will keep well for three to four weeks. Do not keep in the refrigerator, as they will go soft. Do not keep cut onions, as their aroma will contaminate any food with which they come into contact.

Yellow onion

Red onion

White onion

Shallots

Pickling onions

Yellow onions
The most commonly available onions with golden brown papery skins. They have a strong onion flavour. They are ideal for using in any cooked dish.

Vidalia onions
A popular American onion that grows in south-east Georgia. The Vidalia is very sweet, crisp and juicy with a hint of heat. Good raw, thinly sliced in salads. Also very good roasted.

Bermuda onions
Another large onion, slightly more squat than the Spanish onion. Mild flavour. Good raw in salads.

Red onions
Sometimes called Italian onions. Below the beautiful deep-red/purple skin, the flesh is white, flecked with lines of red. The flesh is very sweet and juicy. Wonderful raw in salads or cooked in certain recipes where a distinct sweetness is required.

White onions
An American onion with a pure white skin. The flavour is fairly strong and pungent. Mostly used in cooking, where they add an excellent flavour. Good in salads if a strong onion flavour is required.

Shallots
A small onion which divides into two or more cloves when skinned. It has less smell than the common onion and is considered milder and easier to digest. A popular aromatic vegetable in the French kitchen, the shallot is used in a host of classic recipes. Shallots dissolve almost to nothing when cooked, but do not brown them when sautéeing, as they will become bitter.

Pickling onions
Tiny white or pale onions. The Paris Silverskin is pure white and about the size of a marble. The Giant Zittau is larger and has a darker skin. Mostly used for pickling, but also useful for kebabs, and for any recipe where you need a small onion.

Pearl onions
Larger than pickling onions, these are also known as baby or button onions. They have a delicious, delicate flavour. Pearl onions are particularly sweet and can be used in a wide variety of dishes.

COOKING ONIONS

Although cooked onions are never as strong as raw onion, since their volatile acids are driven off during cooking, different cooking will affect their flavour and, of course, the flavour of the dish you are making.

▶ **Boiling** gives a strong, slightly raw onion flavour, but the longer the onion is cooked, the milder it becomes. Shallots are often used in this way and will eventually disintegrate altogether, leaving behind a subtle onion taste.

◀ **Sautéeing** sliced or chopped onions produce a softer onion and if not allowed to brown, then the flavour will be good but unassertive.

▶ **Frying** onions will brown them and they will develop a delicious caramelised flavour that is both sweet and savoury.

◀ **Roasting** by themselves or with other vegetables produces a superb flavour, the roasting bringing out their natural sweetness.

PREVENTING TEARS

The volatile oils in onions can sting the eyes and make them water. One trick is to leave the root end intact during chopping. Or, you can try peeling onions while they are submerged in a bowl of cold water.

REMOVING ONION SKINS

It is easier to remove the skin of small onions, such as pearl onions, if you let them steep in hot water for a few minutes. The skin will then slip off easily.

Recipes

Pissaladière parcel A variation on the traditional speciality of Nice, made of pastry filled with a layer of slow-cooked onions, topped with anchovies and goat's cheese.

French onion soup The hearty traditional soup of onions served topped with slices of toasted bread and grated Gruyère cheese.

Warm stuffed onion salad Peeled whole onions have their insides hollowed out and are then filled with a ham, cheese, tomato and breadcrumb stuffing before being baked.

Onion bhaji Spicy balls of sliced onion and flour deep-fried. Served as a starter or accompaniment.

Fried onion rings Flour-coated slices of onion deep-fried in hot oil. A popular side dish with beefburgers.

onions

leeks and spring onions

Leeks are related to both garlic and onions but have a milder flavour and a subtle sweetness. Of all the onion family, leeks alone need thorough cleaning. They should be well cooked to avoid an unpleasant raw taste. They can, however, be eaten hot or cold. Spring onions, or scallions, have a mild, delicate flavour. They can be used in salads or cooked dishes where regular onions are too strong. Their stalks are often used as flavouring.

ASIAN SLICING

In many Eastern style dishes both the white and green parts of spring onions are used. Cut at an angle starting at the dark green top and working your way down to the root. Use the line of your knuckles as a guide for the knife.

Spring onions are simply young onions that have been harvested before the bulb has swollen and while the stalks are still green and fresh.

Leeks should have bright, lively looking leaves, with no blemishes or soft spots. Small to medium-sized leeks (less than 2.5 cm/1 in in diameter) are the most tender.

WASHING LEEKS

Separate the leaves and rinse thoroughly under cold water as sand and grit often lodge in the vegetable.

STORING

Spring onions should be stored in the salad drawer of the fridge for up to three days. Leeks can be stored, wrapped in a polythene bag, at the bottom of the fridge, or kept in a cool, dark place where they will keep for up to one week.

NUTRITIONAL INFORMATION

Leeks and spring onions contain useful amounts of vitamin C, together with calcium and iron. Garlic is believed to lower blood cholesterol, thus reducing heart disease. Raw garlic also contains a powerful antibiotic and is said to increase the absorption of vitamins, and there is some indication that it has a beneficial effect against cancer and also strokes. Some authorities, however, say evidence of garlic's health-giving properties is inconclusive and that it would mean having to eat up to seven cloves a day to achieve this effect.

garlic

Garlic is one of the magic ingredients in the kitchen, adding a wonderful pungency and aroma to so many of our savoury dishes. Garlic is related to leeks, onions and chives and like them it is a member of the lily family. The bulb, encased in a parchment like skin, consists of sections, called cloves, which also come in paper skins.

The heat of garlic is said to be due to the climate it grows in. Southern Spain, Portugal and Turkey, where days are long and hot, and nights cold, produce the hottest garlic.

Choose plump, succulent cloves with clear skins. Avoid any garlic bulbs with sprouts.

Fresh garlic
Demand for fresh garlic is increasing and it is becoming a more familiar sight in our supermarkets at the beginning of summer. The flavour of fresh garlic is softer and less pungent than mature garlic.

Purple garlic
Unless you shop in specialist stores you are unlikely to have much choice when buying garlic. However the pink or purple tinged garlic, which comes from the French area of Lautrec and is available at the end of August, is a wonderful garlic, with large juicy cloves and a good potency.

New season garlic
Harvested before maturity, the stalks remain green and fresh. Roast whole, or slice the bulb and leaves and use in salads.

CRUSHING GARLIC

The traditional way to release garlic's pungent oils and make it easier to peel, is to lay the flat side of a chef's knife over a garlic clove and strike it firmly with your fist.

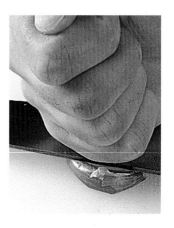

GARLIC PRESS

This is a convenient way of crushing garlic, simpler than crushing with the blade of a knife, and less messy than using a pestle and mortar. Buy a strong aluminium or stainless steel garlic press. Some have reverse prongs for easy cleaning.

STORING

Keep in a cool, dark, airy place. If the air is damp, garlic will begin to sprout, or if it is too warm, the cloves will turn to a grey powder. Whole bulbs can be kept in small earthenware pots; whole strings of garlic can be hung in a larder or any cool, dark place.

ROASTED GARLIC

Garlic mellows and its flavour sweetens when roasted. It is useful as a flavouring, accompaniment or garnish. You can create garlic 'flowers' by slicing off the top of each head of garlic, brushing with oil and cooking in the oven.

leeks, spring onions and garlic

159

shoots and stems

Among nature's most tender vegetables, shoots and stems are considered by some to be the elite of the vegetable kingdom.

Choosing

Celery should look moist and crisp and be tight and compact with unblemished stalks and fresh leaves. The darker the colour the stronger the taste. White celery is generally considered superior to green celery, being more tender and less bitter but is only available during the winter months.

Look for compact, uncracked, whitish-green fennel bulbs free of discoloration; the leaves should look fresh and green. Older, tougher vegetables have bulbs that spread at the top.

Cardoon Looking like a bunch of wild celery, it is prepared by stripping away the outer leaves and ribs, leaving behind the inner ribs and heart. The flavour is rather elusive, said by some to be a cross between artichoke, celery and salsify, while others find it more like asparagus. It can be eaten raw or baked for 30–40 minutes until tender.

Samphire Marsh samphire, although not cultivated, is often found in fishmongers when it is in season in late summer and early autumn. It grows in estuaries and salt marshes and has a distinctly sea-salty, iodine flavour.

Fennel All parts are edible, from the bulb to the celery-like stalks and feathery leaves. Fennel can be eaten raw or cooked; slow-cooking by roasting or braising brings out its sweetness and tames the liquorice flavour.

White celery Sometimes known as blanched or winter celery, the white flesh occurs as earth is banked up against the shoots during growing, so that the stalks are not exposed to sunlight and they remain pale and white.

Green celery is available all year round and is allowed to grow naturally.

PREPARING FENNEL

Rinse the bulbs with cold water; cut off root ends and stalks. Slice each bulb lengthways in half.

Recipes

Fennel au gratin In this dish, fennel is poached until soft and served in a creamy sauce browned under the grill.

Sweet roasted fennel Flavoured with lemon juice and thyme and sweetened with sugar, the fennel is oven roasted.

Asparagus with aioli sauce A Provençal mayonnaise, this sauce is a thick garlic-based accompaniment for asparagus.

Asparagus accompaniments Generally served warm or hot, it is traditionally paired with a mustard or vinaigrette sauce, clarified melted butter, hollandaise or mousseline.

ASPARAGUS

Universally admired, asparagus comes in three types: white, green and purple. Small, thin spears, known as sprue, are also sold. Served either hot or cold, asparagus should always be cooked first. Allow 300 g (11 oz) per person as a first course serving.

Choosing

No matter the type, look for brightly coloured, firm spears with tight buds; avoid those with woody stems. Select roughly even-sized spears for uniform cooking.

STORING

Celery can be stored in the salad drawer of the fridge and will keep for up to 2 weeks. If it turns limp, revive it by standing in a jar of water. Trim the ends of asparagus, stand the spears upright, loosely covered, in a tall glass with 2–3 cm (¾–1¼ in) of water in the bottom.

COOKING ASPARAGUS

▼ **Steaming** If you don't have an asparagus steamer (see page 31), put a bundle of asparagus spears upright into a deep saucepan containing 10 cm (4 in) of simmering water. Wedge the bundle into place with balls of foil. Cover with a dome of foil and simmer for 5–7 minutes until tender.

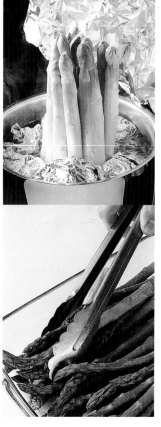

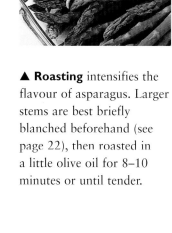

▲ **Roasting** intensifies the flavour of asparagus. Larger stems are best briefly blanched beforehand (see page 22), then roasted in a little olive oil for 8–10 minutes or until tender.

Purple asparagus, which is allowed to grow several centimetres high, has a full-flavoured, delicious taste.

Green asparagus is harvested when the stalks are about 15 cm (6 in) high and said to have the best flavour of all.

White asparagus is harvested as soon as it appears above the ground. It is large and tender with little flavour.

shoots and stems

161

globe artichokes

Unlike other shoots and stems, which require the barest minimum in terms of preparation and cooking, globe artichokes do call for a little work on the part of the cook, and sometimes on the part of the diner too! After cutting and trimming into shape, they take ages to cook, and then need further attention, as the inner leaves and the hairy choke must be removed. However, artichokes are well worth the effort and are loved for their unique texture and luxurious flavour.

Choosing

Only buy artichokes in their season between July and the end of the year. A good specimen should feel heavy for its size, with a good bloom on the leaves. Check its top to make sure that the inner leaves are wrapped tightly round the choke and the heart inside.

STORING

Artichokes can be wrapped loosely and kept in the fridge for 3–4 days. If you do have the opportunity of buying a large quantity, blanch the hearts for 8–10 minutes and then freeze for up to 1 year.

A CLOSER LOOK AT AN ARTICHOKE

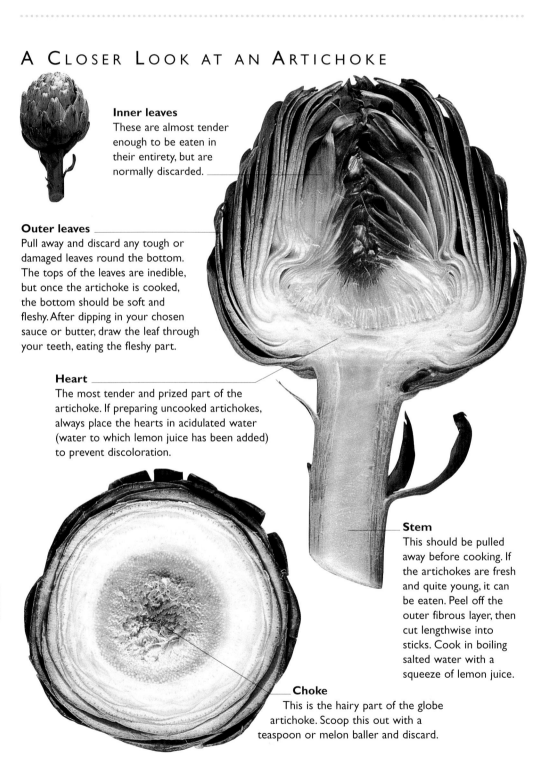

Inner leaves
These are almost tender enough to be eaten in their entirety, but are normally discarded.

Outer leaves
Pull away and discard any tough or damaged leaves round the bottom. The tops of the leaves are inedible, but once the artichoke is cooked, the bottom should be soft and fleshy. After dipping in your chosen sauce or butter, draw the leaf through your teeth, eating the fleshy part.

Heart
The most tender and prized part of the artichoke. If preparing uncooked artichokes, always place the hearts in acidulated water (water to which lemon juice has been added) to prevent discoloration.

Stem
This should be pulled away before cooking. If the artichokes are fresh and quite young, it can be eaten. Peel off the outer fibrous layer, then cut lengthwise into sticks. Cook in boiling salted water with a squeeze of lemon juice.

Choke
This is the hairy part of the globe artichoke. Scoop this out with a teaspoon or melon baller and discard.

Baby artichokes are a particular delicacy and are becoming more readily available in our own supermarkets and greengrocers. They can be eaten whole, including the stalk and outer leaves and even the choke, which is barely developed. In Mediterranean countries, baby artichokes may be served as parts of a salad or side dish, but more frequently form part of an hors d'oeuvre or antipasto.

PREPARING AND COOKING WHOLE ARTICHOKES

Mature artichokes are always served cooked. They should be prepared as below then placed in a pan of boiling salted water with the juice of 1 lemon.

Weight down with a plate and simmer for 30–40 minutes until tender. There are also special artichoke holders to keep them upright during cooking.

The artichoke is done when the bottom leaves come away easily. Let them cool, and if you like, you can now remove the central cone and choke.

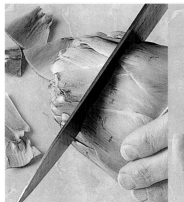

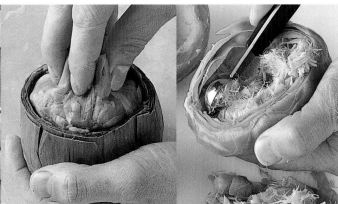

▲ Remove outer leaves Twist off the stalk at the bottom, pulling out the tough fibres. Cut off the top third of the artichoke and trim any tough outer leaves.

▲ Take away central core Once cooled, lift out the soft central cone of leaves and discard.

▲ Remove choke Using a melon baller or small spoon, scrape off the hairy choke, being careful not to waste any of the heart below.

potatoes

Long white

Russet

Round red

New

NUTRITIONAL INFORMATION

Potatoes are an excellent source of carbohydrate. They are high in vitamin C, beta-carotene and potassium. The skin contains a large amount of nutrients, although the majority are in the rest of the vegetable, particularly just below the skin. So, if you're peeling potatoes, only remove a thin layer of flesh with the peelings. To preserve the nutrients of new potatoes, lightly scrub skins and then boil or, if you want to eat them without skins, rub these off once the potatoes are cooked.

YIELD

3 MEDIUM POTATOES

=

500 G (1¼ LB)

=

about 2 cups mashed

=

about 3 cups sliced

=

about 2¼ cups diced

Choosing

Potato varieties are classified by shape (long or round) and skin colour, which can be white, russet or red. A new potato is not a variety but one sold right after harvest. Select your potato according to the recipe you want to cook – waxy or floury (see below). If in doubt, select an all-purpose variety such as Cara.

Make sure the potato is firm, smooth-skinned and solid without any noticeable blemishes or eyes. Reject any with a greenish cast. New potatoes need to be absolutely fresh when buying as they quickly lose their vitamin C and deteriorate more rapidly than old potatoes.

Waxy or floury?

The many varieties of potato fall into two categories: waxy types with a high water, low starch content and floury with a low water, high starch content. The former keeps its shape better when cooking so is ideal for boiling and using in salads; the latter becomes fluffy when cooked so is best baked or mashed. New potatoes, like Jerseys, are generally waxy while older potatoes, such as Maris Pipers and King Edwards, are floury. If you are unsure about the kind you have and want to know before cooking, add one part salt to 11 parts water and drop in the potato. A waxy potato will almost always float to the top while a floury one will sink to the bottom.

STORING

Both old and new potatoes should only ever be stored in a dark, cool, well-ventilated and dry place such as a larder or vegetable rack. If potatoes are exposed to light, they will develop green patches, which can be poisonous. They will go mouldy if stored in a damp place. You can cut away small amounts of green but if the green is widespread, discard the potato. Do not store potatoes in the fridge.

If you are buying potatoes in bulk, you can keep them in their paper sacks. But do take potatoes out of plastic bags, as they encourage the humid conditions that cause mould.

Old potatoes can be stored for several months although they will gradually lose their nutritional value and become floury. Eat new potatoes within two or three days of purchase.

Tools for the Perfect Mash

Never mash potatoes using a food processor; the potatoes will become soupy; for perfect mashed potatoes use one of the following:

POTATO MASHER

Found in various forms, the most popular are a flat steel mesh circle held between two long prongs or a thick wire zigzag that fits into a central handle. A spring-action masher has two mashing heads; when you press on the handle, the upper head comes down next to the lower head.

POTATO RICER

Made of stainless steel or aluminium, it consists of a small pierced basket and two handles, one of which contains a flat disc that presses onto cooked potato forcing it through the holes.

MOULI

For the smoothest, fluffiest mash, place cooked potatoes in the Mouli set over a bowl and turn the handle to force them through.

French Fries

Deep-fried potatoes are characterised by different names depending on their shapes. Among the most popular are the stick-shaped potatoes, which come in different sizes.

• When preparing potatoes for frying, place in a bowl of acidulated water (see page 169) and dry thoroughly before use.

• Don't add too many potatoes to the pan as the oil temperature will lower, making the chips greasy.

• Salt the fries after frying otherwise the potatoes will become soggy.

Straw potatoes
(Pommes pailles) Very fine strips, 7.5 cm (3 in) long

Matchstick potatoes
(Pommes allumettes)
3 mm x 6 cm (⅛ x 2½ in)

Chips (Pommes frites)
5 mm x 7.5 cm (¼ x 3 in)

Straight cut (Pont Neuf)
1 cm x 7.5 cm (½ x 3 in), with trimmed ends and sides; serve stacked.

Recipes

Pommes Anna Named after the French lady of fashion Anna Deslions, this potato dish was created to accompany roast meat and poultry.

Gratin dauphinois Sliced and buttered potatoes with a creamy egg mix and cheese and then baked in a shallow dish.

Duchesse potatoes Potatoes puréed with butter and egg, piped into a decorative shape and baked in the oven; used as an accompaniment or garnish.

Château potatoes New potatoes gently cooked in butter until golden and tender, traditionally served with steak.

Potato rösti This Swiss speciality is made from parboiled potatoes, grated and fried to form a golden cake. Traditionally left out overnight in the snow to dry out.

Lyonnaise potatoes Rounds of par-cooked potatoes sautéed with thinly sliced onions.

Perfect Roast Potatoes

Parboil the potatoes first to help them cook evenly. Drain well and leave in a covered pot with the heat turned off until the potatoes are thoroughly dry. Shake the pot to roughen the potato edges or scratch each one with a fork.

potatoes

other root vegetables

Turnip Members of the cabbage family and closely related to the swede, turnips have a good texture and pleasant peppery flavour if not overcooked. Young turnips, the ones to choose, are small and white and tinged with green at the top; navets, a popular continental version, are tinged with purple. Select turnips that feel heavy for their size, with smooth, unbruised skins.

Parsnips Sweet with nutty overtones. Choose small and medium parsnips for the best flavour; large ones will contain a woody centre. Avoid those with soft spots, rough skin or cracks.

Beetroot Related to the sugar beet, this vegetable has the highest sugar content of any vegetable, and is very low in calories. Choose firm, unblemished, small to medium-sized beetroots. If possible, buy bunches with the green tops on, which can be cooked like spinach. The leaves should look fresh and healthy.

Swede Belonging to the same cabbage family as turnips, these are older, larger and less reputable. Originally known as turnip-rooted cabbages, they acquired their current name when Sweden began exporting them to Britain. Choose firm, heavy swedes with smooth skin and no decay.

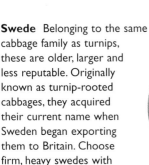

Carrot Highly nutritious, a single carrot supplies enough vitamin A for the entire day. Select firm, crisp carrots with a bright colour and a smooth skin. Baby carrots look attractive on a plate, and young carrots are often sold with their tops but mature ones are sweetest and contain the most vitamins.

TURNED VEGETABLES

Most root vegetables, cucumbers and courgettes can be transformed into neat barrel or olive shapes to resemble baby versions. Traditionally turned

vegetables have seven sides, but they can have five or fewer sides provided the pieces are all uniform in size.

◄ Cut turnips and other round vegetables into quarters, carrots and other tubular vegetables into 5 cm (2 in) lengths.

▼ Using a small paring knife, carefully trim off all sharp edges. Work from top to bottom paring down the vegetable and turn after each cut until it becomes barrel shaped.

KNOBBLY VEGETABLES

Once you remove the tough outer skin of celeriac, Jerusalem artichokes and kohlrabi, you will be left with a trio of very versatile vegetables which can be sliced, chopped, shredded or grated. Use a small sharp knife to remove the peel and work methodically, cutting the vegetable into manageable pieces. The flesh will discolour on exposure to the air so keep pieces in acidulated water (see page 169).

Kohlrabi A member of the cabbage family, this pale green or purple bulb has leafy shoots at the top. The bulb tastes like turnip, while the leaves have a spinach flavour. Choose small, heavy bulbs with dark green leaves; larger bulbs can be woody.

Celeriac
Prized for its knobbly, round root, it is at its best in winter, when it has a pronounced celery flavour and a firm, dense texture similar to that of turnips. Choose small, firm bulbs (under 10 cm/4 in diameter) without any sprouts on top of the bulb and with the minimum of knobs. The roots, if attached, should be clean. Larger vegetables are likely to be woody.

Jerusalem artichoke
Related to the sunflower, these have a crisp, nutty and slightly sweet taste. Choose firm, unblemished tubers free of soft spots and green-tinged portions. and with the minimum of knobs.

RADISHES

Round or long, red, white, black, lavender, pale green or candystriped, this root vegetable also comes in a variety of shapes – round, oval or elongated. The bright red radish is the smallest and most peppery; black radishes have a stronger flavour than more colourful varieties and radishes can grow more than 30 cm (1 ft) long. Always look for smooth radishes that feel firm, not spongy. Radishes are usually eaten raw but can be cooked or used as a garnish.

RADISH GARNISHES

▼ **Radish spiral** Thread a large chunk of radish onto a skewer. Cut, spiralling along the length, turning the vegetable as you go.

▲ **Radish rose** Cut off the tops then cut thin criss-cross slices without cutting into the stem. Chill in iced water to open.

other root vegetables

unusual and exotic roots

STORING

Store in a cool, dark place. Those vegetables marked with an * can be refrigerated.

Cassava	1–2 weeks
Jicama *pieces*	1–2 weeks*
Jicama *whole*	1–2 weeks
Salsify	up to **3** days*
Sweet potato	**3–4** days
Taro	**3–5** days
Yam	**2–3** weeks

PREPARING TARO, YAM AND CASSAVA

Taro, yam and cassava contain a poisonous substance under their skins, which cooking destroys. If using peeled, however, always remove a thick scraping of skin. Discard the peel carefully and wash hands after preparation.

Salsify and scorzonera Two closely related roots, both are thin, long, earthy and hard to clean. They have a distinct flavour, some say similar to oysters though others say it is more similar to asparagus and artichokes. Though they have different coloured skins, both have snowy white flesh. They can be cooked in many of the ways for other root vegetables – puréed, sautéed or boiled.
Black salsify (scorzonera) has a dark brown or black skin, with a pale flesh.
White salsify, sometimes called 'oyster plant', is said to have the superior flavour. It has a paler skin.

Sweet potatoes
Unrelated to the common potato, there are two commonly available varieties: one has an orange-red skin and deep pink flesh, the other has a darker red skin and paler flesh. Both have a sweet, slightly pungent flavour. Choose dry, smooth potatoes without sprouts. Once peeled, keep in acidulated water.

Jicama
The tuber of a plant that also produces beans, it is sold whole, ranging in size from 500 g–3 kg (1¼–7 lb), and in pieces. It is turnip shaped with thin brown skin and white flesh. In taste and texture, jicama resembles the water chestnut and it can be sliced thin and eaten raw. Choose smaller specimens to avoid woodiness; a thick skin indicates it is too old. Scrub under running cold water before peeling and slicing thinly.

Taro Widely used in Africa, Asia and the Caribbean, it is valued for its carbohydrates. The smaller variety, known as eddo or dasheen, may be the size of a new potato, or it can be found as a large barrel-shaped vegetable. All have a bristly, coarse skin with a pale radish-like flesh. Its flavour is said to be evocative of potato and chestnut. Taros soak up a great deal of liquid during cooking and are best included in soups and stews. They also can be deep-fried, boiled and mashed and used for fritters. Serve hot as taro becomes sticky when cold.

vegetables

168

Cassava A popular root vegetable from the West Indies and used in numerous Caribbean and African dishes, it is eaten as a vegetable, either baked or fried, or pounded into a flour from which fufu, a traditional African dish, is made. Tapioca is made from it and it also is used as a thickener for stews and dumplings. An intoxicating liquor can be made from the root.

Tapioca

A flavouring for pies and puddings and a thickener for sauces and soups, it comes as flour, tiny balls or flakes made from the dried paste of grated cassava root.

Yam There are many varieties varying in shape and size but most have a rough brown, russetted skin and a pale flesh. When preparing, peel away the skin thickly. Place in acidulated water (see below right) to prevent discoloration. Yam has a fairly bland flavour, but like potatoes they are versatile, so can be used to bulk out dishes. They are extremely good deep-fried.

PREPARING EXOTIC ROOTS

▼ Most roots should be washed thoroughly and peeled before cooking. Cut or scrape away the skin and a layer of flesh underneath.

▼ Remove any woody centres before you cut into slices, lengths or dice. Once peeled, keep in acidulated water (see below).

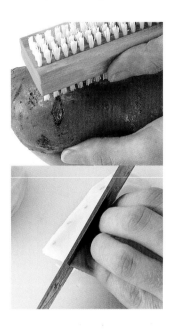

Acidulated water To stop vegetables discolouring when peeled, place in 45 ml (3 tbsp) white wine vinegar or lemon juice mixed with 1 litre (1¾ pints) water.

MANDOLIN

The essential tool for slicing and cutting firm vegetables such as roots and tubers, a mandolin comes in either wood or stainless steel. The more professional ones have guards to hold vegetables for cutting and supports so they can stand at an angle on worktops. Mandolins come with a straight blade, coarse and fine shredder, and a rippled cutter. All can be set to different thicknesses.

Effective cutting
Mandolins are most effective when used at an angle, so ones with legs are the best buys. With some models, the legs can be screwed to a worktop.

leafy greens

Versatile and highly nutritional, these greens have a unique flavour and texture, and they add colour to all sorts of dishes. They are delicious stir-fried or steamed and some, like spinach and dandelion, can be eaten uncooked in salads (see page 190). Most, however, benefit from being cooked – and usually in plenty of butter. They lose almost half their volume during cooking, so calculate portions on weight rather than bulk. If cooking spinach, for example, 225 g (8 oz) shredded spinach, makes a generous serving for one.

A la florentine

In France, any dish à la florentine – in the style of Florence – means it is made with spinach. Among the most famous dishes is Oeufs mollets à la florentine. Soft-boiled eggs are served on a bed of spinach. This is then topped with a cheese sauce and grilled.

Swiss chard either has crinkly green leaves attached to an enlarged white stem, or dark green leaves and a bright red stem. Choose crisp and unblemished leaves.

Beetroot greens are often sold still attached to the vegetable. Leaves should be fresh and springy to the touch.

Spinach wilts quickly so it is important that you buy it when it is very fresh. Check that the leaves are crisp and dark green and the stalks are still crisp. Avoid spinach that looks limp or has yellow spots.

Sorrel has a sour bite but it combines well with spinach. Look for smooth, arrow-shaped bright green leaves that are crisp without signs of yellowing.

Spring greens are actually young cabbage leaves. Their thick green leaves should look crisp and free of blemishes.

Dandelion greens have thick, jagged-edged leaves and a slightly bitter, biting flavour. Choose healthy-looking specimens with dark green leaves and no brown spots.

Kale has frilly dark green leaves and a cabbage-like taste. Buy small bunches with crispy leaves.

ORIENTAL GREENS

Many of these greens are related to cabbages, or greens like spinach and beet. Others come from totally different families, yet, like our own greens, they play an important part in Asian cuisines, adding colour, texture and flavour to soups and stir-fries. Many are now available in our own supermarkets, but failing that, look in Asian or Indian stores, where there is normally a bewildering choice of vegetables. The following is a small selection of the best known.

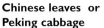

Chinese leaves or Peking cabbage (Pe-Tsai) This is the most familiar oriental cabbage. It has a rather bland, faint cabbage flavour and is mostly popular for its good crunchy texture. Unlike many greens, Chinese cabbage is available all year round.

Chinese mustard greens (Gaai choy) These are hugely popular in India and Asia, though only grown in Europe for the mustard seed. The leaves can be roughly sliced and make an excellent addition to stir-fries, providing a distinct mustard flavour. Young leaves can also be used to perk up salads.

Mustard greens add a peppery bite to salads and can be served cooked. Choose young leaves with a bright green colour and no brown spots.

CUTTING GREENS

Spinach, spring greens and Swiss chard should have their central ribs removed and a few leaves at a time should be stacked and rolled lengthwise into a cylinder. This should be cut across to create thin strips or chiffonade.

Chinese broccoli This looks a little like our own purple sprouting broccoli, except the flowers are yellow or white and the leaves are more slender and coarse. To cook, trim away the outer leaves and tough stalks, and then cut into lengths.

Bok choy Now widely available in our supermarkets, its paddle-shaped leaves make it easily identifiable. Bok choy has a pleasant mild flavour, yet with more character than Chinese cabbage. Both the leaves and the stalk can be eaten; the leaves need only be washed, and the stalk trimmed and sliced if large.

leafy greens

CAULIFLOWER AND BROCCOLI

Cauliflower and broccoli are among our most easily recognisable and popular winter vegetables. As well as the large, creamy white cauliflowers, look out for Romanescoes, which can be pale green or white, with pagoda-type florets, looking a little like a cross between broccoli and cauliflower, and baby cauliflowers, which are simply 'one-person' portions. Green cauliflowers are sometimes available in the shops. Their pale green colouring makes them something of a novelty, but they have a similar flavour to ordinary cauliflowers.

Purple sprouting broccoli is the original version of broccoli, before the plant was tamed to the more familiar calabrese with its blue-green and sometimes purple heads on short succulent stalks. Purple sprouting broccoli is a far more straggly vegetable, with long stalks and small purple flower heads. The tender leaves, stalks and heads are all edible. Look for purplish green heads that are tightly packed.

Cauliflowers should always be creamy white in colour, with the inner green leaves curled round the flower. Avoid those with brown or discoloured patches.

Broccoli similarly should look fresh. Avoid buying broccoli if the flower heads are turning yellow.

Cook's tip

The heads of both these brassicas are tenderer than their thicker stems so are best cooked at different times. Cut the florets from the stalks, dividing larger ones. Then remove the leaves from the stalks and peel away any tough, outer layer; trim off both ends. Cut the stalks in half lengthwise then cut them into slices and sticks.

STORING

All greens can be kept for up to three days in the refrigerator if washed first in cold water, patted dry and then stored in a plastic bag lined with kitchen roll.

Cauliflowers and broccoli will keep for up to four days in the salad drawer of the fridge.

Place cabbage and Brussels sprouts in a plastic bag for storing. Cabbages may be kept in the refrigerator crisper for at least two weeks; Brussels sprouts keep for three to five days.

NUTRITIONAL INFORMATION

Broccoli, though a far more 'modern' vegetable than cauliflower, has overtaken cauliflower in popularity, partly because of its versatility, partly because it contains high levels of vitamin C, carotene, folate, iron, potassium, chromium and calcium, and partly since it has less tendency to become 'rank' if slightly overcooked.

Cabbage is an excellent source of the vitamins A, C, B$_1$, B$_2$, B$_3$ and D. It is also a good source of the minerals iron, potassium and calcium.

CABBAGES

Available in different colours and shapes, they are crisp and mild when raw and slightly sweet when cooked.

Choosing

When selecting a cabbage, feel its weight in the palm of your hand. It should be firm and heavy for its size. Look for healthy, bright leaves. Avoid any cabbage with yellowing or curling leaves, blemishes or discoloured patches or that is beginning to smell 'cabbagy'.

Savoy cabbage is a green cabbage with crinkly or curled leaves. It is particularly tender and has a pleasant mild flavour.

Red cabbage is enjoyed for its beautiful wine-red colour and robust flavour. The colour fades once it has been cut unless a little vinegar is used to 'set' it. Most recipes suggest using 60–75 ml (4–5 tbsp) red wine vinegar when cooking.

Spring cabbage So-called as they are the first cabbages of the year, these green cabbages have loose heads with a pale yellow-green heart.

White cabbage Also known as Dutch cabbage, this is one of the most versatile of cabbages, good for serving raw, or cooking sliced or in wedges. Alternatively, the large leaves can be blanched and then used as wrappers for a variety of stuffings.

Brussels sprouts So-called because they were first cultivated in Flanders (now in Belgium), smaller, greener ones have the sweetest taste. They smell and taste rank if overcooked. Choose firm, compact ones.

▼ **Whole** Remove two large leaves from the cabbage and hollow out the centre, leaving a 2–3 cm (¾–1¼ in) shell. Fill as desired and cover with reserved leaves, overlapping

▲ **Leaves** Use individual leaves for small fillings and overlap two or more if you are wrapping a roast. Place the filling in the centre and bring the sides of the leaves over it before tucking in the top and bottom. Small rolls can be left as is; large rolls can be secured with strips of spring onion.

PREPARING CABBAGES

Slicing and grating Use a stainless steel knife; carbon steel may react with the cabbage causing its cut edges to discolour. Or, use a hand grater, an adjustable-blade slicer or a shredding disc in a food processor

▶ **Coring** The centres of cabbages are tough and inedible and, if kept, will prevent even cooking of the leaves. Cut your cabbage lengthwise into quarters. Then cut off the base of each quarter at an angle to remove the hard white core.

pods, seeds and beans

These are among our most sweet and succulent vegetables. They mostly need little or no preparation, and are probably the most popular of the simple accompaniments, needing only a knob of butter or sprig of mint before serving. Most beans and pods are eaten when they are young and tender. Peas, sweetcorn and, for the most part, broad beans, are podded to remove the seeds, but in the case of green beans and some varieties of garden pea, the whole vegetable is eaten, pod and all.

GARDEN PEAS

No vegetable has quite the taste of summer as garden peas, and if absolutely fresh they are delicious eaten straight from the pod. Once cooked, garden peas can be dressed up with creamy sauces, puréed for soups or added to other vegetables. However, when at their best, peas need very little attention, and are excellent simply served with fresh mint and a knob of butter.

Choosing

Select fresh peas with plump, firm, bright green shiny pods. As the sugars in peas turn to starch soon after picking, buy and cook them as fresh as possible. Shell just before using. Sugar snaps should not be bursting at the seams.

Mangetouts
This variety of pea is eaten pod and all. More translucent than sugar snaps, they are simple to prepare and need the minimum cooking; preferably just blanch or stir-fry quickly.

Sugar snaps
Like mangetouts, sugar snaps are eaten pod and all but they are plumper and rounder. They have a good fresh flavour, are delicious in salads and stir-fries, or they can be briefly cooked. Like mangetouts, take care not to overcook.

Petit pois
The name petit pois refers to a dwarf variety of pea and not, as you might expect, a young pea. Petit pois are mainly grown commercially for freezing, but gardeners are, of course, able to grow their own and they are worth looking out for in farm shops.

YIELD

450 G (I LB) PEAS IN THE POD

two servings of shelled peas

PREPARING PEAS

Peas need to be shelled, mangetouts and sugar snaps need only to have their thick string removed and topped and tailed, if desired.

▶ **Peas** To shell peas, press the base of pea pods to open, then push your thumb up the pod, letting peas fall into a bowl.

▲ **Mangetouts** To string mangetouts and sugar snaps, break off the stalk and pull off the string.

Recipes

Broad beans in a creamy herb sauce Broad beans cooked until tender and served with a smooth creamy sauce flavoured with herbs.

Minted peas with cucumber Peas served with mint, fried vegetables and a crème fraîche and vermouth sauce.

SWEETCORN

Every part of this vegetable may be used. Traditionally the husked corn is boiled and served 'on the cob' with butter or the kernels are scraped off and cooked. In Mexican cooking, the husks are used to make tamales.

Choosing

Corn is naturally sweet, but as soon as it is picked the sugars turn to starch, so it is important that corn is bought when absolutely fresh, and eaten quickly. Choose ears that feel full and heavy for their size. The tassels should be moist and golden without any signs of drying or decay. The kernels should be relatively small and milky when pierced.

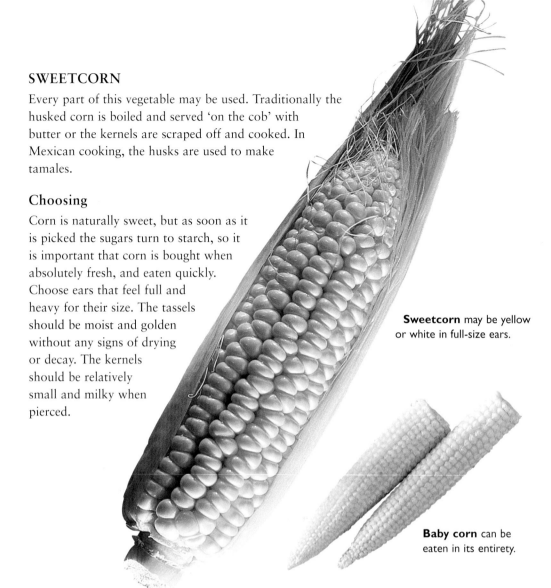

Sweetcorn may be yellow or white in full-size ears.

Baby corn can be eaten in its entirety.

▼ **Removing the husks**
Peel the husks back from the cob and cut off the base. Remove the silk.

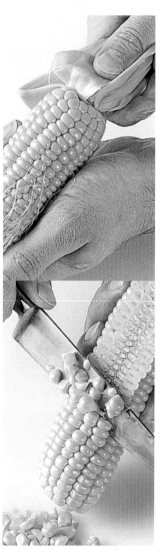

▲ **Cutting**
Some recipes call for sweetcorn kernels and these can be stripped from the cob by holding the cob stalk-end down and cutting down it with a sharp knife in smooth strokes.

STORING

Keep peas in their pods (both peas to be shelled and edible-podded peas) in a plastic bag in the refrigerator crisper and use within one or two days.

Keep fresh sweetcorn in a plastic bag in the refrigerator and use as soon as possible. Remove husk and silk just before cooking.

USING THE HUSKS

The husks are generally left on when roasting or barbecuing corn and they also can be used as a wrapping. If used in an oven or on a barbecue, they are generally first soaked in water for 20 minutes to ensure they don't burn. If they are used as a wrapping, as with tamales, then they are dried at 150°C (300°F) oven for about 30 minutes.

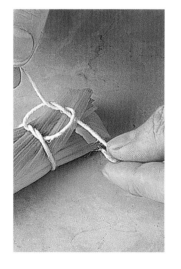

pods, seeds and beans

175

BEANS

Most beans consist of a pod with a single section that holds one row of seeds. Those with edible pods include runner beans, green beans, yellow wax beans and French beans.

Choosing

Beans should have a good colour and firm, unblemished pods that snap crisply when bent (French beans tend to be less crisp).

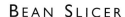

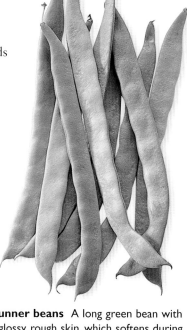

French beans Also known as haricot verts, these are the most prized of the green beans. They are very straight and are plumper and fleshier than the Kenyan green bean. The skin is soft and tender when cooked and they have a pleasant fresh flavour.

Runner beans A long green bean with a glossy, rough skin, which softens during cooking. Runner beans have a good robust flavour and a meltingly tender texture if fresh. Beans that have been on display too long become tough. Because of their distinctive flavour, runner beans are mostly enjoyed by themselves as an accompaniment.

BEAN SLICER

A hand-sized device that removes strings as well as cutting into pieces. It has two cutting blades; one snaps off the end of the bean, the other cuts the bean into four pieces.

Broad beans Also known as fava beans, these are normally sold when the pods are relatively large. Inside the pale green pods, the tightly packed beans lie as if on velvet cushions. Fresh broad beans have a superb texture and sweet flavour. Older ones acquire a bitter flavour and the outer skin of the bean becomes tough. Always shell mature beans before cooking.

Thai bean There are a variety of long thin beans, known variously as yard-long beans, asparagus bean and Chinese beans. They are similar in flavour and texture to green beans.

Green beans A general term for numerous types of beans. Most green beans (and yellow beans) are referred to in the United States as snap beans.

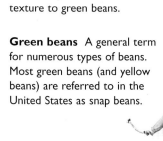

STORING

Refrigerate fresh beans with edible pods in a perforated plastic bag for 3–4 days. Store fresh shell beans with inedible pods in a similar way and use within 2–3 days; shell just before using.

Okra will keep for 3–4 days in the salad drawer of the fridge.

Did you know?

Broad beans should always be cooked, otherwise they can induce favism, an inherited disorder that can result in anaemia. People taking certain anti-depressant drugs are also warned to avoid broad beans.

SKINNING BROAD BEANS

Mature beans can be tough and are best skinned before serving. Although fiddly, it is worth the effort, especially for soups or when making pâtés. Blanch the beans (see page 22) until tender, then slit the skin around one end, using a small knife. Press the other end between your fingers and squeeze the bean out.

PREPARING RUNNER BEANS

Top and tail, and remove the tough threads along the length, if necessary. They are best if thinly sliced using a bean slicer.

OKRA

Native to Africa and still considered by most of us in the west as somewhat exotic, okra is surprisingly well-travelled, being an important part of cuisines as diverse as India and the southern United States. The slender green pods are lantern shaped and contain rows of seeds that ooze a viscous liquid when cooked.

Choosing

Choose small, firm pods, avoiding any that look shrivelled or feel soft when gently squeezed.

NUTRITIONAL INFORMATION

Broad beans are an excellent source of protein, complex carbohydrates, fibre and beta-carotene (which the body converts to vitamin A). They also contain phosphorus, iron, niacin, vitamin C and E.

Green beans are a source of carbohydrates and some protein. They are a good source of vitamins C and A and also contain calcium, potassium and iron.

Peas are an excellent source of vitamin B and a good source of vitamin C. They also contain protein, niacin and folate.

Sweetcorn is a good source of vitamin C and also contains some vitamin A and iron. It is an important carbohydrate food and contains some protein.

Okra contains vitamin C and A, together with folate, thiamine and magnesium.

Natural thickener

Okra's gelatinous substance acts as a natural thickener in spicy curries and soups, the most famous of which is the Louisiana gumbo. To release the viscous liquid, top and tail the pod then slice during preparation.

PREPARING OKRA

For soups and Creole-type stews, that are traditionally thickened with okra, slice the pod into even sized pieces having first topped and tailed it. If you do not particularly like the gloopy characteristic of okra, trim the tops without exposing the seeds, and then boil or steam whole. Okra can also be gently fried – sliced or whole, preferably with garlic, onions and other spices that go well with this mildly flavoured vegetable.

pods, seeds and beans

squashes

Choosing

Squashes are classified into summer and winter varieties. Summer squashes have tender flesh and seeds and soft edible skins; choose those that feel firm. Winter squashes have hard, thick skins and seeds and firm flesh. Select ones with hard, blemish-free skin. Both varieties are available year round and the best specimens are dry and well-shaped, should feel heavy for their size and have a good colour.

Pattypan can be white, yellow or pale green. Perfect for grilling or stuffing, if large.

Courgette and marrow courgettes are basically baby marrows: the smaller they are, the sweeter they come. In addition to green courgettes there are yellow and grey ones – all of which can be eaten raw as well as cooked. Marrow should be firm, heavy and longer than 30 cm (12 in). It can be steamed, boiled and stuffed as well as baked au gratin.

Pumpkin Smaller ones contain more flesh and are best for eating. Cut in half or into wedges, remove the seeds and bake.

What's in a name?

One of those few vegetables known by two different names, though of similar derivation. Courgette is the diminutive of the French word for marrow 'courge'. Likewise, zucchini is the diminutive of the Italian word 'zucca', meaning gourd.

STORING

Summer squashes can be stored in the refrigerator for a few weeks although it is generally better to store them at room temperature for up to one week. Winter squashes have thicker skins and can therefore be kept in a cool, dry place for several months.

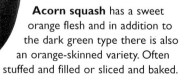

Acorn squash has a sweet orange flesh and in addition to the dark green type there is also an orange-skinned variety. Often stuffed and filled or sliced and baked.

Spaghetti squash So-called because its yellow-gold flesh separates into strands when cooked. Look for pale yellow skin; greenish skin indicates the squash is under-ripe.

Butternut squash has a deep orange flesh that is moist and sweet. Should be peeled before cooking and used in soups and as a vegetable.

NUTRITIONAL INFORMATION

Squashes contain carbohydrate, calcium, iron and potassium and are a reasonable source of vitamin A and C.

Chayote
Also called christophine, this has a large central seed and a slight apple taste. Can be prepared as courgettes.

PREPARATION TECHNIQUES

▼ Acorn squash
Cut squash in half lengthwise through the stalk. Scoop out seeds and fibrous pulp with a spoon, then peel off skin. Cut into smaller pieces before cooking.

▼ Spaghetti squash
Cut in half lengthwise and remove the seeds. Boil or bake. Once cooked, use a fork to rake out the stringy flesh. It comes away in spaghetti-like strands.

▲ Butternut squash
Cut in half, peel or carve off the skin from each half and then cut flesh into chunks.

squashes

179

A Closer Look at a Courgette

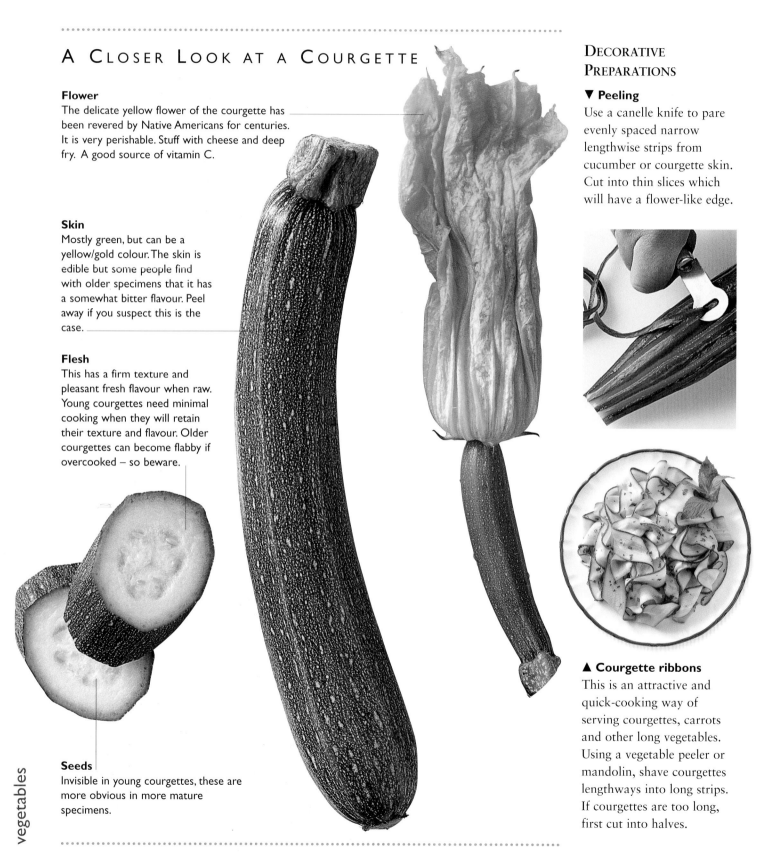

Flower
The delicate yellow flower of the courgette has been revered by Native Americans for centuries. It is very perishable. Stuff with cheese and deep fry. A good source of vitamin C.

Skin
Mostly green, but can be a yellow/gold colour. The skin is edible but some people find with older specimens that it has a somewhat bitter flavour. Peel away if you suspect this is the case.

Flesh
This has a firm texture and pleasant fresh flavour when raw. Young courgettes need minimal cooking when they will retain their texture and flavour. Older courgettes can become flabby if overcooked – so beware.

Seeds
Invisible in young courgettes, these are more obvious in more mature specimens.

DECORATIVE PREPARATIONS

▼ Peeling
Use a canelle knife to pare evenly spaced narrow lengthwise strips from cucumber or courgette skin. Cut into thin slices which will have a flower-like edge.

▲ Courgette ribbons
This is an attractive and quick-cooking way of serving courgettes, carrots and other long vegetables. Using a vegetable peeler or mandolin, shave courgettes lengthways into long strips. If courgettes are too long, first cut into halves.

CUCUMBERS

These perennial favourites for sandwiches and salads are of the slicing variety; the pickling ones are smaller. Both have dark green skin; a crisp texture; moist, cool flesh; and a mild flavour. Slicing cucumbers are available all year round. Choose firm ones without soft spots. They can be kept for up to one week in the fridge. If you buy unwaxed cucumbers, keep wrapped in cling film to seal in moisture.

English cucumbers Thin skinned and virtually seedless, these long cucumbers are frequently sold waxed to seal in moisture.

Gherkins A variety of cucumber whose small fruits are picked while still unripe and are then pickled in vinegar to use as a condiment.

Did you know?

In the past, cucumbers often caused indigestion in certain people; today gourmet cucumbers, sometimes called burpless cucumbers, are grown by producers which contain no or only very small seeds. Kirby cucumbers are similar and for most do not have unpleasant side effects.

Ridged cucumbers
Not widely available in the UK, these are the favourite cucumbers in France. They tend to be smaller and firmer than English cucumbers, have a bumpy skin and a more robust flavour.

Kirby cucumber One of the varieties most often used for pickling. Usually available in summer only.

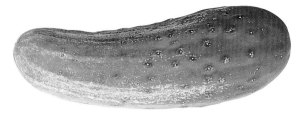

CUCUMBER GARNISHES

Because of their contrasting coloration, cucumbers make attractive decorations.

▼ Cucumber chevrons
Quarter a cucumber lengthwise. Cut into chunks. Cut two V-shaped wedges in flesh, one deeper than the other. Fan the pieces out.

▲ Cucumber twirls
Peel a cucumber using a canelle knife (see opposite page). Cut into wafer-thin slices. Then make a cut halfway into each slice. Gently twist the pieces in opposite directions.

squashes

peppers and chillies

STORING

Keep sweet peppers in a cool place, such as the salad drawer in the refrigerator, where they will keep for a few days. You can freeze sliced or chopped fresh peppers in plastic containers or freezer bags for up to six months. Fresh chillies will keep for one to two weeks in a cool place. Put them in a plastic bag and store them in the chiller compartment in the fridge. Alternatively, wash and dry the chilli and it can be stored indefinitely in a clean screw-top jar.

SKINNING PEPPERS

Cut peppers in half lengthwise, discarding stalks and seeds. Place skin-side up in pan and grill close to heat until charred. Wrap in foil, let stand for 15 minutes then peel off the skin.

Sweet peppers Although classified as fruits, peppers are used by the cook as a vegetable. Red peppers are simply green peppers that have been left on the vine to ripen. Peppers may also be yellow and purplish black. The sweetest pepper is the pimiento, sold tinned or bottled.

Choosing

Peppers should have a glossy skin and should feel firm. Chillies sometimes have a wrinkled skin even when fresh, so don't be put off by a chilli's appearance. However, avoid any peppers that are bruised or have obvious blemishes.

Jalapeño

Scotch bonnet

Serrano

Bird's eye

Caribe chilli

Chilli peppers As a broad rule, the smaller the chilli, the hotter it is. Bird's eye chillies, habaneros and Scotch bonnets are searingly hot; jalapeños and serranos are milder.

Habanero

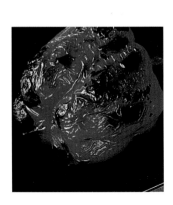

vegetables

REHYDRATING DRIED CHILLIES

To use as a substitute for fresh in cooking, you can either crush or crumble them or soak them for an hour in a bowl of warm water. Drain and grind to a paste and then rub through a sieve to remove the skins.

REMOVING SEEDS AND PITH

The heat of chillies is caused by the presence of a volatile oil called capsaicin, which can burn the skin and eyes. This is present in the whole of the chilli but is very concentrated in the seeds and pith that surrounds the seeds. For this reason, most people prefer to remove the seeds and cut away the pith.
• Wear rubber gloves and use your fingers, or cut and seed chillies using a knife.
• If you do use bare fingers, make sure you wash your hands afterwards.

A CLOSER LOOK AT A CHILLI

Flesh
The thin flesh of a chilli carries a powerful punch, but not so much as the seeds and pith.

Pith
The hottest part of a chilli containing the highest concentration of capsaicin. Remove unless you want maximum heat.

Seeds
The seeds also contain a concentrated amount of capsaicin.

Skin
Chillies can be red, yellow, green or variegated, but the colour is no guide to its heat.

Type	Description	Heat index	Use for	Quantities
Anaheim or California	These large slender chillies can be red or green	Mild to medium hot with an underlying sweet flavour	Can be stuffed and cooked whole, or used sliced for any recipe where a moderate amount of heat is required	Use whole or 2–3 per dish according to taste
Ancho	Small, pepper-shaped chillies that can be green or red	Mild with a pleasant sweet flavour	Thai or Indian curries or mildly spiced salsas and sauces	2–3 per dish according to taste and recipe
Bird's eye	Small long thin red chillies with bright glossy skins	Fiery hot	Mexican dishes	Use sparingly
Cascabel	Plum-shaped chilli	Relatively mild with a nutty flavour	Roast or grill whole or use for milder-flavoured salsas	Use whole or chopped according to recipes
Jalapeño	A green chilli to begin with but turning red as it matures	Hot	Chutneys, relishes and salsas	2–3 per dish according to taste
Ethiopian	A long thin chilli, a pale red when young, but becoming redder	Hot to very hot	Sauces, curries and rice dishes	Use sparingly
Habanero and Scotch bonnets	The habanero is a squat, box-shaped chilli from Mexico that can be green, yellow or red in colour, though this is not a guide to its heat. Scotch bonnets are similar	The hottest of all chillies and eye-wateringly hot	Mexican and Caribbean dishes where intense heat is required	Use very sparingly
Hot gold spike	Pale-yellow or green chilli, grown in the south-western United States	Very hot	Mexican or Tex-Mex dishes or any recipe where heat is required	Use sparingly
Poblano	A small, dark green chilli, that comes from Mexico and is popular in Spain	Normally mild with a sweet, spicy flavour, however, occasionally the odd poblano chilli will be fiercely hot	Can be served whole roasted or grilled. Often used for tapas in Spain	Use whole
Thai	Tiny red, green or yellow chillies	Very hot	Thai sauces, curries and rice dishes	Use sparingly
Serrano	A long slender chilli which can be green or red	Fairly hot	Mexican, Caribbean or Thai dishes	Use 2–3 per recipe according to taste
Yellow wax	Small, pepper-shaped chilli, wide at the top and with a tapering end. Can be pale yellow or green	Varies from mild to very hot	Curries or Thai dishes	Use with care as it is difficult to tell the difference in heat

vegetables

Dried chillies are used for a range of powders, sauces and oils that can be used to spice up all sorts of savoury dishes.

Chilli flakes

Made from whole red chillies, chilli flakes contain the seeds and pith and are likely therefore to be very spicy. Use chilli flakes carefully when adding to a recipe.

Cayenne pepper

The ground powder of a particular variety of chilli that came originally from the Cayenne region of French Guiana. It is a particularly fiery condiment, made using the pith and seeds of the dried chilli, and should be used sparingly. It has a distinctive flavour and providing it is used judiciously, can be added to sauces, biscuits and pastries as well as curries, tagines and other dishes where spiciness is required.

Chilli powder

Made from a variety of dried chillies that range from mild to fiery hot, chilli powder is hot, though neither as hot nor fragrant as cayenne pepper. It is normally deep red in colour and is less finely ground than cayenne. Use for curries, marinades, cooked sauces and salsas, and for Caribbean and Mexican dishes. Check the packet when buying chilli powder, as some contain herbs and other spices. To make your own chilli powder, remove the seeds and pith from red chillies and dry-fry until crisp or dry in the oven. When completely dry, grind in a coffee mill or herb grinder.

Tabasco

Made from hot red chillies, vinegar and salt, Tabasco is hot, spicy and peppery. It is a useful storecupboard ingredient, as it adds instant spiciness to various dishes. It can be used like pepper and salt, for an added spiciness in tagines, curries and other meat or fish dishes.

Chilli sauce

There is a huge number of chilli sauces, ranging from mild and sweet to Vindaloo hot. They are all thick and bright red and often contain other ingredients depending on their country of origin. Chinese and oriental chilli sauce is often called Szechaun chilli or sambal ulek. Mexican chilli sauces are plainer, but no less fiery. Use chilli sauces sparingly in marinades, or in stews and casseroles.

peppers and chillies

185

tomatoes

Choosing

Tomatoes taste best when allowed to ripen slowly on the plant. Ripe tomatoes have a rich sweet flavour, which under-ripe tomatoes lack. Home-grown tomatoes picked at the point of perfection inevitably have the best and sweetest flavour. Where this is not an option, choose locally grown produce, from a farm shop or a supermarket or greengrocer with a fast turnover. Organic tomatoes have a fuller flavour.

Check when buying tomatoes that they are firm and bright red or reddish-orange. They should have a sweet, subtle aroma and will give slightly when gentle pressure is applied.

Beefsteak tomatoes are large (as much as 10 cm/4 in across) and ridged. They are deep red or orange and have a good flavour. They are best eaten raw in salads or sandwiches and are excellent for stuffing.

YIELD

3 MEDIUM-SIZED TOMATOES

=

500 G (1¼ LB)

=

about 1½ cups chopped

Cherry tomatoes have a delicate sweet flavour with a low acidity. There are numerous types available – red, yellow and even white. Plum cherry tomatoes are also available.

Green tomatoes are picked before having time to ripen. They are used famously for pickle, their acidity going particularly well with the sweet-sour flavour of onions, spices and sugars.

Yellow tomatoes are normally less acidic than red tomatoes, with a sweet, delicate and mild flavour. They tend to be medium to large in size, and are often very juicy.

Vine tomatoes that are left on the vine to ripen have considerably more flavour than others. They are dearer, but are worth the extra expense for salads, appetizers and for fresh tomato soups.

Salad tomatoes are very versatile but generally less flavourful. Early tomatoes come from the Canary Islands, Spain, southern Europe and the Channel Islands. In summer, there is a wider variety of home-produced tomatoes.

Plum tomatoes have a good, rich, rounded flavour and are less acidic than most round tomatoes. With fewer seeds, they are also less watery, so are ideal for long cooking in sauces and stews.

NUTRITIONAL INFORMATION

Tomatoes are a good source of vitamin C, especially vine-ripened fruit. A medium-sized tomato contains 40 per cent of the RDA for vitamin C; the soft jelly that surrounds the pips contains the largest concentration. Tomatoes also contain vitamin E, beta-carotene, potassium, magnesium, calcium and phosphorus. Recent research indicates that lycopene, the pigment that turns tomatoes red, may help prevent some forms of cancer by lessening the damage caused by free radicals.

vegetables

Tomato products and preparations

Packaged or tinned tomatoes are processed at the height of the season when they are at their best and have a good flavour. In winter, use them instead of fresh vegetables. Plum tomatoes are the most popular canning tomato, owing to their good pulp and relatively few seeds.

Passata Italian smooth, sieved tomatoes sold in jars or cartons.

Tomato paste A thick liquid made of unseasoned cooked tomatoes strained for uniform consistency.

Tomato purée A thick concentrate with an intense flavour made from unseasoned cooked tomatoes.

Tomato sauce Puréed tomatoes seasoned with salt and usually other herbs and spices.

Sun-dried tomatoes Have a strong smoky flavour and pleasantly chewy texture. Those in oil can be used straight from the jar, while the dried must be rehydrated.

Concassé Roughly chopped tomato flesh often called for in recipes. For a smooth concassé, peel, seed and coarsely chop the tomato and season with salt and pepper. Use as a sauce with vegetables or pasta or as a base for other sauces.

▼ **Peeling** Core tomatoes and with a sharp knife mark a cross in the skin. Blanch them in boiling water for 10 seconds. Drain, then immerse in cold water.

Using the tip of your knife, peel off the loosened skin, starting at the cross.

STORING

Tomatoes are best stored at room temperature, between 13–21°C (55–70°F). Never keep under-ripe tomatoes in the fridge, as the cold temperatures destroy flavour and stop the ripening process. Eat ripe tomatoes within a day or two and cook any that you cannot use. Or, you can freeze them whole to use in sauces; their skins will slide right off when they are thawed. Once a tomato is fully ripe it can be kept in the fridge, but only for one to two days: any longer means the flavour will deteriorate. If tomatoes become over-ripe, cook immediately and freeze. Cut out stalk ends and remove any evidence of decay.

Type of tomato	Under-ripe tomatoes	Ripe
Salad tomatoes, beefsteak	Room temperature **4–5** days	Room temperature **2–3** days or in the fridge for **3–4** days
Plum tomatoes	Room temperature **4–5** days or until soft but not squashy	Room temperature **2–3** days or in the fridge for **3–4** days
Cherry tomatoes	Room temperature **3–4** days or until bright red	Room temperature **2** days or in the fridge for **3** days

▶ **Ripening tomatoes** Under-ripe tomatoes will ripen if left in a dark place for a few days; keep in a brown paper bag and add an apple to speed ripening. As the fruit ripens, it emits a natural gas which speeds up the process.

▲ **Deseeding** Cut tomato in half. Over a bowl, squeeze each half until the seeds fall out.

other vegetable fruits

AUBERGINES

Related to the tomato and pepper, it is, like its relatives, thought of as a vegetable but is actually a fruit. Outside of Britain and Europe in the English speaking world it is known as the eggplant, probably earning its name from the white varieties which look exactly like large decorated eggs. There are many different varieties of aubergine, ranging in size from tiny berries to huge marrow-sized specimens, and in colour from white to rich purple. They all have a similar spongy texture and the same bland flavour. All aubergines need to be cooked – they are unpalatable raw – and their main virtue is their ability to absorb other flavours. They are therefore hugely popular in India, and the Middle and Far East where they are cooked or served with a variety of onions and spices.

Choosing

Look for plump, glossy, heavy aubergines; avoid any with scarred, bruised or dull surfaces. The calyx (cap) should be fresh-looking, tight and free of mould.

Japanese aubergine

Purple aubergine

Baby aubergine

Baby white aubergine

Thai pea aubergines

PREPARING AUBERGINES

▼ Preparing for roasting
To ensure the flesh cooks evenly, cross-hatch the halves cutting deeply with a sharp pointed knife. Then sprinkle with salt.

▲ Preparing for frying
Salting firms the flesh a little and stops aubergines absorbing too much oil (although they will still absorb copious amounts). Slice the aubergine. Spread the slices in a single layer in a colander. Sprinkle salt evenly over the cut surfaces. Leave for about 30 minutes, then rinse under cold running water and pat dry before cooking.

Pinkerton, Ettinger and Fuerte
Smooth skinned, pear-shaped avocado, with pale green flesh.

Aubergines keep in the fridge for 2–3 days. Keep very firm avocados at room temperature until they soften (3–4 days); to speed ripen, place in a brown paper bag. Refrigerate ripe ones and use within 2–3 days.

STONING AN AVOCADO

Cut the avocado lengthwise in half all around the stone. Twist the halves in opposite directions until separated. Carefully strike the stone with a chef's knife. Twist to dislodge the stone.

AVOCADOS

Choosing

Select firm-ripe avocados for slicing and chopping for use in salads, and very ripe fruit for mashing and making guacamole. Firm-ripe avocados yield to gentle pressure; very ripe ones feel soft without pressing. Reject any with bruises, gouges or broken skin.

Hass A small purple-black avocado with a knobbly skin. The thick skin turns black as it ripens. The flesh is a pale golden yellow with a rich buttery texture.

NUTRITIONAL INFORMATION

The avocado is a rich source of protein and carbohydrates, which is why it is considered a good baby food. It is one of the few fruits that contains fat, and is also rich in potassium, vitamin C, some B vitamins and vitamin E.

TOMATILLOS

Small, pale green or yellow, tart-tasting fruits encased in a slightly sticky papery husk, which is taken off before cooking. They are an essential ingredient of Mexican cooking, and can be used raw in salads or cooked in sauces and relishes. Look for those with tight-fitting, dry husks; avoid any that are shrivelled or bruised. Store, covered, in a refrigerator for up to ten days.

PREVENTING DISCOLORATION

Avocados discolour quickly when exposed to the air. Brush slices with lemon juice or add 15 ml (1 tbsp) lemon juice to dishes that call for cut-up avocado such as salads, purées or dips.

other vegetable fruits

189

salads

Salad vegetables are a culinary classification, rather than anything else. They do not belong to any one family. Many of our favourite salad leaves, like radicchio and endive, come from the same family as chicory; others are near or distant relatives of many of our garden weeds and flowers. Their principle common denominator is that they are mostly (although not invariably) served raw. For this reason it is essential that whatever salad ingredient you choose, it must be absolutely fresh.

LETTUCE

There is a huge variety of lettuces, all members of a large and diverse family: *Lactuca sativa*. Since commercially they are grown under glass, there is never a time in the year when there isn't a wide choice available, although the best lettuces for flavour and freshness are the home-grown variety or those grown locally on organic farms, when the season will limit your choices.

Butterheads
The classic soft lettuce, beloved of kitchen gardens. They have a mild flavour and are good in salads if fresh.

Round lettuce These are the soft-leafed lettuces that are sometimes called head or cabbage lettuce. They have loose leaves with cabbage-like heads.

STORING

To keep lettuce crisp, place clean, dry leaves in a food storage bag, along with a few damp kitchen towels and seal. Most varieties, including butterhead and cos, keep for two to three days. Iceberg, Little Gem and other sturdier heads keep for up to a week.

Cos lettuces These are long-leafed lettuces with a pleasant bite and a delicious flavour. Cos is generally considered the most delicious lettuce and is the correct choice for Caesar salad. Little Gems are small and compact, with crumpled leaves. They have a good flavour, but not quite the same excellent texture of cos.

YIELDS*

1 MEDIUM CRISPHEAD LETTUCE

500 g (1¼ lb) prepared leaves

1 MEDIUM BUTTERHEAD LETTUCE

250 g (9 oz) prepared leaves

1 MEDIUM COS LETTUCE

450 g (1 lb) prepared leaves

* allow about 115 g (4 oz) prepared leaves per serving

SALAD SPINNER

This makes short work of drying lettuce; choose the kind with a pull cord. Be careful not to overload the spinner or the leaves will become bruised.

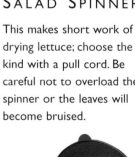

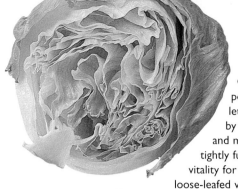

Crispheads These include popular varieties like Iceberg lettuce. They are characterised by their fresh crunchy texture and mild flavour. Their leaves are tightly furled and they retain their vitality for far longer than the loose-leafed varieties.

Looseheads As the name suggests, these are loose-leafed. They have no heart, but become more tightly packed towards the centre. Many looseheads, such as Oak Leaf lettuce and Lollo Rosso, have attractive variegated reddish leaves.

PREPARING

Gently break off leaves at the stem end or cut all the way round the core in a cone shape. Remove and discard any wilted outer leaves along with any that are bruised, or spotted leaves which will deteriorate rapidly.

Wash leaves briefly in cold water, gently removing them from the head so any grit sinks to the bottom of the bowl. Place on a clean tea towel and carefully pat dry with another.

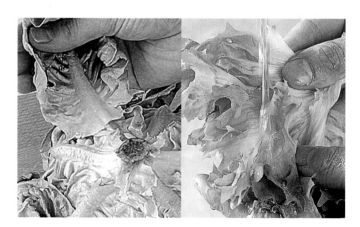

DRESSINGS

Dressings are a vital element of a good salad, adding a richness that contrasts and enhances the flavours and textures of the salad itself. Dressings are almost invariably made using oil, which should be of top quality, and are sharpened with lemon or lime juice, or, as is most frequently used, a wine or cider vinegar.

- Use good quality ingredients for dressings – extra virgin olive oil makes a wonderful dressing, but if you find it too rich, blend with half quantities of sunflower or groundnut oil, which are bland and light.
- As a rule, make dressings in the proportion of five parts oil to one part vinegar, lemon or lime juice.
- Don't drown a salad in dressing. Add just enough to coat the ingredients, without leaving a pool of dressing at the bottom of the bowl.
- For green and mixed salads, add the dressing just before serving. Salads made using cooked ingredients, like rice, pasta and cooked vegetables, can be dressed in advance, so that the flavours have time to blend.

MAKING VINAIGRETTE

To blend the ingredients evenly, they should all be at room temperature. Use a whisk to combine and thicken the vinegar and mustard. Slowly add the oil, whisking constantly until the dressing is smooth, thickened and well blended.

Recipes

Orange and honey dressing A deliciously sweet, citrus dressing to accompany salads.

Lime dressing A fresh mixture of coconut cream, grapeseed oil and sharpened with the juice and zest of a lime.

Lemon vinaigrette Lemon juice, seasoning and honey whisked together with olive oil.

Vinaigrette dressing The famous, versatile dressing based on an oil and vinegar mixture. Dijon mustard is often added.

salads

191

A jumble of leafy greens looks best in a bowl. Choose one to set off your salad to best effect. China, glass, earthenware and ceramic bowls all look good. Wooden bowls are attractive too, but be aware that the wood tends to absorb some of the dressing, so you will have to dedicate the bowl for salads or other savoury foods. Choose a dressing to suit the salad and the other parts of the meal. They should be well-flavoured with a hint of sharpness, either from vinegar or from lemon or lime. Add the dressing just before serving.

Chicory	This adds a distinct bitter/spicy flavour, so use sparingly. Trim the root, remove the core and slice thinly
Cucumber	Gives a cool flavour and crisp texture. Peel if liked. Add to the salad at the last minute, thinly sliced or cut into chunks
Endive or curly endive	A member of the chicory family, endive adds a distinct flavour to any salad
Escarole	Has green frizzy and broad leaves. Trim off the root and remove the outer leaves; separate the leaves and wash and dry well. Tear into bite-sized pieces
Herbs	Choose leafy herbs according to taste: chervil, flat-leaf parsley, fennel, chives and mint work well. Fresh coriander works well in oriental-style salads
Lamb's lettuce	Also known as corn salad, or mâche in France. It adds a pleasant nutty flavour to salads. To prepare, simply pull leaves away from the root; wash and dry if necessary
Lettuce	The favourite salad ingredient. There is a wide range to choose from. Choose a lettuce for its colour and texture. Remove root and any damaged leaves. Wash and dry leaves and tear into bite-sized pieces
Radicchio	Another relative to chicory, though with a less marked bitter flavour, with its pink and wine-red leaves it adds colour to a salad. Remove root and separate, wash and dry leaves. Tear into pieces
Rocket	Often sold as a herb, rocket has an excellent peppery flavour. Rinse thoroughly as it tends to be gritty and discard any discoloured leaves. Add whole to salads
Radish	Adds good crunchy texture and a peppery flavour to salads. Trim root and slice before adding
Spinach	Sweet and earthy-tasting, both flat or crinkly leaves can be used but need thorough rinsing before use
Watercress	Robustly flavoured, with a peppery, pungent taste. Discard any damaged or yellow leaves and add directly to salads

Once you have made a salad, there is still plenty of scope for adding a little extra something, either to give another dimension of flavour, or simply as a garnish. Many of the world's most famous salads are well known because they please the eye as much as the palate. The Indonesian salad gado gado is a riot of colour, the simple basic green salad enlivened with exotic vegetables, fruit and seafood.

Herbs

As well as leafy herbs, like parsley and chervil, choose herbs for their flavour. Tarragon, whole or shredded, gives its distinctive anise-like flavour. Mint, dill, chives and basil can add a finishing decorative flourish, or chop finely and sprinkle over a salad just before serving

Fruit

Orange segments, apples, pears and grapes look and taste good in all sorts of salads. Exotic fruits like mango, papaya, carambolas (star fruit) and lychees are among the many fruits that will add colour and texture to your salad

Flowers

Flowers look pretty in salads and add their own unique flavour. All the flowers shown here are edible; don't raid your garden indiscriminately, however, as some flowers are best not eaten and some are highly toxic. In addition, don't pick flowers for consumption if you suspect they have been treated with chemical pesticides. This also goes for flowers from florists, unless they are labelled 'organic'

Borage

These pretty blue flowers, which are popularly used for Pimm's, can be scattered over a green salad

Marigolds

Use the petals whole to dramatic effect or chop finely. They have a mild mustard and pepper aroma and flavour

Nasturtiums

The whole or shredded petals look good in any salad. They have a pleasant peppery flavour

Pansies

Pansies' bright vibrant colours look superb in salads. Their flavour is mild. Violets and violas, belonging to the same family, are more delicate; violets have a more noticeably perfumed flavour

Sweet peas

Sweet peas look pretty in salads and add a faintly fresh pea flavour

salads

herbs

Fresh (and dried) herbs bring a distinctive taste and personality to food. Western chefs traditionally use specific herb combinations to flavour certain dishes. The most well-known is the bouquet garni used in a wide range of recipes.

Choosing

Make sure that fresh herbs have a bright colour (normally green) and no wilted leaves. Most are extremely delicate and will only last a day or two. It is best to buy as you need them or grow your own.

Many dried herbs happily retain their aromas if kept stored in tightly closed jars in a cool place away from direct light. You may, however, need to use dried herbs more generously than fresh. This is particularly true with dill and chervil.

A CLOSER LOOK AT FINES HERBES

The traditional French Fines Herbes is a combination of four aromatic herbs – chervil, tarragon, chives and parsley. Take equal amounts of each and chop finely.

Chives
Flowers Pale purple flowers appear in late spring and continue throughout summer. They have a delicate chive flavour and make an attractive garnish for salads.
Stem The green stems look like grass and are hollow. They add a subtle onion-flavour if snipped into dishes after cooking.

Tarragon
Leaves Long and narrow, they are a soft green colour, with a sweet peppery aroma and a slightly pungent, vanilla/anise flavour. The glands under the leaves give tarragon its distinctive aroma.

Chervil
Leaves Fine and delicate, with a fresh flavour, reminiscent of anise and citrus.
Stem This is long and willowy. Use these for stocks and where more intense flavour is required.

Parsley
Leaves The leaves in curly parsley should be bright green and tightly curled. Flat-leaf or Italian parsley has larger fern-like leaves which should look fresh and lively. Ideally choose flat-leaf parsley for fines herbes, as it has a more cutting flavour.
Stem Use parsley stems for stocks or in a bouquet garni.

Gremolada
A Milanese flavouring usually made with finely chopped lemon zest, garlic and parsley. Commonly used with osso bucco.

Herbes de Provence
A mixture of fresh (or dried) thyme, bay, rosemary, basil, savory and, occasionally, lavender.

Persillade
A mixture of chopped parsley and garlic, usually added to dishes just before the end of cooking.

STORING

Most fresh herbs are best kept fresh by keeping in a plastic bag and storing at the bottom of the refrigerator.

Coriander is best stored by placing the stems in a glass of cold water. It should keep for three to four days in this way.

Parsley can be kept in the fridge, or sprinkled with water and wrapped in paper towels.

Rosemary will keep for several days by standing the stems in water.

Bouquet garni
This is a selection of aromatic herbs to flavour sauces or stocks; the most common include parsley, thyme, rosemary and bay leaves. They can be secured with the green part of a leek and tied with string.

PREPARING AND USING FRESH HERBS

Exept for chives (see below), you need to strip the leaves of herbs from their stalks and chop coarsely. Hold the herb upright and, using a fork, push the leaves down the stem. With some herb mixtures, you may need to crush the leaves using a mortar and pestle. Soft leaves such as basil, sage and sorrel can be stacked and rolled tightly then sliced crosswise into shreds. This is called a chiffonade. In addition to being added directly to dishes, either singly or as a herb mixture or bundle, herb stems make ideal skewers for small pieces of meat, such as baby lamb chops or for small, delicate vegetable pieces. They also can be formed into herb brushes.

FREEZING HERBS

Basil, chives, coriander, dill, fennel, marjoram, mint, parsley, tarragon and thyme all freeze successfully though there will inevitably be a loss of flavour, especially for the more delicate ones.
▼ Clean and dry them and then open freeze on a baking tray.

▲ When frozen, pack into individual bags or into favourite combinations, such as for bouquet garni. Label and store in the freezer for up to six months.

Alternatively finely chop the herbs (individually or in combinations) and half-fill ice-cube trays. Top up with water and freeze. Once frozen store in labelled freezer bags.

PREPARING CHIVES

A pair of scissors are the best tool for cutting the delicate leaves of this herb. Snip them over a small bowl. Add at the last minute as long cooking destroys their flavour.

HERB BRUSH

This is a pretty and tasty way to impart flavour to grilled or barbecued foods, focaccia and corn on the cob and to brush vinaigrette over salads and steamed vegetables. Rosemary, sage and thyme are good choices.
• Tie a small bouquet of the sprigs together at the stalk end.
• Dip in olive oil or melted butter and use to brush over food on the barbecue.

herbs

195

Type	Description	Affinity with	Notes and tips
Basil	A delicate, aromatic herb, esecially popular in Italian cooking and in Thai cuisine. Basil has a sweet, slightly pungent aroma and a distinct, faintly aniseed flavour. There are several varieties of basil but all have a similar aroma and flavour. Purple basil has deep wine-red leaves; Greek basil has tiny green leaves	Parsley, rosemary, thyme, oregano	The sweetest leaves are those at the top of the plant. Add to cooked dishes at the very end of cooking, as heat destroys the flavour
Bay	An attractive herb sold normally in packets of whole leaves or on small sprigs. Bay leaves have an intense heady aroma and strong flavour, adding a distinct pungency to food	Other bouquet garni ingredients – parsley and thyme – and with rosemary and sage	Crumble or shred leaves to release flavour. Leaves dry well but will eventually lose their flavour. Bay's pungency will overwhelm delicately flavoured food. Use fresh or dried leaves sparingly with well-flavoured dishes
Chervil	A delicate-looking herb, with a sweet, faintly aniseed flavour	Tarragon, parsley, chives	Add at the end of cooking to avoid destroying delicate flavour
Chives	A member of the onion family, with the familiar but much fainter onion flavour	Most delicately flavoured herbs – parsley, chervil, tarragon, basil	Add at the very end of cooking. Chives make an attractive garnish, tied into bundles or snipped and sprinkled over dishes. Dried chives have very little flavour. Use fresh chives or spring onion tops whenever possible
Coriander	A hugely popular herb in cuisines throughout the world, particular those of India, the Middle and Far East and eastern Mediterranean. The flavour is fresh but distinctly pungent and spicy, and goes best with well-flavoured, spicy food	Mint, parsley, thyme	Check recipe when adding: coriander can be very dominating. Use finely chopped roots for curries and meat dishes; the chopped leaves are best added towards the end of cooking. Whole leaves make an attractive garnish
Dill	A pretty feathery herb with a sweet, aniseed flavour	Chives, parsley, thyme, oregano	Use the feathery leaves as a garnish. They are best used uncooked or added at the end of cooking
Fennel	You may often find this feathery herb sprouting from bulbs of Florence fennel. It has the same, though fainter, anise flavour as the vegetable	Chives, parsley, thyme	This is best used in fish dishes, sauces, mayonnaise, salads and as a garnish
Lemon grass	Lemon grass grows throughout southeast Asia, and many of the tropical parts of India, Africa and South America. The bulbous root of the grass is valued for its distinctive citrus flavour, which has the clean sharpness of lemon, but without the bitterness. It is used widely in Thai and Vietnamese cooking	Coriander, basil	If lemon grass is not available, substitute lime or lemon peel with grated fresh root ginger

Type	Description	Affinity with	Notes and tips
Marjoram and oregano	These two herbs are closely related and are interchangeable if necessary. Marjoram is sweeter and less heady than its wild cousin, oregano. Both herbs are popular in the southern Mediterranean, particularly Italy and Greece, both having an affinity with tomato-based dishes. Oregano is the herb that gives pizza its distinctive flavour, and is also one of the ingredients in Mexican chilli powder	Thyme, parsley, chervil	If possible, use fresh marjoram. Oregano, which is less widely available fresh, is good dried
Mint	One of the most common herbs, used in both savoury and sweet dishes. Its unique menthol flavour adds a liveliness to sauces, while its astringency cuts fattiness in meat dishes, notably lamb. There are numerous varieties: apple mint is sweet and mellow; spearmint is piquant and good for mint sauce; peppermint is mostly used for desserts and confectionery	Coriander, parsley, basil, thyme, marjoram	If picking mint, choose young leaves near the top of the plant, which will be sweeter with a better flavour
Parsley	There are two types of parsley – curly and flat-leaf. Both have a mild, fresh flavour, the flat-leaf parsley having a little more 'bite'	Almost any herb can be teamed with parsley, including chives, tarragon, chervil, basil, coriander, marjoram and thyme	Ideally, use curly parsley for garnishing; use flat-leaf parsley for cooking and for salads, where flavour is more important. If adding to cooked dishes, stir in at the very end of cooking in order to retain the flavour
Rosemary	An aromatic herb with an intense pungent flavour that goes well with meat dishes, particularly lamb and game. It is native to the Mediterranean and is widely used in Italian and Greek dishes	Rosemary tends to overpower the delicate herbs but can be used with other robust herbs, like bay and thyme	Use sparingly, and remove sprigs from casseroles before serving. Tuck sprigs inside roasts, or strip stems of rosemary, leaving leaves at one end and use the twigs as skewers for cutlets of lamb for grilling or barbecuing
Sage	Another strongly flavoured herb, with an affinity for meat, particularly pork and goose. It is popular in Italy, used in stuffings and for serving with veal and calf's liver	Thyme, oregano, bay	Use with discretion for stuffings, and for adding to sauces. It is good for flavouring oils and vinegar
Tarragon	Among the most popular and versatile of herbs, with a superb and delicate aniseed/vanilla flavour. It is frequently the herb of choice for fish and poultry dishes, but also has an affinity with egg and cheese dishes	Parsley, chervil, chives, marjoram	Use tarragon sparingly, as the flavour, though subtle, can be intense and disperses quickly
Thyme	An aromatic herb that grows wild in most warm climates. The heady aroma and sweet pungent flavour is closely associated with the cooking of provençal France, Italy and other parts of the Mediterranean	Rosemary, parsley, marjoram or oregano, bay leaves, coriander	Lemon thyme with its delicious citrus flavour is good for herb tea, as well as in cooking

mushrooms

Mushroom is the rather loose term we use to describe edible fungi. Fungus is the scientific classification given to any plant that obtains its energy from the decomposing life around it rather than processing sunlight through its leaves. There are two main categories of edible mushrooms: wild ones like chanterelles, ceps and morels, and cultivated ones, such as button, chestnut and flat mushrooms. Oyster mushrooms, while occasionally found wild in our woodlands, are mostly cultivated, as are shiitake, enoki and other Asian mushrooms and are normally categorised as exotic cultivated mushrooms.

Choosing

Wild mushrooms should be firm but moist without any damp patches. A heady smell is a sign of freshness; a dried stem means it's been stored for several days. Common cultivated types should have white or light tan caps and no discoloration.

Fresh mushrooms are very perishable and should be used within one or two days of purchase. They should be wrapped in kitchen roll and refrigerated; do not store them in a plastic bag, which will trap moisture and cause them to deteriorate rapidly. Clean just before using.

Shiitake With a slightly floury-looking medium to dark grey-brown cap, these have a firm meaty texture which becomes silky when cooked. They go well with soy sauce and other southeast Asian flavours. Discard the tough stalks.

CULTIVATED MUSHROOMS

Enoki Sometimes known as golden needles in Japan, these are fine and pale with pin-head tops. They are edible raw, and are mostly used in salads or as a garnish. The flavour is sweet and almost fruity with hints of rice. Trim bottoms, if necessary, to separate.

Button/white Youngest and tiniest mushrooms are called button; larger ones are closed cap; larger still are open cap. Caps are ivory or white, gills are pink when fresh, darkening as they mature. Wipe with a damp cloth. Peel only if skins are very discoloured.

Chestnut Darker mushroom than button mushroom, with a more pronounced flavour.

A CLOSER LOOK AT MUSHROOMS

Cap
This is the meatiest and best-tasting part. It can be used whole and when large, it can be stuffed and grilled or baked, or coated with batter and fried. Alternatively it is cut up into slices or pieces.

Stalk
Often removed if dry and woody, it can be chopped and used with the cap if in good condition.

Gills
Differing in fineness, depending on the variety, dirt and grit can lodge in the folds and need careful removal.

vegetables

WILD MUSHROOMS

Morels Known in Scandinavia as the 'truffles of the north', these are much prized by collectors. They are cone-shaped, with a distinctive honeycomb-like cap that ranges from pale to dark brown. The cap and stem are completely hollow. Note that morels should not be eaten raw. Cut in half and use a brush or gently running water to remove any debris.

Chanterelles
Frilly, trumpet-shaped mushrooms. Chanterelles have a faint apricot aroma and a pleasant, mild fruity flavour. Rinse carefully under gently running water and shake dry.

Flat/field Field mushrooms are the wild variety, flat mushrooms are a cultivated variety. Caps can range from 3 to 12 cm (1¼–5 in), silky white when young, ageing to light brown. Gills are deep pink, but darken as the mushroom matures. Cut off bottom of stem. Only peel if skin is discoloured. Wipe them with a damp cloth.

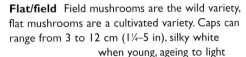

Ceps (France – cèpes; Italy – porcini). One of the largest wild mushrooms, it can weigh up to 1 kg (2½ lb). It is bun-shaped, hence its other name, Penny bun. Much prized for its fine, suede-like texture and excellent flavour. Cut the mushroom in half to check for maggots. Brush stem and cut off bottom, then slice thinly.

Pied bleu Firm, suede-like texture. Cream coloured caps with unusual pale purple-coloured stalks. A mild, fruity flavour.

Duxelles

Duxelles is a classic French combination of finely chopped mushrooms and shallots or onions sautéed in butter until quite dry. Used as a stuffing or garnish, it is said to have been created by La Varenne, chef of the Marquis d'Uxelles.

FINELY CHOPPING MUSHROOMS

To finely chop mushrooms for duxelles, use two chef's knives held together in one hand with the tips of the blades held by your other hand. Chop using a rocking motion.

MUSHROOM BRUSH

This small brush with delicate, very soft 2.5 cm (1 in) long bristles, is used to remove dirt from dry mushrooms.

PREPARING MUSHROOMS

Cultivated white mushrooms are grown in pasteurised compost, so need only wiping, either with a damp cloth or with dampened kitchen roll. Do not wash them as they absorb water and will become soggy. Very sandy mushrooms can be plunged into a bowl of cold water and shaken to loosen the sand. Drain them in a colander.

mushrooms

DRIED MUSHROOMS

Many different varieties are available, including morels, ceps, chanterelles, shiitake and oyster mushrooms. Their flavour is highly concentrated, so even a very small quantity will add richness and depth. They need to be reconstituted before use.

Dried morel

Dried porcini

Dried shiitake

RECONSTITUTING DRIED MUSHROOMS

Put mushrooms in a bowl and cover with warm water, leaving to soak for 35–40 minutes or until they have softened. Drain, then squeeze to extract the liquid. Strain the liquid (to remove any dirt or grit) and use with the mushrooms.

TRUFFLES

There are two main types of truffle. The summer truffle is found in the ground near beech trees and is blackish-brown on the outside, with a marbled reddish-brown interior. It has a distinctive aroma with a strong, slightly nutty flavour.

The Piedmont or white truffle is a far rarer species and is the most valued of all wild mushrooms. It looks something like a small Jerusalem artichoke, with a knobbly brown exterior and pretty claret-coloured marbled flesh. It has an even stronger smell than the summer truffle, that is sweet and distinctive. Its flavour, too, is distinctive. Both varieties are used in stuffings and sauces and with egg and rice dishes.

PREPARING TRUFFLES

▼ Cleaning a truffle
Carefully scrub with a brush. Use a vegetable peeler to remove knobbly skin. Finely chop peelings and use in cooked dishes.

▲ Slicing a truffle
Shave truffles as thinly as possible. Use the shavings in cooking, or else raw on pasta, risottos or omelettes.

seaweed and sea vegetables

PREPARING DRIED SEAWEED

▼ **Nori** To enhance its sweet delicate flavour, nori should be toasted before being used. Check the packets, as some nori available in the shops is ready-toasted. Toast sheets over a flame for a few seconds, or place on a baking sheet and put in a hot oven for 30–60 seconds.

▲ **Wakame** Wakame comes in dried shreds and needs to be reconstituted before use. Soak the shreds in warm water for 2–3 minutes; drain thoroughly and use in soups, salads and stir-fries.

Seaweed is among the strangest of vegetables and one, in the West, that we are not entirely comfortable about eating. Seaweed's association with the euphemistic 'fresh sea air' of the seaside tends to linger. Yet seaweed can be extremely delicious and it is also extremely nutritious, being rich in protein, vitamins and minerals. Seaweeds have been a popular part of Eastern cuisine for centuries, and in Japan particularly, many species are so important that they are cultivated commercially.

Nori Famous in the West as the traditional wrapper for sushi, it is made from a red seaweed, but when dried into sheets turns a dark green/black. The flavour is delicate and mild. Nori doesn't need soaking, but should be toasted if using as a wrapping for sushi (see left). It can also be cut into strips and cooked with rice, or crumbled to garnish rice dishes.

Nori

Wakame This comes in long, dark curly strands. It has a mild slightly sweet flavour. Soak well for a few hours before using in salads or stir-fries, or sprinkle over rice dishes.

Kombu In the West, kombu or kombull is known as giant sea kelp. Rarely used in any Western-type recipes, it is massively popular in Japan and Korea. It is the principal ingredient of the Japanese stock, dashi, and also features in many other dishes as a vegetable or a flavouring. It has a distinctive flavour and is best used in slow-cooked dishes where, as well as adding flavour, it also helps to soften other ingredients.

Wakame

Kombu

MAKING SEAWEED STOCK

Called dashi in Japan, this clear seaweed stock has a delicate fishy flavour. It is very quick and easy to prepare and will keep refrigerated for up to three days. Add kombu seaweed to bonito flakes in a pan of water and bring to the boil. Remove from the heat and let the flakes settle. Slowly strain the liquid through a muslin-lined sieve set over a bowl. Return to the clean pan and simmer for ten minutes.

To concentrate the flavour, return the bonito flakes and kombu seaweed to the stock and repeat as above.

mushrooms, seaweed and sea vegetables

olives and capers

These savoury 'fruits' are two of the most popular products grown in the Mediterranean. They both have very distinctive flavours. Capers are usually incorporated into recipes and olives are either served with drinks or included in many traditional Italian, French, Spanish or Greek dishes. Olives are also pressed to make a wide variety of different grades of olive oil.

Available in a wide variety of colours and flavours, olives are best bought fresh or packed in oil rather than cured in brine. The colour of olives is related to the ripeness of the fruit – from green to yellow green initially and then on to purple and black.

Capers Capers are the small green flower buds from a bush that grows all round the Mediterranean. They are used only in their preserved form and are mostly available preserved in vinegar, brine or olive oil, but can be found layered in salt in Italian shops. Either way, rinse before use to remove excess salt. Capers keep well for months, but make sure they are completely covered with liquid or they will spoil. They add a salty, sour flavour and go well with smooth-textured or delicately flavoured foods, such as veal. They feature in a number of classic dishes.

Caper berries Caper berries are larger than capers, but have a similar taste and can be used in recipes instead of capers. Nasturtium seeds can also be substituted for capers although they have a slight mustard flavour.

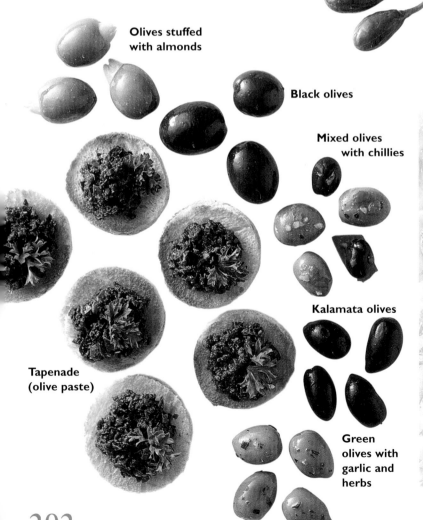

Olives stuffed with almonds

Black olives

Mixed olives with chillies

Kalamata olives

Tapenade (olive paste)

Green olives with garlic and herbs

Recipes

Tomato and caper salsa Made with finely chopped capers, chillies, tomato and olive oil, this salsa is an ideal accompaniment for fish.

Marinated olives An important element of Italian, Greek and Spanish cooking where they grow in profusion, olives can be marinated in a variety of ways. In this recipe, black and green olives are split, mixed with stuffed olives, coriander seeds and orange zest, covered in olive oil and left to mature for one month.

Salsa verde Spanish for green sauce, this is a smooth mixture of breadcrumbs, capers, gherkin, chives, lemon juice and olive oil. The ingredients are blended together and then seasoned with salt and pepper. Perfect with grilled fish.

fruits and nuts

apples and pears

Apples and pears are among the most versatile of fruits. Eaten raw they need no preparation beyond being washed – simply a case of grab and go! They also cook superbly, being a central component of some of our most famous dishes – from a sauce to serve with a main course to an old-time favourite like apple pie.

APPLES

Cooking apples There are a variety of cooking apples available, but by far the most popular is Bramley's Seedlings. These are large, green apples, occasionally with red flushing, with a white juicy flesh. Too tart for eating, the flesh when cooked disintegrates to a fluffy purée, making it ideal for apple sauce and other cooked apple recipes where a soft texture is required.

Cox The Cox, or Cox's Orange Pippin, is one of the best-known and best-loved apples. Mostly small or medium-sized, it has a firm juicy flesh and excellent flavour, balancing sweetness and acidity.

Empire The Empire is a popular American apple with a dark-red skin and creamy white flesh. It is tart-sweet in flavour with a good crisp texture.

Golden Delicious A popular apple that tends to be rather tasteless and grainy in texture when over-ripe. Good-quality Golden Delicious apples should be firm with smooth, pale yellow/green skin. The more mature fruit has a yellowish, slightly pitted skin and it is best avoided.

Granny Smith Granny Smith apples are grown throughout Europe and America, but were first grown in Australia by a English émigré, 'Annie Smith'. They have a uniformly green skin and clear bright white flesh. Their tart flavour and crisp texture make them a good eating apple but they are also popular for cooking.

Red Delicious A large American apple enjoyed for its sweet flavour. The skin is tough, but the flesh is juicy and sweet.

Spartan A Canadian apple with a delicious aromatic flavour but rather tough skin.

CORING

Core apples by pushing a corer into the stalk end. Twist to cut around the core, then gently pull it out.

APPLE CRESCENTS

Core and peel an apple, keeping it whole. Cut in half lengthwise. Put each half cut-side down and cut crosswise into half moons.

PEARS

Pears are related to the apple. It is best to buy them unripe and let them ripen at room temperature. For this reason they were traditionally only ever used for cooking, either for making jams, or baked, braised or stewed and served as a dessert. Varieties to look out for include Conference, Kieffer, Bartlett and Wildemann.

ASIAN PEARS

There are a variety pears from Asia which, with their round shape and russet skin, look more like apples than pears. Bite into one, however, and you will find that while it is crisp and juicy, it also has the typical granular pear-like texture. They are best eaten raw, preferably straight from the fridge, when they have the taste and texture of a sweet fragrant iced lolly.

Shandong A good firm texture and a flavour that is a cross between an apple and a pear.

Tientsin pears These Chinese and Korean pears are small and plump. Their pale yellow mottled skin encloses a bright white flesh. They are sweet, juicy and crunchy and like other Asian pears, should be eaten raw, ideally straight from the fridge.

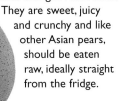

Nashi Pears Small, golden-brown skin, with a sweet white juicy flesh.

DISCOLORATION

The flesh of apples and pears quickly discolours after peeling. To prevent this, paint with lemon or lime juice immediately after peeling or cutting.

PEAR FANS

Peel, halve and core the pear, leaving the stalk intact. Put the cut side down and slice from stalk to bottom. Press with your hand to fan out the slices.

Recipes

Almond baked apples Peeled apples are covered with butter, ground almonds and sugar, filled with a mixture of dried figs and citrus zest, then baked until soft and sweet.

Flambéed apples Triberg-style Dessert apples cooked with butter, sugar, lemon and honey until tender. Kirsch is then spooned over the apples and set alight. Served with whipped cream while still slightly flaming.

Pears in red wine Pears poached in claret or other red wine with sugar and cloves; serve with toasted almonds and yogurt or cream.

Tarte des demoiselles tatin This upside-down apple pie is cooked in a metal pan. Sugar caramelises on the bottom to make a rich topping when the tart is unmoulded.

Pear sorbet Poached pears, puréed with a little of the poaching syrup and frozen. Poire Williams – a spirit distilled from pears – is added in some recipes.

Poires belle Hélène Pears poached in a sugar syrup and served with a hot chocolate and orange sauce.

stone fruits

Choosing

Peaches and nectarines that are picked for export (which includes all fruit sold in our own shops) are picked when firm. They will soften but will not get sweeter, so choose with care, selecting fruit with a good rosy bloom, avoiding any that have a greenish tinge or feel particularly hard.

Home-grown plums are best picked just before they are ripe. Shop-bought ones should be slightly firm but with a little 'give'. They should be unblemished with a good bloom.

Whenever possible, buy cherries that are on their stalks, as this is the best guide to freshness. These should be green and pliant; woody, withered stalks suggest the cherry has been picked for some time. (And if the stalks have been removed, then you have reason to be suspicious.) The cherries themselves should be plump and unblemished. If possible, try one to test for sweetness.

PEACHES AND NECTARINES

There are hundreds, probably thousands of different varieties of peach, but in Britain they are normally classified simply as those with white or yellow flesh, of which the white-fleshed are normally best for eating and the yellow for cooking. Nectarines are a type of peach native to China. Although some people detect a touch more acidity, they have a similar flavour and texture to a peach, and in North America, where the soft down is removed from peach skin, the fruits are virtually indistinguishable.

A CLOSER LOOK AT A PEACH

Skin
By brushing the soft downy skin you can test for ripeness. Under-ripe peaches have a green tinge to the skin and are best avoided – they will never ripen.

Stone
In some peaches, the flesh is firmly attached to the stone (known as 'clingstones'); in others the flesh comes away easily ('freestones'). The latter are best for baking.

Flesh
Normally the same colour as the palest colour on the skin. Fine juicy texture and sweet flavour. As the peach ripens, so the flesh around the stone becomes dappled with red or pink.

500 G (¼ LB) PEACHES

=

3 medium or 4 small

=

about 3 cups sliced

=

about 2¼ cups chopped

The kernels of peach and apricot stones can be poisonous. They contain a chemical compound, glucoside, which can react to form prussic acid or hydrogen cyanide. These can be driven off if the kernels are roasted, but do not eat kernels raw.

NUTRITIONAL INFORMATION

Peaches are a good source of vitamin A, although not as good as apricots. They also provide vitamin C.

Apricots are a very valuable source of vitamin A in the form of beta-carotene. One serving of three apricots provides nearly half of an adult's daily requirement of this vitamin. They are also a good source of vitamin C and potassium and provide some iron and calcium.

Plums contain some vitamin A and are also a good source of vitamin C.

Cherries are a source of vitamin C and are also rich in dietary fibre.

STONING PEACHES

Cut around the fruit with a small knife, following the seam and cutting right down to the stone. Holding the cut fruit, twist each half quite sharply in opposite directions to expose the stone. Carefully prise the stone out of the fruit with the top of the knife, then lift it out with your fingers.

APRICOTS

Native to China where they have been cultivated for thousands of years, most of the fruit found for sale in our shops is orange/yellow in colour, flushed with red. Apricots have an excellent balance of sweetness and acidity, and are good eaten by themselves or cooked. They are used extensively in the Middle and Near East for sweet and savoury dishes.

Apricots have a short 'peak' when they are at their best, and unfortunately they do not travel well, so while a perfect apricot is a wonderful thing, they are often disappointing, being dry and rather woolly if unripe, and lacking in flavour once past their best. Choose apricots with a rich colour and smooth skin.

PLUMS

Whatever the season, there are usually several varieties available in supermarkets suitable for cooking if not for eating. Plums vary in colour, size, flavour and sweetness. Yet in spite of their many differences, they all have smooth skins and a juicy flesh with good acidity.

Czar These are large, dark blue-black plums with orange flesh.

Damsons The cultivated form of the wild plum, damsons have dark, blue-black skins with a soft white bloom. They have a strong tart flavour and can be stewed for pies and tarts, but are most commonly used for making jellies and jams.

Mirabelles These are small yellow-green or red plums that grow on long stalks like cherries. They have a bitter skin, but a sweet flesh and are mostly used for stewing or jam.

stone fruits

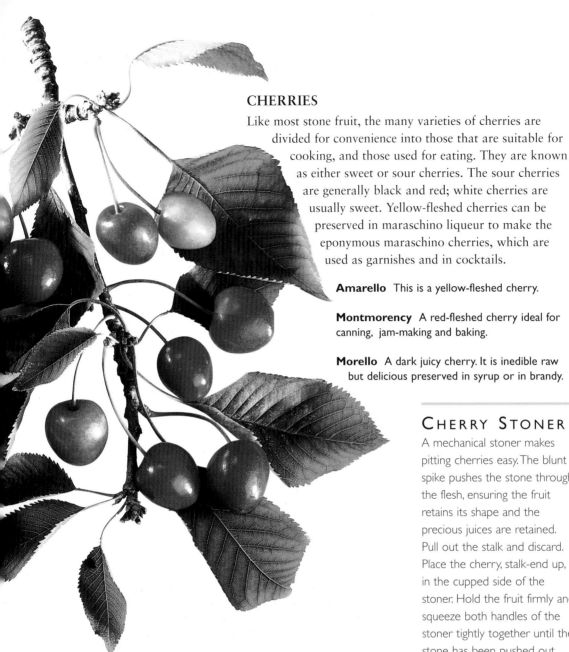

CHERRIES

Like most stone fruit, the many varieties of cherries are divided for convenience into those that are suitable for cooking, and those used for eating. They are known as either sweet or sour cherries. The sour cherries are generally black and red; white cherries are usually sweet. Yellow-fleshed cherries can be preserved in maraschino liqueur to make the eponymous maraschino cherries, which are used as garnishes and in cocktails.

Amarello This is a yellow-fleshed cherry.

Montmorency A red-fleshed cherry ideal for canning, jam-making and baking.

Morello A dark juicy cherry. It is inedible raw but delicious preserved in syrup or in brandy.

CHERRY STONER

A mechanical stoner makes pitting cherries easy. The blunt spike pushes the stone through the flesh, ensuring the fruit retains its shape and the precious juices are retained. Pull out the stalk and discard. Place the cherry, stalk-end up, in the cupped side of the stoner. Hold the fruit firmly and squeeze both handles of the stoner tightly together until the stone has been pushed out. The same technique can be used for stoning olives.

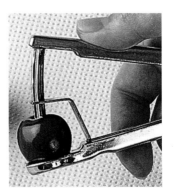

STORING

Kept at room temperature for a day or two, peaches and nectarines will gradually soften. Once fully ripe, keep in the fridge for up to two days.

Apricots will keep for one to two days at room temperature if under-ripe, but then store in the fridge and eat within three to four days once fully ripened.

Once ripe, keep plums in the fridge and eat within two days.

Cherries keep for one to two days in the fridge. Wash before use.

Recipes

Brandied cherries
Cherries poached gently in a light, cinnamon-flavoured syrup and stored in brandy.

Black Forest gâteau A favourite recipe where sponge layers are filled with a cherry mixture and topped with cream and more cherries.

Cherry brûlées
Cherries are soaked in Kirsch and baked with a creamy custard mixture. Served chilled with a thin layer of caramel and a fresh cherry on top.

Warm peaches and blueberries with mascarpone ice cream
Peaches, blueberries, citrus zests and cardamom seeds heated gently in butter and brown sugar until soft. Served with a creamy Italian-style ice cream.

berries

STRAWBERRIES

These soft fruits have a wide range of uses in the kitchen. They are served fresh in fruit salads and used to top cakes and pavlovas but they also are cooked in cakes, tartlets, pies, crumbles, puddings, sauces and jams.

Choosing

If possible, buy from a local grower or, better still, pick your own, which is cheaper and the fruit is fresher. If buying from stores, always check punnets carefully. The fruit should be plump and shiny, without any sign of mould or rot and there should be no sign of staining or leakage on the bottom of the punnet, which would suggest that the fruit at the bottom of the pack was squashed.

PREPARING STRAWBERRIES

Strawberry hulls are usually removed, although you can leave them intact if the berries are to be used for decoration. Prise out the leafy top (hull) with the tip of a small knife. You can then slice the whole fruit in half lengthwise with a chef's knife.

Strawberries
Wonderful served by themselves with a sprinkling of sugar, if liked, and cream, they are also superb in various desserts like pavlova, shortcakes and tartlets. They have an affinity with chocolate and can be dipped whole into melted chocolate and used as a decoration or as an after-dinner treat. Lightly poached strawberries can go into summer pudding. Ripe strawberries are popular for jam.

Recipes

Summer pudding
A bread-lined basin is filled with a compote of berries and left to let the juices to soak the bread.

Blueberry fritters with apple sauce Blueberries coated in sweet almond batter and apple sauce.

WILD STRAWBERRIES

Miniature, slender versions of the normal strawberry, they have a sweet fragrant flavour.

Fraises des bois or Alpine strawberries These grow wild in Britain and Europe, although certain varieties are cultivated and are sold commercially. The cultivated ones are slightly larger than their wild cousins and you may find white and yellow varieties as well as red, which look pretty and have a wonderful vanilla flavour.

Gooseberries A relative of the blackcurrant, the best-known variety is bright green. Though they have a reputation for being impossibly sour, some types of gooseberries are sweet enough to be eaten raw. They can be cooked in a little water and sugar, and then used to make fools, ice creams or sorbets. They have a high pectin content which makes them a good choice for jellies and jam, either on their own or with other fruits. Gooseberry sauce is also good served with oily fish such as trout and mackerel.

Raspberries Superb by themselves with sugar and cream, they also can be used in fruit salads, and for pavlovas and tartlets. A coulis of puréed, sieved and sweetened raspberries is an essential part of Peach Melba. The purée can also be used for making ice creams, sorbets and also fruit fools.

Cranberries
These can be served with meat and game, and most traditionally of all, with turkey at Christmas or Thanksgiving. Cranberries can be used for sweet and savoury dishes. However, they must always be cooked and are normally stewed in water with sugar and a piece of lemon peel, until tender.

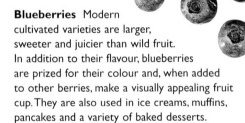

Blueberries Modern cultivated varieties are larger, sweeter and juicier than wild fruit. In addition to their flavour, blueberries are prized for their colour and, when added to other berries, make a visually appealing fruit cup. They are also used in ice creams, muffins, pancakes and a variety of baked desserts.

Blackberries
A free food of the countryside, they also are grown commercially along with their close relations, dewberries. Although good uncooked in fruit salads, blackberries are popular teamed with apples for pies and crumbles and are an excellent addition to summer puddings. Blackberries are also good for ice creams, fools, coulis and jam.

What's in a name?

Blackberries and raspberries are both members of the rose family (the thorns give it away). There are numerous hybrids, some deliberately bred, others occurring naturally. They include the dewberry, the loganberry, boysenberry and the tayberry.

STORING

Most soft fruits are highly perishable and should be eaten as soon as possible after purchase. Strawberries, raspberries and blackberries are prone to mould, and one spoiled fruit will quickly contaminate the rest, so discard any mouldy fruit straight away.

Strawberries do not freeze well, but other soft fruits can be frozen and this is recommended if you have a glut and would like a good supply throughout the winter. Open freeze fruit like raspberries and blackberries having first removed stalks from currants, and topped and tailed gooseberries. Cranberries and blueberries can be popped straight into the freezer in plastic bags.

Harder berries, like gooseberries and blueberries, will keep for up to a week at the bottom of the fridge. Cranberries will keep for longer – up to four weeks.

REDCURRANTS, BLACKCURRANTS AND WHITECURRANTS

These small versatile fruits are all closely related. A popular garden fruit in Britain, Germany and northern Europe, they are almost unheard of in Mediterranean countries.

Blackcurrants are the most acidic of the currants and are rarely eaten raw. Red and white currants, which are a variety of the same plant, are sweeter and contain less pectin (which causes the mouth-puckering reaction) and can be eaten uncooked.

Blackcurrants can be used in all sorts of tarts, for making ice cream, sorbets, or as an addition to summer pudding. They are often used for making cordials.

Redcurrants As well as using for decoration, redcurrants can be added to summer puddings, for making coulis, and most famously of all for redcurrant jelly, traditionally served with lamb and venison.

Whitecurrants make an attractive decoration.

STRIPPING CURRANTS

Currants need to have their stalks removed before use by stripping. The only tool you need for this clever technique is an ordinary kitchen fork. Run the tines of a fork down the stalk – the currants will come away easily.

PURÉEING IN A MOULI

Strawberries, raspberries or, as here, redcurrants, can be worked through a food mill to make a smooth purée. The seeds are left behind in the mill, so there is no need to sieve afterwards.

Fit the fine disc into the mouli and set it over a large bowl. Put berries of your choice in the bowl. Hold the handle firmly and turn the crank so that the blade pushes the fruit into the bowl beneath.

berries

211

citrus fruits

ORANGES

These come in both bitter and sweet varieties; sweet oranges may be further divided into blood, common and navel oranges. In addition to being eaten raw and as a garnish, oranges and orange juice are used in savoury dishes, marinades and a wide variety of desserts, including sorbets, cakes, curds, tarts, gelatin moulds and puddings. The ones shown here are those most used in cooking.

Choosing

Oranges should feel heavy for their size and be firm, without any soft spots. Avoid oranges with dull colouring or rough, grooved or wrinkled skin; select those with bright-looking skins.

Blood orange A very juicy, thin-skinned orange with a sweet red flesh. Blood oranges owe their colour to the orange tree being once crossed with a pomegranate tree. They make excellent refreshing juice and can be used in salads and compotes.

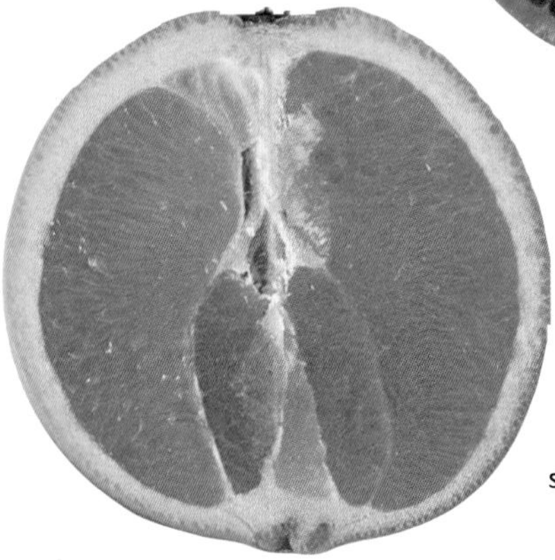

Navelina/ Washington navel A sweet seedless orange, with characteristic navel shape at the bottom or flower end. Excellent flavour with a good balance of acidity and sweetness.

Jaffa orange From Israel this is a variety of the navel orange. It can be used in salads, compotes, cooking and baking.

Valencia A sweet, thick-skinned orange that is easy to peel. If in its prime, the fruit is sweet and juicy. It is valued for the quality and quantity of its juice and is a good cooking and baking orange.

A CLOSER LOOK AT AN ORANGE

Zest Coloured outer layer of peel contains essential oils; see page 11 for advice on how to remove this layer using a zester.

Pith Bitter-flavoured white layer surrounding the fruit.

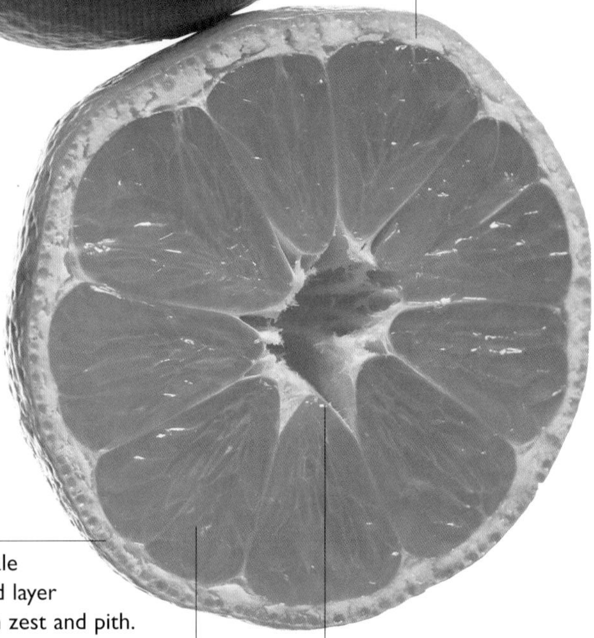

Rind Thick pale coloured layer between zest and pith.

Segments Juicy flesh of the citrus fruit.

Membrane Transparent thin layer that separates the segments.

BITTER ORANGES

Sometimes called sour oranges, bitter oranges have a tough, dark skin which is extremely sour and bitter.

Seville The fruit, together with the skin, is used for marmalade and also for making orange-flavoured liqueurs like Curaçao, Grand Marnier and Cointreau.

Kumquats A close relative of the orange, they are much smaller, only about 2–4 cm (¾–1½ in) in diameter. They are juicy with a distinct citrus-sour flavour, and although they can be eaten as they are, skin and all, they are more commonly used in cooking, or candied. When buying, choose unblemished specimens.

Tangerines Clementines, mandarins and satsumas are all types of tangerine. Small and easy-to-peel, they are most often eaten uncooked, but they are delicious served in sugar or liqueur syrup.

STORING

Oranges keep for several days at room temperature or for one to two weeks in the fridge.

Kumquats will keep for up to ten days in the fridge.

NUTRITIONAL INFORMATION

Oranges are an excellent source of vitamin C, providing twice the adult daily requirement. They also contain calcium.
Lemons are rich in vitamin C.
Limes are rich in vitamin C, and are also a source of potassium, calcium and phosphorus.
Grapefruits are an excellent source of vitamin C.
Kumquats are rich in vitamins C and A. They are also a source of calcium, phosphorous and riboflavin.

PEELING AND SLICING A CITRUS FRUIT

When cutting the peel from oranges, it is important to cut away the bitter pith, leaving the flesh intact.

▼ Cut a slice of peel from both ends of the fruit to expose the flesh. Stand it up and cut away the peel and white pith, following the curve of the fruit.

▼ Hold the fruit firmly on its side and cut the flesh crosswise into slices about 3 mm (⅛ in) thick, using a gentle sawing action with the knife.

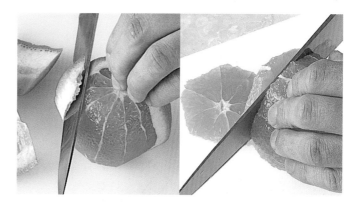

SEGMENTING CITRUS FRUITS

This simple technique cuts citrus fruits into neat segments so that none of the tough membrane is included. Work over a bowl to collect the juice as it drips from the fruit.

▼ Hold the peeled fruit in one hand. Cut down both sides of one white membrane to the core. Leave as little flesh as possible attached.

▼ Work around the fruit, continuing to cut along the membranes and remove segments; fold the membranes back as you cut.

LEMONS

They are, with oranges, the most important citrus fruit and are arguably the most important fruit in the kitchen, because its tart flavour enhances sweet and savoury foods alike. The juice of a lemon will add lift to just about any recipe, but as important is the skin of the lemon which contains aromatic essential oils.

Lemons are the major ingredient in lemon tarts, either made with whole candied slices or the juice and zest, and in lemon curds. Otherwise lemons – juice and zest – are used for adding sharpness to sauces, soups, custards, and in fact an almost endless list of sweet and savoury dishes.

Choosing

When buying lemons, choose fruit that is heavy for its size. Many lemons are treated with wax and sprays to give a glossy appearance, so if you intend to use lemon zest, buy unwaxed lemons if you can.

LIMES

Smaller than lemons, they also, like lemons, add a superb sharpness to sweet and savoury foods. A little sourer than lemons, they are also more aromatic, a feature that is particularly suited to Thai and Indonesian cookery. They are also used widely in Mexican and other Central American and Caribbean cuisines. Limes are mostly used for perking up all types of food, but also star in Key lime pie. Lime juice is the classic ingredient with tequila in a Margarita cocktail.

Choosing

Select unblemished fruit, which has a good colour and feels heavy for its size. Avoid any that are beginning to shrivel and look dry. Limes will keep for up to a week in a cool place.

CITRUS CUPS

Oranges, lemons and limes make attractive containers for sorbets of the same flavour. Hollow out the fruits and use the flesh to make the filling and slice off the bottom so the cup will sit level. Then freeze the shell until it is ready to use.

CRYSTALLISED PEEL

The peel of oranges, lemons and limes can be cooked in a sugar syrup and used as a decorative garnish. Cut thin strips of citrus peel, making sure to remove all pith. Place rind in a pan, cover with sugar and water and cook until syrup has evaporated. Spread out the rinds and dredge with caster sugar. Leave until cold.

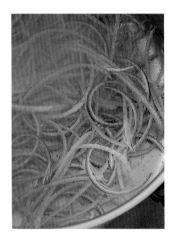

Recipes

Lemon meringue pie
Pastry shell filled with a lemon cream and topped with stiffly whisked egg whites and sugar.

Crêpes Suzette
Pancakes are coated in a sweet butter and orange sauce, then flambéed in an orange liqueur.

Caramelised citrus tart with dark berry ice Pastry case filled with a gently whisked mixture of egg, sugar, cream and citrus juices. This is baked and served with a caramelised topping, accompanied by a berry sorbet and candied limes, and drizzled with syrup.

GRAPEFRUIT

Hugely popular and, after oranges, the most grown citrus fruit in the world, there are numerous different types, varying in size, colour and sweetness. Most grapefruits have deep yellow skins, but their flesh ranges from pale yellow, through pink to a deep ruby red. The pinker the grapefruit, the sweeter they are likely to be. Unlike lemons, limes and oranges, grapefruit juice and zest is hardly ever used in cooking – the flavour is too assertive. For this reason, grapefruit is best served by itself, or with neutrally flavoured foods, where it does not matter if the grapefruit flavour dominates.

Choosing

Buy grapefruit that feels heavy for its size, avoiding any that look wrinkled or have soft, spongy skins.

Pomelos These look rather like an old relative to the grapefruit, which is exactly what they are, being larger and coarser, with a thicker rind. The flavour is fairly similar too, although the pomelo is juicy and more spicy.

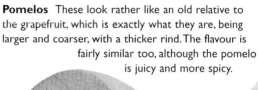

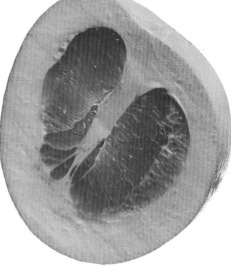

Ugli fruit This is a hybrid of a grapefruit, orange and tangerine. It is large and normally rather hefty-looking, but it has a good sweet flavour.

CITRUS GARNISHES

Citrus knots These are good on petits fours. Peel the citrus fruit avoiding the pith, then cut the peel into fine strips. Tie a knot in each strip.

Citrus twists Cut the fruit neatly into thin slices with a sharp knife, then cut from the edge into the centre of each slice. Twist the slice from the cut in opposite directions.

Zig-zags Draw a zig-zag pattern round the centre of a lemon. Using a sharp knife, cut through pattern to halve the lemon.

Scalloped slices Use a zester to cut lengthways strips of rind from lemon or orange to give a striped effect. Cut fruit crossways into thin slices.

citrus fruits

exotic fruits

Choosing and storing

Bananas continue to ripen once they are picked, and it is possible to buy them at almost every stage of ripeness. A perfectly ripe fruit will be uniformly yellow and, as it continues to ripen, brown speckles will appear; unripe bananas are varying shades of green, while if over-ripe, the banana becomes increasingly dark.

Look for fresh-looking, unwrinkled kiwi fruit that feels heavy for its size. Unripe fruit will ripen if stored at room temperature, but do not keep alongside other fruit, as the enzymes in the fruit (which also help tenderise meat), will cause it to ripen too quickly.

Choose unblemished papaya that are slightly yielding when gently squeezed in the palm of the hand. Unripe fruit will ripen if kept at room temperature; once ripe, keep in the fridge.

When perfectly ripe, mangoes should be soft to the touch, like avocados, and have a sweet aroma. If the skin has many black patches, it may be over-ripe and the flesh will be too soft and overly sweet.

A perfectly ripe custard apple should be firm, but with a little 'give', and have a green quilted skin, with patches of brown developing. It should feel heavy for its size. If the fruit is hard and uniformly pale green it is likely to be unripe; overly soft and brown and it will be past its best.

Fresh dates should be plump with smooth, shiny skins. Avoid any dates that are shrivelled or have sugar crystals on the skin.

Look for figs that are soft and smell sweet, but avoid any that look too soft. Once ripe, they should be eaten as soon as possible; if still unripe, keep at room temperature for a day or two, and then store in the fridge for up to three days.

Bananas Baked as a dessert or used to flavour cakes, quick breads, puddings, pies and ice cream, bananas also can be used in fruit salads or as a topping. Use slightly underripe bananas for baking with butter and sugar; overripe bananas are best in cakes and breads.

Plantains or green bananas are a close relative of the banana, although they are much heftier and it is easy to discern the difference. They cannot be eaten raw but are excellent cooked, either fried or boiled in their skins and sliced.

Kiwi fruit Rough-skinned ovoid fruit with brilliant green flesh, surrounding tiny black edible seeds. The flesh is delicate and sweet/sour. It is best eaten raw or in fruit salads.

YIELD

3 MEDIUM BANANAS

=

4 small bananas

=

500 g (1¼ lb)

=

1 cup mashed

Passion fruit A hard, wrinkled fruit that contains numerous small edible seeds inside its intensely fragrant pulp. It can be used for making ice cream, sorbets, for drinks, or adding to fruit salads. The seeds are edible, and passion fruit can be eaten on its own, or the pulp can be sieved. Choose fruit that is heavy for its size. It will naturally wrinkle when ripe and will keep in the fridge for up to one week.

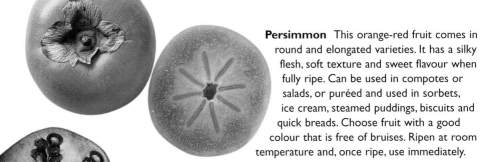

Persimmon This orange-red fruit comes in round and elongated varieties. It has a silky flesh, soft texture and sweet flavour when fully ripe. Can be used in compotes or salads, or puréed and used in sorbets, ice cream, steamed puddings, biscuits and quick breads. Choose fruit with a good colour that is free of bruises. Ripen at room temperature and, once ripe, use immediately.

Star fruit Also known as carambolas, they have a sweet but rather watery taste. Mostly used for decorative purposes in fruit salads and pavlovas. Choose bright-looking, undamaged fruit.

Pomegranate The tough, shiny red-skinned fruit contains tightly packed seeds with deep pink, intensely sweet flesh. Use seeds to garnish fruit salads, desserts and main courses or press through a sieve and use juice as a flavouring. Choose colourful fruit without cracks or splits and that gives slightly to pressure.

Loquat Also known as Japanese medlar, this sweet, slightly resinous Mediterranean fruit is peeled and eaten raw, made into preserves and cooked with roast pork and chicken. Choose firm, unblemished ones that give slightly to pressure. They will last for up to two weeks in the fridge.

Guavas The pale green skin covers a flesh that varies from white to a deep pink. It has a sweet perfumed aroma, and a tart flavour. Good eaten raw or poached gently and puréed to make ice creams. Guava is also used for making fragrant jams and jellies.

Pepino Peel and discard the bitter skin and slice the flesh thinly. Use in fruit salads; purée for sorbets; and, if sautéed in butter, use as a garnish. Fruit should have a good yellow skin colour and give slightly when pressed.

NUTRITIONAL INFORMATION

Bananas are great energy food, which is why athletes eat them. They are also rich in potassium, riboflavin, niacin and are a good source of vitamins A, B_6 and C.

Kiwi fruit is exceptionally high in vitamin C, a single fruit providing more than the average daily requirement for an adult. They also contain vitamins E, A and some potassium.

Passion fruit is an excellent source of vitamins A and C, and also provides potassium, iron and some calcium.

Papayas are an extremely good source of vitamin C. They also provide vitamin A, calcium and iron.

Mangoes are an extremely good source of vitamin A and beta-carotene. They also contain vitamin C.

Figs are a source of calcium, iron and copper, and also provide dietary fibre.

Prickly pear This can be eaten raw or cooked, but use gloves to remove the spiny skin. The flesh has the texture of melon and it can be served with smoked or cured meat. Choose unblemished fruit. Ripe fruit has pink skin. The fruit will ripen at room temperature, and will keep for four to five days in the fridge.

exotic fruits

Papayas A tropical, pear-shaped fruit with a green flesh that turns yellow/orange when ripe. The golden orange flesh is sweet, juicy and silky smooth. Also known as a pawpaw, its black seeds are edible with a slightly peppery flavour and they are sometimes used as a garnish. Papayas are excellent served by themselves or added to fruit salads. Like melons they go well with cured meats, or the cubed flesh can go into fish or chicken curries, or served in elegant main course salads like gado gado.

STORING

Wrapped in paper or plastic, dates will keep in the fridge for up to two weeks.

Leave unripe custard apples to soften at room temperature and then store in the fridge for up to four days.

Pineapples These should only ever be picked once ripe, as the starch will not convert to sugar once it is off the plant. Over-ripe or bruised fruit has a strong aroma and tends to have soft patches.

Mangoes A large and luscious tropical fruit with variously green, yellow, pink-gold and red skin. The flesh is golden yellow with a unique aroma and flavour said by some to be a spicy combination of peach and pineapple. Best eaten raw, either alone or in fruit salads. The fruit can also be puréed for ice creams, sorbets and frozen yogurts.

Dates The skin is thin and papery and the flesh is soft and sweet. They are probably the most calorific of all fruits, containing 230 kilocalories per 90 g (3½ oz). Dates can be used to make savoury appetizers or chopped and used to sweeten cakes, biscuits, breads, muffins, fruit salads and stuffings.

Figs Can have a green or purple-black skin, filled with a soft succulent pink or red flesh with tiny seeds. They can be served fresh as an appetizer or dessert, or baked. There are three varieties – dark purple skinned with deep red flesh, yellow-green with a pink flesh and green skinned, with an amber-coloured flesh.

Custard apples
A heart or oval-shaped fruit with a soft, sweet custard-like pulp, that tastes like a combination of pineapple, papaya, and banana. Also known as cherimoya, its fruit may be added to salads or puréed for ice cream or sorbet.

Lychees A small pink/red fruit, whose scaly skin encloses a succulent soft white flesh. The skin and dark brown seed are inedible, but the flesh is delicious, with a grape-like texture and a sweet perfumed flavour. Serve by themselves or add, peeled and stoned, to fruit salads. They can also be poached, Chinese-style, in flower-scented syrup. Choose fruit that is pink or red. They will keep in the fridge for up to one week.

Physalis Small, orange-gold fruit encased in a papery flower, also known as Cape gooseberry. Their flavour is sweet with slightly tart undertones. Physalis are always sold in their papery husks and it is a good idea to check one or two to make sure the fruit is not over-ripe. Excellent served raw either by themselves or as a decoration. They are also good cooked to make jams and jellies.

fruits and nuts

PREPARING PINEAPPLE

▼ Removing the skin
Cut off the plume and the bottom of the pineapple. Stand the fruit upright and slice off the skin from top to bottom using a large knife.

▼ Removing eyes Dig out any spikes or eyes left in the flesh with the point of a small knife. Then slice the fruit crosswise using a chef's knife.

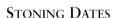

▲ Coring Lay each pineapple slice flat and then stamp out the core with a small cutter.

DICING A MANGO

Fibrous mango flesh sticks to the central stone, making it difficult to remove. This method, called the hedgehog method, is good when serving the mango as a dessert or for removing the flesh for a fruit salad.

Slice the fruit lengthwise on either side of the flat stone, cutting as close to the stone as possible.

▲ Slice the flesh of the two stoneless sections in a lattice pattern, cutting down to the peel but not piercing it.

▲ Push the peel inside out with your thumbs. Cut away cubes with a knife.

MAKING A FIG FLOWER

Trim the stalk end with a knife. Cut a deep cross in the top of the fig and open it out by pushing the sides slightly with your fingers. Fig flowers can be served plain, or alternatively with a filling spooned or piped into the centre.

STONING DATES

Hold the date firmly in one hand and pull the stone out by the attached stalk, using the tip of a small knife to help you get a good grip.

PREPARING A LYCHEE

Starting at the stalk end, carefully cut through the rough, brittle skin with a knife; it will peel off cleanly. The pearly white flesh contains a long, brown inedible seed. Ripe fruit has a pink blush on its skin.

CARAMEL-COATED PHYSALIS

Gently peel back the leaves and twist at the base. Dip into a sugar syrup, and allow excess to drip off. Place upright on greased backing parchment and allow to set.

exotic fruits

219

other fruits

Rhubarb, grapes and melons do not fall into any particular category; rhubarb is now judged to be a fruit though it is, in fact, a vegetable! Rhubarb is also an exception in the fruit world, because it needs to be cooked before becoming edible. Grapes are mostly enjoyed as a dessert fruit, but can be added to sauces served with duck, veal or fish. Melons, with their delicate flavour and texture, are never cooked. They can be used in chilled soups, sorbets, fruit salads and to accompany thinly sliced ham.

Choosing

Buy rhubarb with crisp, firm stalks that release sap if snapped in half.

Buy grapes with care. They should look firm, with a good bloom, and should taste sweet. It is easy to check by tasting a stray fruit. Avoid over-ripe fruit that is beginning to brown or show signs of mould.

You will need to handle a melon when buying. It should feel heavy for its size, and have a fragrant aroma. The more mature the fruit, the sweeter the aroma, but it should not smell musky which is sign that it is over-ripe. Press the stalk end gently with your thumb; it should have a little 'give'. Avoid any fruit with soft patches.

Grapes Those grown specifically for the table are known as dessert grapes and there are numerous varieties. White grapes can be anything from pale yellow to vivid green; black grapes are purple, bluish or deep wine red. The best grapes are considered to be muscat grapes, which are large with a richly perfumed flesh and may be black, red or white. Among the popular seedless varieties are Thompson seedless and Flame seedless. They contain less tannin than other varieties, and are sweet and juicy. Grapes need to be washed before serving.

Rhubarb The best rhubarb is available in early spring and has been forced; its stems are sweet and tender. Older rhubarb, with its thick green and red stems and large dark green leaves, is much tougher. Rhubarb must always be cooked in order to be palatable and will usually need to be sweetened.

PREPARING RHUBARB

Early season rhubarb is tender and requires little preparation, but main crop rhubarb needs peeling. Cut off the leaves and discard, then pare away the skin in long strips using a vegetable peeler. Trim the base of each stalk. Slice crosswise on the diagonal into neat chunks before cooking.

PEELING AND DESEEDING GRAPES

When used in a sauce or as a garnish, the chewy skin and the pips need removing.
- **Peeling** Blanch for 10 seconds, then strip off the skin with a paring knife, starting at the stalk end.
- **Deseeding** Open out a sterilised paperclip and use one hooked end to pull out pips. To remove the pips from grape halves, flick them out with the tip of a small pointed knife.

Honeydew melon A winter melon which, at its best, is deliciously sweet and juicy. Honeydews have a smooth yellow skin, with a pale green ripening to orange flesh.

Watermelon is sweet and thirst quenching, with a cool, juicy flesh. Most watermelons have a smooth glossy skin, dark green in colour with pale green stripes. The flesh is usually a deep wine-red with black seeds dotted throughout the flesh. It belongs to a different genus of the cucumber family than other sweet melons.

Galia melon Medium-sweet, highly fragrant, moist and juicy, this melon is round with a pale green flesh and green to golden rind.

Charentais melon A cantaloupe variety. Small and highly scented with a deep orange flesh.

Cantaloupe melon is a small round variety with a ribbed, golden brown russetted skin. The flesh is pale orange with a delicious aromatic flavour.

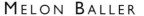

NUTRITIONAL INFORMATION

The nutritional value of melons will vary from type to type; however, most are a good source of vitamin C. Those with orange flesh contain a significant amount of beta-carotene, and most also are a source of vitamin B. They are all very low in calories.

PREPARING MELONS

Small melons make decorative containers for fruit salads and other desserts. Mark a slanted zigzag line in the skin just above the midline, using the tip of a knife. Cut on the marked lines, inserting the knife through to the centre of the fruit each time. Gently pull the melon apart. Scoop out the seeds and fibrous flesh, and discard. Remove balls of flesh from the bottom section with a melon baller.

MELON BALLER

A double-headed device with a large and a smaller head, it is simple to use. Just insert the head into the cut flesh of the melon and twist to remove neat balls of fruit. A melon baller can be used for other fruit as well.

dried fruits

A range of dried fruit is used in sweet and savoury dishes. It is naturally sweeter than fresh fruit as the drying process concentrates its sugars. It can take 5 kg (11 lb) of fresh fruit to make 1 kg (2½ lb) of dried, so if the fruit is measured by volume or weight, dried fruits are much higher in calories than fresh.

Dried apples can be used in fruit compotes or in dishes from Normandy, which traditionally combine apples, cream and Calvados to superb effect.

Prunes Derived from purple or red plums, prunes are available in various forms, including stoned and ready-to-eat. The finest prune is the Agen, which is sold complete with stones and needs to be soaked before cooking.

Dates These are intensely sweet and sticky, with dark wrinkled skins. The most highly prized is the Tunisian Deglet Noor, which means 'date of the light'. The Medjool date is also much loved and has a rich, fudge-like texture. Dates are available in several forms. Semi-dried dates are the best dessert dates; pressed blocks of dates or packets of chopped dates are perfectly adequate for cooking and baking.

Dried pears (left) and **peaches** (below left) are more delicately flavoured than apricots.

Dried apricots are versatile and feature in many sweet and savoury dishes. They have an intense, rich flavour, with a good tartness. They are mostly available ready-to-eat or dried, the latter requiring soaking before use.

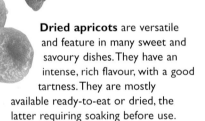

RAISINS, CURRANTS AND SULTANAS

These are all dried grapes – the difference is in the type of grape used – muscatel for raisins, black Corinth grapes for currants and a white, seedless grape for sultanas.

Figs The best dried figs are made from very ripe golden-yellow Smyrna figs dried in the sun and turned occasionally, thus their flattened, cushion shape. To preserve their essential plumpness, figs should be loosely packed. If using in cooking, soak them in wine or water for a few hours.

Currants are smaller, sweeter and tangier than raisins. Can easily substitute for chopped raisins.

Raisins should be plumped up in brandy before cooking.

Sultanas are generally plumper and paler than raisins. They are very sweet and moist and have a mild, slightly fragrant taste.

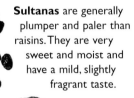

USING DRIED FRUIT

• To keep dried fruits from sinking to the bottom of cake batters, toss them in a little of the measured flour before starting the batter. The flour will help keep the fruit suspended within the cake mixture and stop it from absorbing too much of the liquid.

• Dried fruit will adhere to your knife during chopping. Dip your knife or scissors frequently into hot water while cutting.

• Unless labelled ready-to-eat, prunes should be soaked before using. If you have 'no-soak' prunes and the recipe calls to soak them in brandy, simply cut the soaking time by half. If prunes are cooked, it is not necessary to soak them.

fruits and nuts

222

preserves and condiments

Jam is made from whole fruit that is crushed or mashed and cooked with sugar.

Chutneys are fruits or vegetables cooked very slowly with sugar, vinegar and spices.

Conserves are two or more fruits cooked with sugar and raisins or nuts.

Marmalade is the term used for conserves made from oranges or other citrus fruits like grapefruit, lemons, limes or tangerines.

Fruit essence is extracted from the skins of citrus fruit, which contains the essential oil.

Fruit butters are spiced, puréed fruits simmered slowly in an oven or open pan until thick and creamy.

Jelly is made from fruit juice that has been strained or sieved to remove any particles and then cooked with sugar.

Preserves are similar to jams but contain larger and more distinct pieces of fruit.

SOFTENING JAM

This technique will prevent jam used as a filling from tearing cakes when it is spread over layers. Put the seedless or sieved jam on a worktop or clean, smooth, chopping board, and work it back and forth with a palette knife until it has a very soft, spreading consistency. Then use the same palette knife to apply jam to the cake layers.

FRUIT GLAZE

To give cakes a smooth finish and add moisture to cakes, tarts and tartlets, prepare a glaze made from jam. Use apricot jam for chocolate cakes, and red fruit jam for fruit tarts. Melt 90 g (3½ oz) jam, then work it through a sieve to remove lumps. Return to pan, add 50 ml (2 fl oz) water and bring to the boil, stirring. Brush over the cake or tart.

nuts and seeds

Choosing

Nuts come in a wide variety of forms and are sold in many different types of packaging. It's best to buy nuts in the shell as shelled nuts can go rancid very quickly. If buying nuts in the shell, look for unbroken, clean shells without any holes, cracks, splits or stains. The nuts should feel heavy for their size; if they are light, the nuts inside may be old and shrivelled. If you buy shelled nuts, they should be plump, firm and uniform in size and colour.

REMOVING THE SKINS FROM NUTS

▲ **Hazelnuts and Brazil nuts** These are best roasted before skinning. Spread the nuts evenly on a baking sheet and roast at 180°C (350°F/gas 4) for 10 minutes, occasionally shaking. Wrap the nuts in a teatowel for a few minutes, then rub to remove skins.

▲ **Almonds and pistachios** Their skin is bitter and will spoil the nut's delicate flavour if left on. To remove the skin, blanch (see page 22) and pinch the softened skin between your thumb and index finger and slip it off. The skins are easiest to remove when still warm.

GRINDING NUTS

Some recipes, particularly those for flourless tortes, call for ground nuts, and these have to be ground very fine and dry. If ground too much, however, nuts can form a paste. To prevent this, use a food processor, blender or grinder and process the nuts in small batches. With each cupful, add 15 ml (1 tbsp) of the sugar from the recipe. Then, using the pulse button, start and stop the processor frequently until all the nuts are ground.

Substitution

Pecans and walnuts are versatile and can substitute for most other nuts; almonds and hazelnuts also can be interchanged. As most dessert recipes are formulated for a specific type of nut, it is best not to substitute except as above.

PEELING CHESTNUTS

These sweet, starchy nuts have a hard brittle shell and papery skin, both of which need to be removed. Don't try to peel too many at one time, because as the nut cools, the inner skin stubbornly stays put.

Hold the nut between your fingers and cut away the shell using a sharp knife. By piercing the skin, and then blanching the nut in boiling water for 1 minute, the outer skin is even easier to remove.

◀ **Remove the inner skin** Put the chestnuts in a pan of boiling water and simmer for a few minutes. As the skins begin to come away from the chestnuts, take out a few at a time (they must be peeled hot) and pull or rub away the skin.

Type	Description	Yield	Uses	Notes
Almonds	One of the most popular and versatile nuts. Sweet flavour	450 g (1 lb) in the shell = 165 g (5½ oz) whole	Blanched for decoration; toasted in savoury dishes; ground for cakes, tarts, pastry and biscuits	For best flavour, buy whole almonds and blanch
Brazil nuts	Large nut. Sweet, milky flavour	450 g (1 lb) in the shell = 200 g (7 oz) whole	Decoration or as a dessert nut	Brazil nuts go rancid very quickly once exposed to air, so use shelled nuts quickly
Cashew nuts	Plump, grey/white nut with a delicious sweet flavour. 'Short' texture	450 g (1 lb) shelled	Stir-fries, curries, rice dishes or sprinkled over salads; south Indian and Asian dishes; butters	Add cashew nuts, whole or ground, at the end of cooking, to avoid spoiling their flavour
Chestnuts	Delicate, sweet flavour. Starchy with a soft, almost melting texture	450 g (1 lb) in the shell = 350 g (12 oz) whole	In stuffings, soups, purées, cakes, biscuits and ice cream. Added to vegetables, stir-fries and stews	Always use cooked; they contain tannic acid which is unpleasant raw and inhibits iron absorption
Coconut	Juice is extremely sweet; flesh is juicy, less sweet. Desiccated is shredded and dried	1 medium = 450 g (1 lb) shredded	Juice for drinks; milk, cream and creamed coconut in Indian and southeast Asian dishes	When buying a coconut, shake gently to hear the juice. The 'eyes' should be dry and clean
Hazelnut	Crunchy nut with a distinctive, slightly bitter flavour which is less apparent when roasted	450 g (1 lb) in the shell = 200 g (7 oz) whole	Toasted, chopped and grated in cakes and desserts. Widely used in a variety of savoury dishes	Hazelnuts are also known as cobnuts or filberts
Macadamia nuts	Round nut with a flaky, buttery texture and a sweet flavour	450 g (1 lb) in the shell = 165 g (5½ oz) whole	Add whole to salads. Used for butters and satay sauces in Indonesian cooking	Look out for salad oil made from macadamia nuts. It has a light, slightly sweet flavour
Peanuts	Slightly bitter when raw, but roasted have a delicious sweet/savoury flavour	450 g (1 lb) in the shell = 350 g (12 oz) whole	Salads or stir-fries; in southeast Asian cuisine, used whole, ground (for sauces) or for oil	Also known as groundnuts. Ripe peanuts are harvested in the same way as potatoes
Pecans	Elongated nut in a glossy red oval-shaped shell. Sweet, mild flavour. Native to America	500 g (1¼ lb) in the shell = 50 g (2 oz) shelled	Pecan pie; other cakes, pies and ice creams. Add texture to salads. Can be used in stuffings	Pecan nuts are high in fat so should be eaten in moderation
Pine nuts	Tiny, cream-coloured nuts, with a distinct 'tarry' flavour	450 g (1 lb) in the shell = 200 g (7 oz) whole	Key component of pesto. Widely used in Greek, Turkish and Middle Eastern savoury dishes	Because of their high oil content, pinenuts quickly become rancid, so buy only in small quantities
Pistachios	Intense or pale green nuts in a papery red/brown skin with a mild, sweet flavour	500 g (1¼ lb) in the shell = 275 g (10 oz) chopped	Stuffings, pâtés and some festive Indian rice dishes. Sweets and desserts, ice cream	
Walnuts	Dried walnuts have a bitter/sweet flavour	450 g (1 lb) in the shell = 225 g (8 oz) shelled	Desserts, cakes, ice creams; stir-fries or salads (their most famous savoury incarnation is in Waldorf salad)	

PREPARING A WHOLE COCONUT

Pierce a metal skewer through the indentations in the stalk end of the husk. Drain off the juice through the holes. Crack the coconut by tapping it with a hammer all around its girth. Keep turning it around until it splits in half. Prise the flesh out of the shell by working a small knife between flesh and shell. Pare away any dark outer skin with a vegetable peeler and shred or grate the flesh according to the recipe.

COCONUT MILK

Available ready prepared, but you can make it at home, using fresh or desiccated coconut. The grated flesh is steeped in boiling water, then squeezed to extract the coconut milk. You can steep and squeeze it more than once, each time getting a thinner milk.

• Rub the coconut flesh against the coarsest grid of a box grater, or grate it in a food processor fitted with the metal blade.

• Put the grated coconut flesh in a bowl and pour over boiling water to cover. Stir well to mix, then leave to soak for 30 minutes until the water is absorbed.

• Turn into a muslin-lined sieve set over a bowl and let the milk drain through.

• Draw up the muslin and squeeze hard to extract as much milk as possible.

STORING

Nuts and seeds are high in fat, which means they go rancid very quickly when exposed to the air. It is best to buy in small quantities and check use-by dates carefully. It is also recommended buying nuts from a store with a fast turnover.

Whole nuts and seeds should be stored in a cool dark place. Shelled nuts and seeds should be kept in an airtight container in a cool dark place. They can be frozen for up to six months.

Sunflower seeds
Rich in vitamin E, protein, vitamin B_1, iron and niacin, they taste best when dry-roasted, which brings out the nutty flavour.

Poppy seeds have a pleasant flavour and crunchy texture and are normally used for sprinkling over loaves, or adding to cakes and biscuits.

Pumpkin seeds
Larger than many of the other seeds, they have a mild, nutty flavour and a delicious texture with plenty of 'bite'. Like most seeds, they are very nutritious.

Sesame seeds are best if lightly roasted – either dry-fry or roast in the oven for about 4–5 minutes until lightly golden. Ground sesame seeds are used for making tahini.

ROASTING SEEDS

To bring out the 'nutty' flavour of seeds, they are best if lightly roasted in a preheated oven at 160°C (325°F/gas 3) for 4–5 minutes.

• Spread the seeds in a thin layer in a small roasting pan.

• Place in the preheated oven and cook for about 4–5 minutes, shaking the pan occasionally.

• Watch the seeds carefully. They will quickly scorch if roasted for too long.

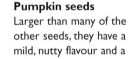

flavourings

spices

GINGER AND GALANGAL

Stem ginger
Deliciously sweet and spicy, preserved or stem ginger is popular in biscuits, cakes and desserts, either finely chopped or sliced.

Crystallized ginger
This is mostly served as a sweet, the candied fruit rolled in fine sugar.

Ground ginger Widely available and is a good choice for cakes, puddings and ginger-bread. The powder is fine and sand-coloured and is distinctly aromatic and pungent.

Fresh root ginger Ginger has a sweet, fragrant aroma and fresh, citric, slightly spicy flavour. The root should be fresh-looking, with a silvery skin. Buy in small quantities. It will keep for up to a week in a cool dry place.

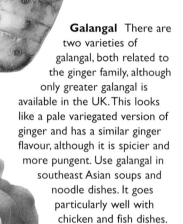

Galangal There are two varieties of galangal, both related to the ginger family, although only greater galangal is available in the UK. This looks like a pale variegated version of ginger and has a similar ginger flavour, although it is spicier and more pungent. Use galangal in southeast Asian soups and noodle dishes. It goes particularly well with chicken and fish dishes. It can be thinly sliced or pounded with onion, garlic, lemon grass and chillies to make a spicy paste for green or red curries.

Pickled ginger Thinly sliced ginger, normally pickled in sweetened vinegar. Japanese pickled ginger is traditionally served with sushi.

PREPARING GINGER

Fresh root ginger is used in a multitude of Asian and Indian dishes. The pale yellow flesh is slightly fibrous. To preserve freshness, peel small amounts of ginger just before using. Peeled ginger can be sliced, chopped, grated or crushed.

▼ **Removing the skin** Use the sharp, heavy blade of a cleaver to scrape away the tough outer skin.

▼ **Grating the flesh** A wooden Japanese grater or oroshigane is authentic, but a metal box grater will do.

PREPARING GALANGAL

Galangal is normally peeled and then thinly sliced. Use in Thai curries and other dishes where a spicy, ginger flavour is required.

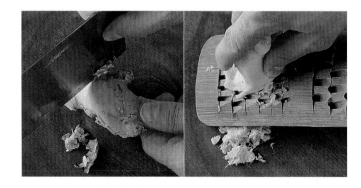

flavourings

CURRY SPICE MIXTURES

There are a wide variety of different curry spice mixtures, many from the Indian sub-continent, but others from Thailand and Indonesia. The Chinese and Japanese also have their own favourite spice mixtures. Here is a selection of some of the more popular mixtures.

Curry powder Coriander, cumin, fenugreek, black mustard, black pepper, turmeric, ginger, red chillies. Use for chicken, lamb or beef curries.

Thai curry For red curry paste: red chillies, red onion, garlic, galangal, lemon grass, cumin, coriander, blachan (dried and fermented shrimp paste), stems of fresh coriander. For green curry paste: substitute green chillies and white onion for the red chillies and onion, and use coriander leaves.

Garam masala Coriander, cumin, black pepper, bay leaves, green cardamom, mace, cloves, cinnamon. Add to curries, vegetable dishes, rice or dhals at the end of cooking.

Chermoula Onion, garlic, chilli, fresh coriander, mint, cumin, paprika, saffron, lemon juice. Use for Moroccan-style recipes, particularly fish dishes.

Cajun spice Garlic, black pepper, mustard, chilli powder, cumin, paprika, thyme, onion. Use for Cajun-style dishes like gumbo.

Chinese five spice powder Star anise, Szechuan pepper, cassia, cloves, fennel seeds. Use in a variety of Chinese-style dishes, particularly duck and poultry dishes.

PREPARING SPICES

The aroma and flavour of any whole spice, like cumin coriander or cardamom, will be enhanced if dry-fried briefly before grinding or adding whole to dishes. Spices can be dry-fried by themselves or with other spices. Preheat a frying pan without oil and add the whole spices. Toss briefly over a moderate heat until they begin to give off a rich aroma. If grinding, allow the spice to cool slightly.

Cloves

Stud an onion with one or two cloves (not too many) and use when making chicken stock, bread sauce or for any slow-cooked casseroles to impart extra flavour.

MORTAR AND PESTLE

A mortar, a small curved bowl, and a pestle, a heavy pounding tool, is essential if you don't possess a spice mill, and wish to grind spices at home rather than buy the ready-ground products. Mortars can be made in stone, marble, wood, glass or unglazed porcelain. They should have a slightly rough interior surface in order to provide the necessary friction to grind the spices. The pestle is normally made of the same material and should feel relatively heavy.

SWEET SPICE MIXTURES

These traditional aromatic blends are greatly favoured by European cooks, who use them for cakes, biscuits and puddings and to flavour meat and poultry dishes, as well. The old-fashioned English pickling spice mixture is used in vinegars and a variety of condiments.

Quatre-épices
A mix of four spices. Combine 1 tbsp black peppercorns, 2 tsp each whole cloves and grated nutmeg and 1 tsp ground ginger. Variations may use allspice and cinnamon.

Pickling spice
Mix 2 tbsp ground ginger with 1 tbsp each white mustard seeds, black peppercorns, dried red chillies, allspice berries, dill seed and crushed mace. Add 1 cinnamon stick, crushed, 2 bay leaves, and 1 tsp whole cloves.

Mixed spice
Also known as pudding spice. Finely grind 1 tbsp coriander seeds, 1 tsp each allspice berries and cloves, and 1 cinnamon stick; mix with 1 tbsp grated nutmeg and 2 tsp ground ginger.

Type	Other names	Description	Use for	Tip
Ajowan	Bishop's weed	Ajowan is an Indian spice. Although related to caraway and cumin, it has a more herbal flavour reminiscent of thyme	Ajowan is popular in dhals and other bean and pulse recipes	
Allspice	Jamaican pepper	Allspice comes from the New World and is mostly associated with Caribbean cuisine. It is very aromatic, with a heady smell reminiscent of cloves, nutmeg and cinnamon. It has a distinct flavour	Allspice is traditionally used in rich fruit cakes, Christmas puddings and biscuits. Use also for pickling, for marinades for fish and shellfish and for game and poultry	Buy the whole spice and grind at home, as the aroma and flavour of ready-ground spice fade quickly
Anise	Aniseed	Anise is related to dill fennel and caraway and has the familiar aniseed flavour	Use in sweet and savoury dishes; it is good in cakes and biscuits and in breads, either kneaded into the dough or sprinkled over loaves. You can also add it to Indian dishes	Buy whole seeds and grind at home. Dry-frying heightens the spiciness and flavour of the seeds
Asafoetida	Stinking gum, Devil's dung	A popular Indian spice with an extremely unpleasant smell in its raw state, which disappears during cooking. In its unprocessed form, the resin comes in large soft lumps, which is how it is mostly used in India. In the West, it is normally available in powdered form	Good in vegetable and pulse dishes	Use extremely sparingly
Caraway		A popular European spice, with a warm, peppery aroma and sharp flavour, reminiscent of eucalyptus and aniseed. It is widely used in Holland, Germany, Austria and Eastern Europe in sweet and savoury dishes	Vegetable dishes and soups, particularly cabbage; in cakes, biscuits and breads	Caraway is mostly used whole, added to or sprinkled over breads. Ground caraway has a very intense flavour so use sparingly
Cardamom		An essential Indian spice, with a warm pungent aroma and a pleasant lemon-like flavour. There are several types: green is the most common; white pods are bleached green pods, used in desserts; and black cardamom, a related variety with a distinct pungency	Cardamom is widely used in sweet and savoury dishes in India. Use for curries, pilafs, dhals, and for cakes and desserts. It is a key ingredient in garam masala	Use green or white cardamom pods only. Brown cardamom seeds are too pungent and rather unpleasant
Cassia and cinnamon	False cinnamon (cassia), quills (cinnamon)	Hugely popular aromatic spices, from related laurel-like trees. Both are made from the inner bark of the tree, cassia being dried into woody strips and cinnamon drying into neat quills. Cinnamon has a wonderful fragrant aroma and a warm spicy flavour. Cassia is quite similar, but is less fragrant and more pungent	Use cassia in savoury dishes like curries, and in pickles. Use cinnamon in sweet dishes: cakes, puddings and biscuits. It can also be used in poultry and game dishes	

Type	Other names	Description	Use for	Tip
Celery seed		These small, grey-brown seeds come from the celery plant. They have a strong, almost bitter flavour and should be used sparingly. Celery seeds are often available in the form of celery salt and celery pepper, which can be made at home by grinding respectively with salt or peppercorns	Soups, sauces, casseroles, egg dishes, fish, poultry and rabbit dishes, tomato juice and sauce, salad dressings, breads, biscuits	
Cloves		Cloves are the unopened buds of an evergreen tree. They have a distinct pungent aroma and flavour. They add a pleasant pungency to dishes but use with discretion as they can be overpowering	Excellent in sweet and savoury dishes. Traditionally used for mulled wine, Christmas cakes and puddings, rich fruit cakes, mincemeat, stewed fruit, gingerbread. Also use in bread sauce, marinades for game, for boiled meats, especially ham, beef, lamb and pork stews; pickles and chutneys	Cloves are a key ingredient in Chinese five spice powder. Note that the ground spice is particularly strong in flavour
Coriander		The small brown seeds from the coriander plant represent, along with cumin and cardamom, one of the great spices of Indian cuisine. Ground coriander has a lovely aromatic flavour, with a slightly citrus flavour	Use ground coriander for curries, meat, poultry dishes and vegetable dishes. Use whole seeds for pickles and chutney	Buy whole and grind at home as flavour fades from ready-ground spice. Dry-fry seeds first to appreciate the full flavour of this spice
Cumin		Another hugely important spice used in a number of important cuisines including India, the Middle East, North Africa and Mexico. The aroma is strong and spicy, and the flavour is warm and pungent	Tastes good with Mexican dishes, cous cous and other North African dishes, curries and meat casseroles. Cumin is an essential ingredient in numerous curry mixes and in garam masala	Buy the whole seeds and grind at home. Dry-frying enhances the nutty flavour and blunts the slight bitterness of the spice
Dill seed		Dill seed is similar in flavour to the fresh herb, with a fragrant aroma and a fresh flavour tasting of caraway	Use whole or crushed seeds in pickles, chutneys, for making flavoured vinegar, in breadmaking and for biscuits. Use crushed seeds in fish and egg dishes, for making mayonnaise and in potato dishes	
Fennel		Fennel seeds are small, olive green and hard, shaped like flattened ovals. Like the herb, they have an anise flavour. Whole seeds, crushed seeds or the ground spice can be used according to the intensity of flavour required	Ground fennel is used in curries and can be added to meat and vegetable dishes. Whole or crushed seeds are used for breads, biscuits and in some cabbage recipes	
Fenugreek	Methi	A golden brown coloured spice that looks like tiny evenly-coloured stones. It has a strong curry aroma and a tangy flavour	Tastes good with meat, poultry and vegetable curries and dhals	Use sparingly, as fenugreek has a strong flavour with a tendency to take over a dish given the chance

spices

231

Type	Other names	Description	Use for	Tip
Juniper		Juniper is the fruit of a relative of the cypress tree. The berries are dark blue, almost black in colour and have a distinct, gin-like flavour	Marinades for meat and game and for casseroles with venison and other game, lamb and pork. Also use for pâtés and terrines	Crush the seeds before use
Nutmeg and mace		Nutmeg and mace come from the same evergreen tree, the nutmeg being the kernel or seed of the fruit, the mace being the bright lacy covering of the seed. Both have a wonderfully fragrant, sweet and warm aroma and a delicious flavour, nutmeg being more fragrant and sweeter than mace	Cakes, puddings, custards and milk sauces. Use nutmeg in pasta, vegetable, poultry and fish dishes	
Saffron	Saffron crocus	An expensive spice which comes from the stigma of a species of crocus. Saffron has a mild aroma but adds a distinct, slightly pungent flavour and a pretty coral-colour to dishes	Tastes good with soups, fish, egg and rice dishes, particularly festive dishes like paella and biryani. Also use in some poultry dishes. Good in cakes, breads and biscuits	
Star anise	Chinese anise	Chinese anise is the signature spice of Chinese cuisine. The whole spice is an eight-pointed star within which are tiny amber-coloured seeds. It has a strong aniseed flavour and aroma	Tastes good with Eastern-style dishes, especially duck and chicken. Also fish and shellfish dishes	Star anise is one of the components of five spice powder, which is used throughout China and Vietnam
Sumac		A red berry from the sumac bush that grows throughout the Middle East. The berry, which is available whole or ground, has an astringent flavour	Use for marinades and with seafood and vegetables and in stuffings, rice and pulse dishes	
Szechuan pepper	Japanese pepper, Chinese pepper, anise pepper	Although called pepper, this is no relation to pepper. It has a pungent aroma with a peppery, slightly citrus flavour	Used widely in Chinese cookery, rubbed over poultry and duck. It is often mixed with salt and used as a condiment	Szechuan pepper is one of the spices in Chinese five spice powder
Tamarind	Indian date	A popular spice in India and parts of southeast Asia, tamarind adds an astringent flavour to numerous curries and Eastern dishes. It normally comes in compressed blocks and as the name suggests, looks very like dates	Use in curries, chutneys, vegetable and pulse dishes	
Turmeric	Indian saffron	A popular Indian spice, adding an intense yellow colour and a warm, musky flavour to food. Fresh turmeric looks like small roots of ginger, but the spice is mostly known in the West in powdered form	Use in curries, in fish, poultry and rice dishes, in pickles and chutneys	
Vanilla		Vanilla is the seedpod of a species of orchid. It is richly scented and has a pleasant sweet flavour	Numerous desserts, chocolate and coffee puddings, ice cream, custards	Vanilla extract is made from the true spice – avoid vanilla essence

PREPARING VANILLA

Both the pod and seeds of the vanilla bean can be used as flavourings; the seeds impart a stronger flavour than the pod.

Cut the pod in half lengthwise; infuse in warm milk for 30 minutes, or store in a jar of caster sugar.

▲ Removing the seeds
Scrape out the seeds from the halved bean with the tip of a knife; use as for pod above.

COOKING IDEAS WITH SPICES

There are countless ways of using spices – here are just a few ideas for giving your favourite spice a starring role.

Cinnamon Use a whole quill for stirring hot chocolate, or add to fruit stews and compotes.

Allspice Use equal quantities of allspice and peppercorns to grind over fish or shellfish dishes.

Caraway Sprinkle caraway seeds over rye loaves.

Cardamom Use to make a refreshing tisane, by infusing whole crushed green cardamom pods in boiling water. Add a strip of orange peel and infuse for 5 minutes, then add green or black tea and infuse for a few more minutes before serving, with sugar, if liked.

Coriander Use whole crushed seeds in pickles.

Saffron Infuse saffron in warm milk and then add to a wine and cream sauce to serve with fish.

Fenugreek Sprout the seeds and use for salads and sandwiches. They will sprout in a covered jar in just a few days. Remember to rinse twice a day.

Juniper Add whole crushed juniper berries and stir into rich sauces and serve with wild duck or other rich game.

Nutmeg Sprinkle grated nutmeg over rice puddings or milk drinks.

Vanilla Make vanilla sugar by storing caster or granulated sugar with a vanilla pod. Use for custards, ice creams and other desserts.

PREPARING SAFFRON AND TAMARIND

Saffron and tamarind both require soaking before use. Tamarind is usually sold in compressed blocks. Break off 2.5 cm (1 in) square and soak in 150 ml (¼ pint) warm water for 10–20 minutes, breaking up and squeezing the tamarind with your fingers. Strain the liquid, discarding the pulp and seeds and add the liquid to curries, rice dishes and dhals. Saffron is sold in thin, wiry threads. Pour warm water or milk over a few threads. Soak for about 10 minutes, stirring occasionally. Strain the liquid or stir directly into the dish you are preparing.

SPICE MILL

An electric spice mill takes the effort out of grinding spices. Spices can be ground coarsely or more finely as required. Coffee grinders can be used, although you will need to clean the equipment carefully both before and after use, as the flavours of both coffee and the spices will linger and will invariably taint anything that is used in the grinder subsequently.

oils

An essential ingredient for all cooks, oils are used as a fat for browning, sautéeing and frying foods as well as a flavouring. Some oils are general purpose but some should only be used for cooking and others, because their tastes are intense, work best as a flavouring.

OLIVE OIL

This is considered the king of all oils. It is versatile, good for frying, cooking and for dressings. What's more, it has an excellent flavour and is the most healthy of all oils, being rich in monounsaturated fat (thought to reduce blood cholesterol).

Virgin and extra virgin olive oils come from the first cold pressing of the olives. The best virgin olive oils come from single estates, where different types of olives are blended with care. Use for salad dressings, stir into pasta, drizzle over cooked vegetables or add to sauces. If frying, dilute the flavour a little with sunflower oil. Cold pressed or pure olive oil is a more refined olive oil. The olives that have been reduced to a paste after the first pressing, are washed with hot water to extract more oil. Use for sautéeing, frying, roasting, and for dressings, preferably blended with virgin or extra virgin olive oil.

The flavour and colour of an olive oil is also dependant on other factors, including the country of origin, the climate, the soil and the blend of olives.

Spain Much loved by Spaniards but considered rather rank by some. Most Spanish olive oil comes from single olive varieties rather than a blend, and is therefore less complex in flavour.

Italy Generally considered to produce the finest olive oils. There are numerous different olive oils, the best being the Tuscan oils. However, there are oils from Sicily, Perugia and Liguria to name but a few. In order to find a wide selection of Italian oils, you will need to visit a specialist shop.

Greece Greek olive oil has a fairly robust flavour. It is noticeably cheaper than Italian and French olive oil.

France There is relatively little olive oil production in France, but visitors may find bottles of locally produced oils in Provence.

California A few olive oils are produced in California's Napa Valley, enjoyed for their slightly sweet flavour.

Australia Australian olive oils tend to be sharp and sweet.

Oils and fats

All oils are made up of fats, the least desirable being the saturated fatty acids found in animal fats like butter or cheese. These are thought to increase blood cholesterol levels. Polyunsaturated and monounsaturated fatty acids are believed to reduce cholesterol, and are preferable for those following a low-cholesterol diet.

Oil	Saturated fat	Polyunsaturated fat	Monounsaturated fat
Coconut	90%		
Corn	13%	60%	27%
Olive	15%	15%	70%
Palm	45%	10%	40%
Rapeseed	7%	33%	60%
Safflower	10%	75%	15%
Sesame	25%	75%	–
Soya	15%	55%	30%
Sunflower	12%	70%	18%
Nut Oils Almond	10%	20%	70%
Hazelnut	Mostly monounsaturated		
Peanut	20%	30%	50%
Walnut	10%	15%	75%

OTHER COOKING OILS

Corn oil This comes from the germ of maize. A widely used cooking oil, it has a noticeable strong flavour and can be used for cooking. Economical but not particularly pleasant.

Sunflower oil An excellent all-purpose oil. It is light with almost no taste at all, making it popular for frying and simple dishes where you do not wish to mask the flavour of other ingredients. It can be blended with other oils – olive or nut oils – for dressings and is good for making mayonnaise, if you want something more unassuming than olive oil. Cold-pressed oils are increasingly available and have more character. Sunflower oil contains a high percentage of polyunsaturated fats and, along with safflower oil, is the best oil for use in cholesterol-reducing diets.

Safflower oil This is a light, general-purpose oil extracted from the seeds of the safflower. It has a more oily texture and nuttier flavour than sunflower but generally can be substituted for this or groundnut oil. Like sunflower oil it is low in saturated fats.

Peanut or groundnut oil A useful mildly flavoured oil, good for all sorts of cooking and for salad dressings. It is the most popular oil in Indian, Chinese and southeast Asian cooking.

Soya oil A useful frying oil because of its high smoking point, soya oil is not normally recommended for dressings as some people find it has a slightly fishy flavour. Commercially, however, this is the most important of all the oils, used widely for margarines. It is also among the more healthy oils, being low in saturated fats.

Rapeseed oil Also known as canola, rapeseed oil is popular in Indian cooking, where it is known as colza.

Coconut oil The most unhealthy oil, it contains up to 90 per cent saturated fat. It is nevertheless popular in recipes from southeast Asia, the West Indies and the Pacific. Coconut cream and milk contain some coconut oil, and the pure oil has a coconut flavour.

Grapeseed oil This is made from the leftover grape pips from wine-making. It has a delicate, mild flavour and is suitable for dressings, especially if combined with more strongly flavoured oils.

Vegetable oil A blend of various oils, most commonly rapeseed, soya, coconut and/or palm. It is highly refined, cheap and generally labelled as an all-purpose oil, but while useful for frying owing to its high smoke point, it has a rather greasy feel, both in taste and texture, and is therefore unpleasant in dressings.

SPECIALITY OILS

Almond oil
A sweetly flavoured oil used for cakes, biscuits, desserts and confectionery.

Walnut oil
A richly flavoured oil with a distinct nutty flavour. Use sparingly; do not overheat. Use for salad dressings and to drizzle over pasta or cooked vegetables.

Sesame oil
Popular in Chinese, Indian and Middle Eastern cooking. There are two varieties, a pale light oil made from untoasted seeds and the toasted version, which is darker and has a strong nutty aroma and rich flavour. Use sparingly. It will burn if heated too fiercely.

Hazelnut oil
A delicious oil with a fine, hazelnut flavour. A little goes a long way; blend with other oils rather than use solo. Add to salad dressings, sprinkle over vegetables or use in cakes, biscuits and pastries.

Mustard seed oil
A very popular Indian cooking oil, but not widely available in the UK. It has a mustard-style flavour but this is driven off when heated. It is often used instead of ghee.

vinegars

Almost every country of the world produces its own style of vinegar. There are almost as many vinegars as there are types of alcohol, a not unreasonable state of affairs, as vinegar is in effect the by-product of wine-making or brewing. Consequently, malt and cider vinegars are popular British vinegars, but the traditional vinegars of France are mostly those made from wine, while in Spain, sherry vinegar is commonly found.

Malt vinegar This is made from malted barley and is the popular choice for chutneys and pickles. The colourless variety is distilled and very strong and is used for pickling baby onions and other vegetables where it is important to preserve the colour of the vegetable. Brown malt vinegar has been coloured with caramel and is used commercially and at home for dark chutneys. Although it is less sour than wine vinegar, its flavour is too assertive for dressings. It is the vinegar of choice for fish and chip connoisseurs.

Spirit or distilled vinegar This is a very strong vinegar used almost exclusively for pickling. It is usually made by distilling a white, malt vinegar.

Cider vinegar This is made from cider or from apple pulp and is particularly popular in the United States. It is normally pale brown in colour with a strong 'bite' and a perceptible apple flavour. Use for Normandy-style recipes and for pickling, particularly fruits like pears.

Wine vinegar There are numerous wine vinegars – red, white and rose – which range in quality. Although most Western countries produce their own wine vinegar, the traditional vinegars come from wine-producing countries like France, Spain and Italy. The best wine vinegars are made by the Orléans method, a process which starts with a good-quality wine as a base and by which the acetic fermentation takes place in a natural and unhurried way. In contrast, cheaper vinegars are made in huge heated vats, a method which is fast, but produces a harsher and less finely flavoured product.

White wine vinegars are extremely versatile and are the best choice for most dressings, mayonnaise and sauces. Use these for adding 'bite' to stews and soups.

Rice vinegar comes from any of the alcoholic rice drinks, the best known of which is sake. There are a number of varieties. Chinese red or black vinegar is dark amber, and has a rich flavour. From Japan, there is a brown rice vinegar, which is rich and heady. There are other milder white vinegars, which have a slightly sweet flavour and a mild astringency. All types of vinegars are used in Eastern cuisines, in savoury and some sweet recipes, and for making dipping sauces. Use in any Eastern recipe, or in place of wine vinegar for dressings.

Champagne vinegar comes in attractive corked bottles. It is made by taking the sediment from Champagne. Champagne vinegar comes in year-old, non-vintage varieties, or three-year-old, vintage types. Use it in dressings.

Balsamic vinegar This is the finest and oldest of all vinegars. It has been made in Modena and Reggio in northern Italy for about 1,000 years but only very recently has it been available in the shops. It is dark in colour with a deep rich flavour reminiscent of port, herbs and wild flowers. Use it in simple dressings or sprinkle over pasta, salads or over roasted or steamed vegetables. A little goes a long way.

There are two categories – artisan-made and commercial. When buying artisan balsamic, look for the word 'tradizionale' on the label. These vinegars will have been aged in wooden barrels for at least four to five years. A Vecchio label indicates a 12-year-old vinegar. Extra Vecchio means that it is 25 years old. The colour on the label denotes the quality: gold being the highest quality, then silver, then red. Commercial balsamic is not regulated, but many vinegars for sale are still very good.

Sherry vinegar is normally made by a long slow process and is consequently rich and mellow, but with enough 'bite' to make it a good addition to sauces and dressings. Sprinkle over steamed or roasted vegetables or add to sauces and stews.

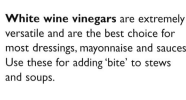

MAKING A FLAVOURED VINEGAR

Herb vinegars are very simple to make and can be used to add a delicious flavour to salad dressings, sauces, soups and marinades. Decide which herbs you are going to use – basil, coriander, parsley and mint go particularly well with white wine vinegar while rosemary and thyme are also delicious in red wine vinegar.

Blanch a large bunch of your chosen herbs and plunge straight into iced water. Drain the herbs and pat dry with kitchen roll. Pour 150 ml (¼ pint) vinegar over the herbs and transfer to a food processor. Process until smooth.

Pour the mixture into a jug, cover and leave in the fridge overnight. Strain the vinegar through muslin (right) into a clean jug and then pour the flavoured vinegar into a clean bottle. You can add blanched herbs to the vinegar for decoration, if required. You can also make garlic and chilli oil using this method – the number of chillies and garlic cloves you use will depend on your taste.

Matching oils and vinegars

When making vinaigrette (see page 191) paired oils and vinegars should complement each other. The rich texture of extra virgin olive oil, for example, is well balanced by balsamic vinegar. Nut oils are good with fruit vinegars, such as raspberry, while chilli or herb oils benefit from the sharp bite of wine vinegar.

USING VINEGAR TO PRESERVE

Vinegar has been used as a preservative for many years. Making chutneys, relishes and pickles with seasonal fruit and vegetables is a delicious way of storing abundant produce. When you choose vinegar for pickling, make sure it is good quality – it needs to have a high acid content to preserve the fruit and vegetables. Brown malt vinegar gives a good flavour but the colourless variety is more often used so the colours of the fruit and vegetables are not tainted. Wine, cider and sherry vinegars can also be used for preserving.

storecupboard extras

A well stocked storecupboard should contain not only everyday basics such as flour and sugar, but a range of easy-to-use extras that can be used either to turn simple dishes into something a little different or for a specific culinary purpose, for example, as a setting agent.

Gelatine An animal product, extracted from bones, it comes in powdered form in small packets, or in sheets. A good gelatine has no taste at all. It is usually dissolved in a warm liquid (after being softened in cold water) and used for setting mousses and jellies.

▼ Worcestershire sauce
Made from tamarind, molasses, anchovies, soy sauce, onions, sugar and lime, along with other secret ingredients, this sauce has a distinct, fiery taste. It is used to make Bloody Marys.

Agar agar is the vegetarian alternative to gelatine. It is available in sticks, in shreds or as a powder and unlike gelatine, needs to be dissolved in boiling water. It makes a very firm jelly, but doesn't react with enzymes in pineapple and papaya making these fruit unsuitable for using with agar agar.

◄ Anchovy essence This is less overwhelming in aroma than Eastern fish and shrimp pastes, but adds a similar flavour. Mixed with soy sauce, it can substitute for nam pla or belacan.

▼ Stock cubes Available in a range of flavours, from lamb to fish, these concentrated cubes are a useful standby if fresh stock is not available. Dilute with boiling water, following the packet instructions, before use. They are often quite salty, so taste and season the dish after adding the made-up stock.

DISSOLVING GELATINE

It is necessary to soak both gelatine powder and leaf gelatine before use so that they blend smoothly with the mixture they are setting. When heating gelatine, never let it boil or it will spoil your mousse or jelly by becoming stringy.

Powder Sprinkle the measured amount of gelatine over 60 ml (4 tbsp) cold water in a bowl and let stand for about 5 minutes until spongy. Place the bowl over a pan of hot water and stir until the liquid is clear.

Leaf Soften leaves in cold water for 5 minutes. Squeeze out excess water. Transfer leaves to your hot liquid to dissolve.

MAKING ASPIC

You can make your own aspic with a well-flavoured clear stock. Soak gelatine leaves for 2–3 minutes in a little cold stock allowing 10 g (¼ oz) gelatine for every 500 ml (17 fl oz) liquid. Warm the remaining stock, then add the gelatine liquid. Stir over a gentle heat until the gelatine has melted. Spoon over cooked and chilled salmon, chicken or cold meats.

Aspic shapes Aspic is a classic garnish for chilled consommé. Having made it (either from a packet or using gelatine), pour a 1–2 cm (½–¾ in) layer into a shallow tin. Chill and cut out petal, diamond or crescent shapes.

Sauce type	Country of origin	Description	Uses
Light soy sauce	China	Light brown in colour with a delicate flavour	Soups, dips, seafood and vegetable dishes
Dark soy sauce	China	Darker and stronger than light soy sauce, it has a slightly sweet edge owing to the caramel which is added during the fermentation process	Dark meat dishes such as beef or duck, or for heartier chicken and pork dishes
Japanese soy sauce	Japan	Like all Japanese soy sauces, this is less salty and sweeter than Chinese soy sauce. Usukuchi is light and fragrant. Others are darker and more strongly flavoured, but not particularly salty	Use light soy sauce for soups, dips and fish dishes and as a table condiment. Dark soy sauce is best for red meat dishes
Tamari	Japan	Dark, with a strong flavour; this soy sauce is brewed without wheat.	Dips, especially sushi
Shoyu	Japan	Rich flavoured sauce	Dips, especially sushi
Ketjap manis	Indonesia	A thick, black soy sauce with a powerful aroma but a sweet flavour. Ketjap asin is thinner and less strongly flavoured	Indonesian rice and noodle dishes
Teriyaki sauce	Japan	This is a soy sauce-based product that is made with wine, sugar and spices	Marinades, basting or seasoning grilled or barbecued dishes
Nam pla	Thailand	Made using salted fermented fish, this is an essential seasoning in Thai cuisine. It is used both in cooking and as a condiment. Although it smells fishy, this is not particularly noticeable when added to dishes, adding an authentic salty taste to numerous dishes	In fish, meat, poultry and noodle dishes, and as a dipping sauce blended with chillies, garlic, sugar and lime juice
Shrimp paste	Belacan (Malaysia), nuoc mam (Vietnam), ngapi (Burma)	Shrimp paste is used extensively all over southeast Asia. Made from tiny salted shrimps that have been pounded and left to ferment. The paste is available in various forms – compressed and dried in a block, or bottled into cans or jars. Like nam pla, shrimp pastes smell revolting, but this vanishes during cooking	Used in the same way as Thailand's nam pla and just as essential
Oyster sauce	China	A thick soy based sauce, coloured a rich brown with caramel and flavoured with oyster juice. The flavour is delicate with, surprisingly, no hint of fish	Oyster sauce can be used in a variety of cooked dishes, adding depth of flavour, as well as colour. Especially good with chicken and beancurd, and with some noodle dishes that need perking up
Hoisin sauce	China	Often known as barbecue sauce, hoisin sauce is sweet and spicy, with a faint anise flavour	Classically served with Peking duck
Plum sauce	China	A type of sweet-and-sour sauce, made from plum juice, vinegar, and flavoured with chilli, ginger and spices	Also served with Peking duck, as a dipping sauce and in numerous other Chinese dishes

storecupboard extras

salt and pepper

SALT

This is a kitchen essential we really do take for granted. Salt can bring out the flavour of almost every food. Although we do tend to eat too much in the West, a little salt adds depth to both sweet and savoury foods. Salt is one of the four basic taste regions of the tongue (the others are sweet, sour and bitter). Without any salt, food can taste bland and insipid.

- Salt is required in bread making to strengthen the gluten and feed the yeast. Too much will make the dough collapse.
- Use a pinch of salt when whisking egg whites for meringues; the salt inhibits the protein in the eggs, making it easier to whisk into stiff peaks.
- When boiling vegetables, add a small pinch of salt at the beginning of the cooking time. The salt will be absorbed and other minerals in the vegetables will be retained.
- A pinch of salt in sweet mixtures, like batters and cakes, sharpens the flavour. Salt reduces the sourness of acids and increases the sweetness of sugars, if used sparingly.
- Do not salt pulses until cooked as it toughens the bean. Similarly, do not rub salt into cut sides of meat.

Table salt Treated to keep it free flowing. A few grains of rice added to the salt cellar help to prevent it becoming damp in steamy atmospheres.

English sea salt This comes from Maldon in Essex and is considered among the best sea salts. The flavour is strong and 'salty'. Use for sprinkling onto biscuits and loaves.

Black salt This is from India where it is used as a seasoning and a spice.

Sea salt This is produced by evaporating sea water, either naturally or by artificial means. It is commonly used for table and cooking use and comes in two grades, a fine salt that can be used at the table, and a coarser version, which is good for cooking or for using in a salt mill.

Rock salt This salt, derived from inland lakes and seas, is the source of kitchen and cooking salt. Once sold in large blocks, it is now most commonly available in refined form kept flowing by the addition of magnesium carbonate to prevent it taking in moisture from the air.

STORING

Salt should be stored in an airtight container in a cool dry place. Avoid keeping it in silver salt cellars which will turn green when chlorine in the salt reacts with the silver.

BAKING SHELLFISH

Rock salt can be used to keep oysters, mussels or clams level when baking or grilling. Pour in enough salt to create a 1 cm (½ in) layer in the bottom of a baking pan and place the oysters on top. Discard salt after cooking.

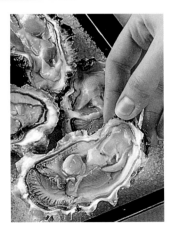

PEPPER

Pepper is the world's most important spice. The name pepper comes from the Sanskrit word, pippali, meaning berry. There are many different varieties of pepper. The plant grows in any tropical or sub-tropical area, grown throughout the Far East, Africa, the South Sea Islands and Brazil. Pepper is one of the most versatile spices, used in virtually all savoury cooking. Both black and white pepper is used in cuisines worldwide, at all stages of the cooking process and as a table condiment. Not only does pepper contribute its own special seasoning, it has the capacity to enhance other flavours.

Pink peppercorns These are not true peppercorns, but come from a tree native to South America. They have a mild flavour.

Fresh green peppercorns These are the berries of the pepper plant that have been canned rather than dried. They have a strong, distinct flavour without being particularly hot. As well as in southeast Asian dishes, use green peppercorns in sauces to serve with game or duck.

Mixed peppercorns These peppercorns come from the same plant, a vine that today is grown in many tropical and sub-tropical regions. For black pepper, the green, unripe berries are picked from the plant and are dried in the sun until wrinkled and black. For white pepper, the berries are allowed to ripen fully on the vine and the outer husk and pulp is then removed. In flavour, black pepper is more aromatic and spicy than white pepper, which is hot with warm, earthy undertones.

PEPPERMILL

A peppermill is one of the essential pieces of equipment in the kitchen, and one that is almost as essential at the table. Peppercorns should be ground as and when they are needed in order to capture fully their aroma and flavour. The setting can normally be adjusted from coarse to fine to suit the recipe and personal taste. A peppermill can be used for grinding spices, although you will need to wash it out each time, to avoid tainting other food. Choose heavy mills with strong grinding mechanisms.

CRUSHING PEPPERCORNS

Coarsely crushed peppercorns are ideal for steaks or for pressing onto a duck breast before cooking. Place the peppercorns in a plastic bag and squash with a rolling pin. They can also be crushed in a mortar, using a pestle, or in a coffee grinder.

COATING WITH PEPPERCORNS

Plain goat's and other soft cheese can be 'dressed up' with a covering of coarsely ground black pepper. Sprinkle about 25 g (1 oz) pepper on greaseproof paper. Roll cheese logs in the pepper then cut individual slices as desired.

sweeteners

SUGAR

When it comes to cakes and biscuits, cheesecakes and sponges, sugar is the one ingredient you will find it very difficult to do without. Fatless sponges, angel food cake, mousses and some biscuits mean that you can at times do without, respectively, butter, flour and eggs, but you will not be able to make a cake without sugar. Treacle and syrup are both forms of sugar.

Brown sugar Natural brown sugar is moist and sticky. There are a number of varieties, muscovado being the darkest and most strongly flavoured. Natural brown sugars come from raw sugar cane, their colour being dependant on the amount of molasses present. Light brown sugar is popular for puddings and cakes, since it creams easily and has only a mild brown sugar taste. Rich brown sugar is darker and has a more pronounced flavour. Use this for rich fruit cakes and for gingerbread and Christmas puddings.

White sugar If you remove all the molasses, you are left with white or refined sugar. There are various grades and all are equally sweet, although the finer the sugar, the sweeter they taste. If in doubt as to which type of white sugar to use, granulated is a good all-purpose choice.

Demerara A partly refined sugar with a small proportion of molasses. Used for adding a sweet crunch to crumbles and cake and biscuit toppings.

Preserving or jam sugar These sugars contain added pectin which, together with their larger crystals, makes them useful for jam-making.

Caster sugar Called superfine sugar in the United States, this sugar has finer crystals that dissolve quickly. It is the best choice for making cakes, custards and meringues.

Icing sugar Icing or powdered sugar (US) dissolves easily when blended with a liquid. Use for making icings and fondants or for dusting onto desserts. You can make your own by grinding caster sugar in a coffee mill.

Cook's tip

Brown sugar has a tendency to go hard once the packet has been opened. To soften, place in a bowl and cover with a damp cloth. The sugar will absorb the moisture from the cloth and will become soft and usable within an hour or two.

SUGAR SYRUPS AND THEIR USES

The two essential techniques for a clear, non-grainy sugar syrup are to make sure the sugar has completely dissolved before raising the heat and boiling the liquid, and never to stir the syrup once boiling. Put the sugar and cold water in a heavy pan; stir over a low heat until the sugar dissolves. For a simple syrup, boil for 1 minute. For other boiled syrups, see below.

- **Light sugar syrup** (250 g/9 oz sugar to 500 ml/17 fl oz water) Use for fruit salads
- **Medium syrup** (250 g/9 oz sugar to 250 ml/8 fl oz water) Use for candying fruits
- **Heavy syrup** (250 g/9 oz sugar to 225 ml/7½ fl oz water) Use for caramel and ice creams
- **Soft ball** (119°C/238°F) For Italian meringue and buttercream icing
- **Hard ball** (138°C/280°F) Use for marzipan, fondant and sweets
- **Soft crack** (151°C/304°F) Use for nougat, some caramels and toffee
- **Hard crack** (168°C/336°F) For pulled and spun, rock or straw sugar and glazed fruit
- **Caramel in liquid form** Use for flavouring sauces and using in desserts like crème caramel. Cracked or crushed caramel is used for brittles and toppings

SUGAR THERMOMETER

This is invaluable for determining the exact temperature of boiled sugar syrups, and the setting points of jams, jellies and sweets. Take care that the tip of the thermometer touches only the liquid – not the pan.

BOILED SUGAR SYRUPS

If a syrup is left on the heat, water will evaporate and the syrup will thicken. During boiling, brush the sides of the pan with water to prevent crystals forming. Once the sugar syrup is at the required setting point, lower the base of the pan into iced water to prevent further cooking.

Soft ball First stage of saturation point; holds its shape but is soft when pressed.

Hard ball Forms a firm and pliable ball, giving a chewy texture.

Soft crack Brittle, but with a soft, pliable texture.

Hard crack Very brittle. Beyond this point sugar will quickly caramelise.

CARAMEL

Amber-coloured caramel forms when heavy sugar syrup is heated beyond the hard crack stage and all the moisture has evaporated. Light caramel is mild; medium caramel is dark golden brown and has a nutty taste. Don't cook over 190°C (375°F) or it will burn. If it sets too quickly, re-warm briefly.

Bring heavy syrup to the boil in a heavy pan. Lower the heat and swirl the pan once or twice so the syrup colours evenly; do not stir. When the caramel is the required colour, plunge the base of the pan into iced water to stop further cooking; remove the pan before the caramel sets.

Drizzled caramel shapes Make a heavy sugar syrup, then cook to a caramel. Line a baking sheet with oiled baking parchment. Take a spoonful of caramel and drizzle it onto the parchment, letting it fall from the tip of the spoon. Let the shapes cool, then lift them off the paper.

sweeteners

243

MAKING ICINGS

▶ **Glacé icing** Sift icing sugar into a bowl. Add a little warm water or flavouring of your choice and whisk vigorously. Continue whisking until smooth, adding more liquids as necessary.

◀ **Royal icing** To delay setting and make icing easy to work with, add glycerine. Put the sifted icing sugar in a bowl and make a well. Add lightly beaten egg whites and lemon juice. Whisk for about 10 minutes until stiff and glossy, and then whisk in the glycerine.

▶ **Chocolate icing** Add chocolate to sugar syrup, then whisk over a moderate heat until well combined and smooth. To test for the thread stage, dip fingers in iced water, then chocolate and pull apart to see thread. Tap pan to knock out air bubbles. Use immediately.

◀ **Buttercream** Boil sugar syrup to the soft ball stage. Add to egg yolks and egg in a thin steady stream, whisking all the time until pale and thick. Add chunks of softened butter to the mixture, then whisk in the flavouring of your choice. Chill for 5–10 minutes to firm up before use.

HONEY

The colour, flavour, consistency and quality of honey depend on the source of the nectar as well as the method of production. In general, the darker the colour, the stronger the flavour. Many commercial brands of honey are pasteurised and blended to give a uniform taste and texture and to prolong the shelf life, but from the point of view of both flavour and health, it is best to buy raw unfiltered honey from a single flower source.

Honeycomb This is honey that is still sealed within the cells. You can buy whole, halved or chunks of honeycomb. It is normally sealed in wax so the honey doesn't run out. More commonly available commercially is cell honey, which comes bottled in jars.

Clear clover Clear honeys have been heat-treated, a process that prevents them from crystallizing, which will happen naturally after a few weeks. Many people prefer clear or runny honey as it is easier to use in cooking. Clover honey is pale straw in colour and has a delightful sweet, mild flavour. It is good for cooking and eating. At one time, clover honey was the most popular and most commonly produced honey in Britain. It has declined in recent years owing to the loss of pastureland.

Orange blossom There are a variety of exotic honeys, imported from the United States and China. Almost a fifth of honey sold in Britain comes from China. Orange Blossom honey from California has a lovely aroma and flavour.

Hymettus This is the most famous of the Greek honeys and is heavily scented.

Scottish heather This is light in flavour and colour with a pleasant aromatic tang.

SYRUPS AND MOLASSES

Derived from natural sources, the syrups and molasses listed below can be a healthy alternative to sugar. The natural stickiness is useful in many recipes, adding richness to baking and sauces. Choose organically produced syrups and molasses, to avoid the chemicals and additives used in the sugar-refining process.

Grain syrups Corn, barley, wheat and rice can be transformed into syrups that are used in place of sugar in baked goods and sauces. Grain syrups are not as sweet as sugar and have a mild subtle flavour. Malt extract, a by-product of barley, has a more intense flavour and is good in breads and other baked goods. Grain syrups tend to be easier to digest and enter the bloodstream more slowly than other forms of refined sugar, which causes swings in blood sugar levels.

Golden syrup The famous Lyle's Golden Syrup was launched over 100 years ago and is still packaged in the same classic green and gold tin. Although it can be eaten neat (it is delicious on warm drop scones), it is one of the most versatile syrups, useful for baking and for fudge and toffee sauces to pour over ice cream.

Black treacle Made by refining molasses, it is thick, black and extremely sticky, less sweet than honey and with a strong flavour. It is used for recipes which call for its colour and distinctive flavour, notably gingerbread, some fruit cakes, Christmas pudding, toffee and Boston baked beans.

Syrup type	Description	Uses	Tips
Maple syrup	Made from the evaporated sap of the maple tree. It has a rich, distinctive flavour and is sweeter than sugar, so less is required in cooking	Glazing carrots or ham. Excellent with pancakes and waffles	Check you're not buying a synthetic maple syrup flavouring
Golden syrup	This is a light golden treacle	In flapjacks and other biscuits, and for making fudge sauces and toffee. Traditionally cooked with sponge to make syrup pudding or for treacle tart	It is the impurities in the syrup which give it both its colour and taste
Grain syrups	Most grains, such as corn, barley and rice, can be used for making syrups	Malt-extract (from barley) has a strong flavour and is used for bread-making; corn syrup, popular in the States, can be used in barbecue sauces and jellies	Grain syrups are less refined than other syrups and therefore enter the bloodstream more slowly
Black treacle	Similar to molasses, treacle is a product of sugar-refining. Thick, black and extremely sticky with a strong flavour. Sweeter than molasses but less sweet than syrup and honey	Use in baking for certain puddings and for gingerbreads, fruit cakes, Christmas pudding and toffee	Use molasses or treacle for Boston baked beans
Palm/date syrup	Obtained from date palms. Very dark, rich and sweet	As an ingredient in some Indian recipes	
Molasses	This rich, syrupy liquid is a by-product of sugar refining and ranges in quality and colour	Use in baking for certain biscuits and fruitcakes. Glazing pork and ham joints	Blackstrap molasses contain less sugar than lighter alternatives and are richer in vitamins and minerals

chocolate

From indulgent Belgian truffles to a simple cup of cocoa, versatile chocolate is one of the most popular sweet flavourings in the world. Made from the beans of the cacao tree, chocolate depends for its taste and quality on the blend of beans used, how the beans are roasted and the proportion of cocoa butter.

Baker's chocolate Also known as unsweetened chocolate, this chocolate does not contain any added sugar or flavourings. It is popular with professional chefs because it has good setting and cutting properties, and it is the best chocolate for making flexible decorations, such as ribbons, but as it can be difficult for the home cook to find, bittersweet chocolate is often used instead,

Couverture This is a fine-quality chocolate with a high percentage of cocoa butter. It is beloved of pastry chefs for its fine flavour and glossy finish, but is more difficult to work with than baker's chocolate and must always be tempered (see right) before use. It is mostly used for decorations or for making hand-made chocolates.

Bittersweet chocolate Also known as 'luxury', 'continental' or 'bitter' chocolate, this is the popular choice for cooking. As a general rule, the higher the percentage of cocoa solids, the better the chocolate. You will need to check the packet, but most plain chocolate nowadays contains at least 50 per cent cocoa solids, with 60–70 per cent the preferred minimum for chocoholics.

Plain The widely available plain chocolate can contain between 30 and 70 per cent cocoa solids. Better quality chocolate also contains a correspondingly smaller proportion of sugar.

Milk This is a popular confection, but is not an ideal choice for baking since, apart from a few expensive brands, it has a relatively low cocoa solid content.

White Not chocolate at all to aficionados, since it does not contain any cocoa solids. Some manufacturers use vegetable fats rather than cocoa butter, so their product shouldn't be called chocolate at all. White chocolate can be used for desserts, providing an attractive colour contrast, but like milk chocolate, it burns easily and should be melted with care.

Cocoa This is the concentrated powder made from chocolate liquor but with all the cocoa butter extracted. Although best known for making beverages, it is also extremely useful in baking, adding a good chocolate hit to cakes and desserts.

Drinking chocolate A sweetened form of cocoa, popular for making drinks but is not recommended for baking.

Chocolate-flavoured cake covering This popular cooking chocolate has its merits, as the high fat content means that it melts well and is satisfyingly pliable. Use for making chocolate curls or ribbons, but add a proportion of plain chocolate when melting to improve the flavour.

Carob A caffeine-free alternative to chocolate, coming from the pod of an evergreen tree that grows in the warmer parts of Europe.

PREPARING CHOCOLATE

It is easiest to chop and grate chocolate when it is cool and firm. In warm weather, refrigerate it first and take the extra precaution of holding it in a piece of baking parchment or foil. All utensils should be absolutely dry.

Chopping Work the blade of a chef's knife backwards and forwards over the chocolate.

Grating Hold the chocolate firmly; work it down against the coarsest grid of the grater.

STORING

Chocolate melts at hand heat. It should be stored in a cool dry place, between 16–18°C (60–64°F). If chocolate has a whitish bloom, it suggests it hasn't been stored properly or has been tempered (see right) at too high a heat.

MELTING CHOCOLATE

Chocolate is best melted in a bain-marie over a very low heat. If it gets too hot it will turn grainy and scorch; if splashed with water, it will harden or 'seize' and acquire a dull finish.

Chop into rough even-sized pieces. Place the pieces in a dry heatproof bowl and set over a pan of hot (not simmering) water. When the chocolate starts to melt, stir it with a wooden spoon until smooth.

TEMPERING

This technique is for chocolate that has a high cocoa butter content. It provides the consistency and sheen required for many decorative items. Melting, cooling and re-warming breaks down the fat to produce glossy, streak-free chocolate that sets very hard.

▶ Slowly melt the chocolate in a bowl over a pan of hot (not simmering) water. Stir it until smooth, and it reaches a temperature of 45°C (113°F).

▶ Set the bowl of chocolate over another bowl filled with ice cubes. Stir until the chocolate cools and the temperature drops to 25°C (77°F). Warm the chocolate again over a pan of hot water for 30–60 seconds, until it reaches a working temperature of 32°C (90°F).

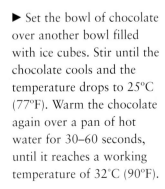

chocolate

MAKING SHAPES FOR DECORATION

When preparing chocolate for cutting or shaving, work quickly so the chocolate does not set hard before you have finished. Once smoothed and settled to an even layer, you can place a second sheet of baking parchment on top of the chocolate and invert the paper sheets so the new sheet is on the bottom. This will stop the chocolate curling up as it dries. Peel off the top sheet before cutting.

The shapes can be used for decorating gateaux or ice creams, or for making boxes or pyramids (below), which can then be filled with fruit, sorbets, or sweets and chocolates.

◀ **Spreading the chocolate** Ladle tempered chocolate onto a baking sheet lined with baking parchment. Quickly spread to a layer about 3 mm (⅛ in) thick, using a paddling motion, with a large angled spatula. Cool until cloudy but not set.

◀ **Cutting shapes** Dip a biscuit cutter in hot water, dry and then cut out rounds. For triangles, squares or rectangles use a knife. Let the shapes set on baking parchment.

DOUBLE-DUSTED CHOCOLATE SHAPES

Cut out triangles or squares. Put a little icing sugar in a sieve and gently tap it over the shapes. Put a little cocoa powder in another sieve and dust on top of the icing sugar. You can vary the effect by using cocoa powder first, or by dusting cocoa powder on white chocolate. When making shapes, always work while the chocolate is still malleable. If it sets and becomes hard, it will be brittle and crack.

MAKING CHOCOLATE CUPS

Pastry chefs make cups by dipping the outside of dariole moulds covered in clingfilm in tempered chocolate. Here are two alternative methods.

▶ **Cake cases** Paint a thin coating of tempered chocolate on the inside of petit four cases. Leave to set, then carefully peel away the paper case.

◀ **Moulded chocolate cups** Trim a disposable plastic cup down to the required height and fill to the brim with melted chocolate. Pour out the excess chocolate and chill to set. Remove from the plastic cup, cutting it off if necessary.

Chocolate Decorations

Half-coated fruits Soft fruits such as strawberries can be dipped half-way into either plain or white chocolate and used to decorate cakes and desserts. Allow the excess chocolate to drip off and place on greaseproof paper until set.

Chocolate quills Spread chocolate over the back of a baking sheet. Once set, rub the chocolate's surface to warm it slightly. Hold the baking sheet steady and slide a pastry scraper under the chocolate to form cigarette shapes.

Chocolate rose leaves Wipe leaves with a damp tea towel and pat dry. Melt 300 g (11 oz) chocolate. Hold the leaf by the stem and brush a generous coating of chocolate on one side of the leaf – the underside gives best results. Refrigerate until firm, then gently peel away the leaf from the chocolate.

Chocolate curls Hold a block of room-temperature white or dark chocolate firmly and run a vegetable peeler along one edge to make curls. For the best results, use chocolate with a low cocoa butter content or baker's chocolate, both of which are less likely to crack as they form curls.

Recipes

Hot chocolate cheesecake This is a delicious, all-chocolate dessert. Cocoa powder is added to the pastry to make a chocolate base, while the filling is flavoured with chocolate nuts.

Sachertorte There are countless wonderful chocolate gateaux. This all-time favourite from Austria is famous for its smooth rich chocolate topping.

Chocolate ganache This is a thick and extremely rich chocolate spread. It is made by pouring hot cream over chocolate and beating with a wooden spoon until the mixture is smooth and glossy. Use ganache as an icing, for filling cakes or for sandwiching together biscuits or meringues.

Chocolate roulade Similar to a chocolate Swiss roll, this sponge-based dessert is baked in a shallow tin, covered with a thick, creamy vanilla filling then rolled up tightly and decorated with chocolate curls and a sprinkling of cocoa powder.

Chocolate brownies A long-standing family favourite, brownies are made with a smooth mixture of chocolate, flour, melted butter, eggs and sugar, with additional flavouring from walnut halves, coffee, vanilla essence and further chunks of chopped, plain chocolate.

Decorative Outlines

Pipe an outline directly onto a serving plate using chocolate ganache (see left). Leave to set, then fill with a white chocolate sauce or fruit coulis.

chocolate

249

coffee and tea

COFFEE

Coffee is mainly prepared as a beverage but it also is used as a flavouring for iced desserts, puddings and cakes. The two main types of coffee bean are *coffea arabica* and *coffea robusta*. Of these, the arabica is considered the superior bean, but robusta is often blended with arabica for a relatively inexpensive coffee, but still with a good flavour.

ROASTS

Unroasted Before roasting, the seeds of the coffee plant are normally pale, varying from very pale, through yellow to green. They can be round or oval in shape. Some 'pods' contain only one seed, which is known as a peaberry bean owing to its pea shape.

Light roasted This type of roast is suitable for mild coffees with a delicate aroma and flavour. The coffee beans are pale to medium brown in colour.

Medium roast This is best for coffees with a well-defined character. The flavour is stronger, yet is still suitable for drinking black or with milk for breakfast as well as after meals.

Dark A dark or full roast gives a full-bodied coffee with a strong aroma and a slightly bitter flavour. The beans are dark and glossy.

High roast This is sometimes called a 'continental roast', giving a strong, bitter coffee. The beans are almost black and glossy.

Espresso Intensely black glossy beans that produce a dark roasted coffee, with a full-bodied bitter flavour.

GRINDS

Medium grind This is suitable for fairly light coffees made in a cafetière or a Neapolitan flip machine.

Omnigrind This comes between fine or filter grind and medium grind. It is supposed to work equally well for both, but in reality is more medium than fine, and providing you know the requirements of your particular coffee

maker, it is better to go with the precise grind. It works quite well with Neapolitan flip machines and other equipment that calls for a medium fine grind.

Fine (filter) Use this grind for glass balloon/vacuum method, and for filter or drip methods of making coffee. It produces a stronger coffee with a good full-bodied flavour.

Espresso This is a very fine grind. Use for espresso machines.

Turkish This is sometimes called pulverised or powdered coffee (not to be confused with instant coffee), and makes an exceptionally strong cup of coffee. The flavour of the beans is intensified by the grinding process.

OTHER COFFEE PRODUCTS

Instant coffee Instant coffee is made by brewing coffee beans into a concentrate. For coffee granules, the concentrate is then freeze-dried and processed to make dry, crisp particles and the best of this type uses arabica coffee. Coffee powder, cheaper generally than granules, is mostly made from robusta beans, the concentrate being dried to a fine powder. Better powders are heated further to make a granular-type of powder.

Coffee essence Sold in familiar flat-faced jars, coffee essence is convenient when using coffee as a flavouring. Make sure to buy pure coffee essence and not chicory and coffee essence.

Coffee liqueur Tia Maria is the most famous, made using Jamaican rum liqueur with coffee extracts and spices. Kahlúa is a Mexican coffee liqueur with a different flavour, suitable for many Italian-style desserts.

COFFEE EQUIPMENT

Make sure to choose the correct grind of coffee to suit the method of brewing. The finer the grain, the greater the surface area that is exposed to water and the slower the length of time for the water to run through it. The coffee will consequently be more full-bodied and stronger. Coffee machines are designed for a particular grind of coffee and if this is not right the coffee will be disappointing, either weak and thin tasting, if the grains are too coarse, or bitter and grainy if the grind is too fine.

FOR COARSE GRINDS
Jug (carafe)

FOR MEDIUM GRINDS
Plunger or cafetière (below), Neapolitan flip machines, glass balloon/vacuum method

FOR FINE GRINDS
Filter/drip method, espresso pots, ibrik (for Turkish coffee using pulverised grinds)

TEA

Black teas Once picked the leaves are dried, bruised and then fermented in the open air, a process which gives black tea its characteristic colour, strength and flavour. Black tea is commonly drunk with milk, but lemon makes a very refreshing brew. Varieties include Assam, Ceylon, Darjeeling, Keemun, Orange Pekoe and Lapsang Souchong.

Blended teas All English teas are a blend of black teas. Blending teas has been an important and skilled job ever since tea was introduced to this country in the 17th century. There are more than 3,000 different blends of tea; to sample more than the typically available teas in supermarkets, you will need to visit a specialist shop. Examples of blended teas are Earl Grey, English Breakfast and Irish Breakfast.

Green teas These come mostly from China and Japan where they are the popular teas for drinking. Because the leaves are dried immediately after picking, unlike black teas which are allowed to ferment, the brew is noticeably fresher with a mild, astringent flavour. Green teas are served alone, or with herbs like mint or lemon verbena, but never with milk. Gunpowder, Jasmine, Hyson and Moyunes are all green teas.

Oolong teas These unusual teas come half-way between green and black teas, the leaf only having been half-fermented.

Tisanes and fruit teas Tisanes are popular healthy beverages, being free of caffeine or tannin. There are numerous tisanes to choose from, with new ones on the supermarket shelves every year. Like ordinary tea, they can be used for making ice creams and sorbets, either used by themselves or blended with fruit juice.

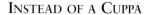

INSTEAD OF A CUPPA

Tea can be used in a surprising number of recipes, adding new dimensions to classic techniques. Tea smoking is used in Chinese dishes to add colour and flavour to foods, such as duck and chicken, but does not cook them. Black tea is mixed with brown sugar and herbs or spices and placed in the bottom of a heavy pan. The food is placed on a rack over this mixture, covered and the pan is left over high heat for approximately 15 minutes while the food smokes. Tea is also used to flavour chocolate ganache and can be made into ice cream.

▶ **Green tea ice cream** In order to obtain the full flavour of the tea, pound green tea leaves. Add, little by little, to softened vanilla ice cream. Serve with a dark chocolate sauce (see right).

index

A

Acidulated water 169
Acorn squash 178
Agar agar 238
Al dente 151
Almonds
  removing skin 22
  toasted 53
  see also Nuts
Anchovy(ies)
  desalting 69
  essence 238
Apples 204
  baking 39
  dried 222
Apricots 207, 208
  dried 222
  removing skin 22
Artichokes 162–3, 167
Asparagus 161
Aspic 238
Aubergines 188
Avocado(s) 189

B

Bacon 96–97
Bain-marie 15
Baking
  apples 39
  beans 17
  beetroot 39
  bread 39
  en papillote 38
  fish 38
  fruit 39
  pastry 19
  potatoes 38, 39
  powder 149
  quick breads 39
  shellfish 240
  vegetables 38
Balsamic vinegar 126
Bananas 216
Barbecuing 42–43
  chicken drumsticks and
    thighs 105
  sweetcorn 175
Barding 34, 35
Basting 35
Batter(s) 131

deep-frying 48, 49
Beancurd 135
Beans, dried *see* Pulses
Beans, green 176, 177
Béarnaise sauce 123
Béchamel sauce 119
Beef 82–85
  roasting times 35–6
Beefsteak tomatoes 186
Beetroot 166
  baking 39
  greens 170
Berries 209–10
  see also name of fruit
Beurre manié 123
Bicarbonate of soda 149
Black treacle 245
Blackberries 210
Blackcurrants 211
Blanching 22–23
Blueberries 210
Boiling 26–27
  onions 157
Bok choy 171
Boning
  flat fish 61
  freshwater fish 67
  leg of lamb 91
  monkfish 62
  oily fish 65
  quail 114
  turkey breast 107
  veal breast 87
Bouquet garni 195
Braising 32–33
Bread 148–9
  baking 39
  -based puddings 149
Breadcrumbs 148
Broad beans 176
Broccoli 172
Brunoise 32
Bruschetta 149
Brussels sprouts 172, 173
Beurre blanc 123
Beurre manié 123
Bulgar wheat 141
Butter 122–3
  sauces 123
Buttercream 244
Butterflying
  leg of lamb 91

prawns 73
Buttermilk 118
Butternut squash 179

C

Cabbage(s) 172, 173
Cake
  equipment 16–17
  making and decorating
    20–21
Calamari *see* Squid
Caper berries 202
Capers 202
Capon, roasting times 37
Caramel 243
Cardoon 160
Carrots 166
Carving 50–51
Cassava 168, 169
Casseroles 32
Cauliflower 172
Cayenne pepper 185
Celeriac 167
Celery 160
Chaudfroid duck 110
Chayote 179
Cheddar 125
Cheese 124–7
Chermoula 229
Cherries 208
Cherry tomatoes 186
Chestnuts, peeling 224
Chicken 102–5
  carving 50
  escalopes 45
  making a pinwheel 29
  poaching 28
  poussin 102
  preparing for stir-frying 47
  roasting times 37
  see also Poultry
Chicory 192
Chilli(es) 183–5
Chinese
  broccoli 171
  leaves 171
  mustard greens 171
Chives 195
Chocolate 246–9
  coated fruits 53
  cups 248

decorations 249
  icing 244
Chopping 11
Chutneys 223
Citrus fruits 213–15
  crystallised peel 214
  garnishes 215
  see also names of fruit
Clams, opening 79
Clarifying butter 123
Clementines 213
Cloves 229
Coating(s)
  for deep-frying 48
  escalopes 45, 87, 104, 147
  with peppercorns 241
Cocoa 246
Coconut 226
Concassé 187
Condensed milk 118
Conserves 223
Corn *see* Sweetcorn
Cos lettuce 190
Coulis, fruit 53
Courgette 178, 180
Court bouillon 67
Cous cous 141
Crab 76–77
  boiling 27
Cranberries 210
Crayfish, boiling 27
Cream 120–1
Creamed cakes 20
Crème fraîche 120, 121
Crevettes 72
Crostini 149
Croutons and croûtes 148
Crustaceans, boiling 27
Crystallised peel 214
Cucumbers 180, 181, 192
Cured meats 100
Currants
  dried fruit 222
  soft fruit 211
Curry spice mixtures 229
Custard apple 216, 218
Custards, making 119

D

Damsons 207
Dandelion greens 170

Dashi 201
Dates 216, 218, 219
Decorating
  cakes 21
  caramel 243
  with cream 121
  desserts 53
  making chocolate shapes
    248, 249
  making outlines 249
Deep-fat fryer 13, 48
Deep-fried potatoes 165
Deep-frying 48–49
Desserts, decorating 53
Dhal see Lentils
Dicing 11
Dried beans see Pulses
Dried fruit 222
Dried peas 138
Dried salt cod 69
Dry-frying 45
Duck 108–10
  breasts
    dry-frying 45
    scoring 45
  carving 50
  chaudfroid 110
  garnishes 110
  roasting times 37
  salmis 110
  wild 112
Duxelles 199

E

Egg(s) 128–32
  batter 131
  meringue 132
  poaching 28
  shallow-frying 45
  soufflés 131
  wash 13
  whites
    folding in 130
    whisking 130
Electrical equipment 13, 121,
  145
  deep-fat fryer 13, 48
  spice mill 233
Emmenthal 125
En papillote, baking fish 38
Endive 192
Equipment 10–17
  balloon whisk 121
  bamboo steamer 30
  barbecue 42
  bean slicer 176
  bulb baster 35

cherry stoner 208
couscousière 141
egg piercer 131
egg timer 131
fish kettle 28
garlic press 159
mandolin 169
for mashed potatoes 165
melon baller 221
mortar and pestle 229
mouli 211
mushroom brush 199
pasta 151
peppermill 241
poultry shears 103
rice 145
rotary grater 127
salad spinner 190
spatula 42
stir-frying 46
see also Cake equipment;
  Electrical equipment;
  Knife(ves);
  Thermometer(s)
Escalopes
  coating and frying 45
  flouring 147
  veal 87
Escarole 192
Evaporated milk 118
Exotic fruit 216

F

Fat(s) 122
Fennel 160
Figs 216, 218, 219
  dried 222
Filleting
  knife 61
  whole flat fish 61
  see also Boning
Fines herbes 194
Fish 58–69
  barbecuing 43
  deep-frying 49
  garnishes 80
  goujons 49, 62
  grilling 41
  marinating 23
  poaching 28
  smoked, cooking chart 70
  steaming 30, 31
  stock 63
  stuffing 25
  tenderising 23
Flavouring
  grilled fish 41

oils 235
  roast meat 34
  vinegars 237
  see also Spices 228–33
Flour 146–7
Flowers, edible 193
Foie gras 111
Food processor 13
French beans 176
French fries 165
French method of deep-frying
  49
Fritters, fruit 49
Fruit(s) 204–15
  baking 39
  butters 223
  chocolate coated 53
  citrus 212–15
  coulis 53
  essence 223
  exotic 216–19
  fritters 49
  glaze 223
  in salads 193
  poaching 29
  see also names of fruit
Frying 44–45
  deep-frying 48–49
  escalopes 45, 87
  onions 157
  sausages 99
  stir-frying 46–47

G

Galangal 228
Game 115–16
Game birds 112–14
  accompaniments for 114
Gammon 96, 97
Garam masala 229
Garlic 159
Garnishes 52–53
  aspic 238
  citrus 215
  cucumber 181
  for duck 110
  for fish and shellfish 80
  radish 167
  see also Decorating
Gelatine 238
Ghee 122
Gherkins 181
Ginger 228
Glaze
  egg wash 131
  fruit 223
Goose 111

preparing for roasting 109
  roasting times 37
  see also Poultry
Gooseberries 210
Gorgonzola 125
Goujons 49, 62
Grains 139–45
Grapefruit 215
  see also Citrus fruits
Grapes 220
Gratin topping 126
Gravy making 35
Green beans 176
Greens, leafy 170–3
Gremolada 194
Grilling 40–41
  sausages 99
  shellfish 240
Grouse 112–14
  casseroling 32
  roasting times 37
Guavas 217
Guinea fowl 112
  roasting times 37
Gutting
  freshwater fish 67
  herring 65

H

Ham 96–97
  carving a whole 51
  roasting times 37
Heart see Offal
Herb(s) 194–7
  in salad 192–3
Herring, scaling, gutting and
  boning 65
Hollandaise sauce 123
Honey 244

I

Ice-cream
  maker 13
  scoop 12
Icing 244
  cakes 21

J

Jam 223
Jelly 223
Jerusalem artichoke 167
Jointing
  chicken 103
  rabbit 116
Julienne 11

Kale 171
Kebabs 42
Kidneys *see* Offal
Kiwi fruit 216
Knife(ves) 10–11
  canelle 180
  cleaver 46
  filleting 61
  oyster 79
  smoked salmon 70
Kohlrabi 167
Kombu 201
Kumquats 213

Lamb 88–91
  carving 51
  roasting times 35–6
Lard 122
Larding meat 34
Lardons 97
Leafy greens *see* Greens, leafy
Leeks 158
Lemons 214
  see also Citrus fruits
Lentils 134
Lettuce 190–91
  see also Salads
Limes 214
  see also Citrus fruits
Lining
  cake tin 16
  pie dish 19
Liver 98
Lobster 74–75
  boiling 27
Loquat 217
Lychees 218, 219

Mandarins 213
Mangetouts 174
Mangoes 216, 218, 219
Margarine 122
Marinating 23
  oily fish 65
Marmalade 223
Measures and measuring 13
Meat
  barbecuing 43
  garnishing 53
  grilling 40
  larding and barding 34
  marinating 23

preparing for stews 33
preparing for stir-frying 47
roasting 34
roasting times 35–37
sealing the juices 33
skimming the fat 33
stewing 32
stuffing 25
tenderising 23
thermometer 35
  see also Beef; Lamb; Pork;
    Veal
Melba toast 148
Melon(s) 220, 221
Meringues 132
Microwave blanching 22
Milk 118–19
Mirepoix 32
Molasses 245
Mozzarella 125
Mushrooms 198–200
Mussels 78, 79
  steaming 31
Mustard greens 171

Nectarines 206, 208
Neufchâtel 125
Noisettes
  of lamb 91
  of pork 94
Noodles 154
  stir-fried 47
Nori 201
Nut(s) 224–6

Offal 98
Oil(s) 44, 234–5
Okra 177
Olive oil 234
Olives 202
Omelette pan 131
Onions 156–7
  see also Spring onions
Oranges 212–13
Oriental sauces 239
Oyster(s) 78–79

Pan-frying 44
Pans 14–15
  casseroles 32
  frying 45
  omelette 131

see also Tins
Papayas 216, 218
Paprika 182
Parboiling 22
Parmesan 125
Parsnips 166
Partridge 112–14
  roasting times 37
Passata 187
Passion fruit 216
Pasta 150–3
  equipment 13
Pastry 18–19
  equipment 16–17
Pattypan squash 178
Paupiettes 62
Peaches 206, 207
  dried 222
  removing skin 22
Pears 205
  dried 222
Peas
  dried 138
  garden varieties 174–5
  split 138
Peeling
  and de-veining prawns 73
  hot water method 22
  onions 157
  and slicing citrus fruit 213
  tomatoes 187
Peking cabbage 171
Peking duck 110
Pepino 217
Pepper and peppercorns 241
Peppers *see* Sweet peppers
Persillade 194
Persimmon 217
Petit pois 174
Pheasants 112–14
  roasting times 37
Physalis 218
  caramel coated 219
Pie edges 19
Pie tins 17
Pigeons 112–13
Pineapples 218, 219
Plantains 216
Plum tomatoes 186
Plums 207, 208
Poaching 28–29
  sausages 99
Polenta 141
Pomegranate 217
Pomelos 215
Poppy seeds 226
Pork 92–95
  roasting 35, 37

Potatoes 164–5
  baking 38, 39
  deep-frying 49, 165
  French deep-frying 49
  sweet 168
Poultry 103–11
  barbecuing 43
  barding 35
  carving 50
  casseroling 32
  grilling 41
  marinating 23
  pounding 23
  roasting temperatures 35
  roasting times 37
  spatchcocking 41
  stuffing 24
  tenderising 23
Pounding meat and poultry
    23, 87
Poussin 102
  roasting times 37
Prawns 72–73
  boiling 27
Preserves 223
Prickly pear 217
Prunes 222
Puddings
  bread-based 149
  steamed 31
Pulses 134–8
Pumpkin 178
  seeds 226
Puréeing soft fruit 211
Purple sprouting broccoli 172

Quail 112–14
  casseroling 32
  eggs 129
  roasting times 37
Quick breads, baking 39

Rabbit 115–16
Radishes 167, 192
Raising agents 149
Raisins 222
Raspberries 210
Redcurrants 211
Rhubarb 220
Rice 142–5
Ricotta 125
Risotto 145
Roasting
  asparagus 161

garlic 159
  meat and poultry 34, 35
  onions 157
  potatoes 165
  preparing duck for 109
  preparing goose for 109
  times, meat and poultry 36–37
  turkey 107
  vegetables 38
Rocket 192
Root vegetables
  exotic 168
  see also Vegetable(s); name of vegetable
Rotisserie grilling 41
Round fish 58
Runner beans 176

Saffron, preparing 233
Salad(s) 190–3
Salmis of duck 110
Salmon, smoked 70
Salsify 168
Salt 240
  crust for baking fish 38
Saltimbocca 87
Samphire 160
Sashimi 65
Satay chicken 105
Satsumas 213
Sauce(s)
  béarnaise 123
  béchamel 119
  butter 123
  cream enriched 121
  hollandaise 123
  oriental 239
  pasta 151
  reducing 27
  white 119
  Worcestershire 238
Saucepans 14–15
Sausages 99
  see also Cured meats
Sautéeing 44
  onions 157
Scaling herring 65
Scallops, preparing 79
Scorzonera 168
Seaweed 201
Seeds 226
Sesame seeds 226
Shallots 156
Shellfish 78–79
  baking or grilling 240

boiling 27
garnishes 80
stuffing 25
Shortening 122
Shrimps 72–73
  boiling 27
Simmering 26
Skinning
  bacon, gammon and ham 97
  broad beans 176
  fish 60–2
  sweet peppers 182
Smetana 120
Smoked fish 70
Snipe 112
Sorrel 170
Soufflés 131
Soups, garnishing 53
Soured cream 120, 121
Soy sauce 239
Soya
  beans 135
  milk 118
Spaghetti squash 179
Spatchcocking 41
Spelt 146
Spice(s) 228–33
  chart 230–2
Spinach 170, 192
Split peas 138
Spring greens 170
Spring onion(s) 158
  garnish 52
Squash 178–81
Squid 71
Star fruit 217
Steaks 83
  testing for doneness 40
Steamed puddings 31
Steaming 30–31
  asparagus 161
Stewing meat 32, 33
Stir-frying 46–47
Stock
  cubes 238
  fish 63
Strawberries 209, 210
Stuffing
  chicken 105
  fish and shellfish 25
  leg of lamb 91
  meat 25
  pork 93
  poultry 24
  quail 114
  turkey 107
  veal joint 87

vegetables 25
Suet 122
Sugar 242–3
Sugar snap peas 174
Sultanas 222
Sun-dried tomatoes 187
Sunflower seeds 226
Sushi 65
  Japanese rolling mat 145
Swedes 166
Sweet peppers 182
Sweet potatoes 168
Sweet spice mixtures 229
Sweetbreads *see* Offal
Sweetcorn 175
Swiss chard 170
Swiss roll, preparing 20
Syrups 245

Tabasco 185
Tamales 175
Tamarind, preparing 233
Tangerines 213
Tapenade 202
Tapioca 169
Taros 168
Tenderising meat and poultry 23
Testing for doneness
  bread 39
  cakes 20
  fish 63
  grilled meat 40
  pasta 151
  poached chicken 28
  pork 96
  prawns 73
  rice 144
  roast meat and poultry 35
  steaks 40
  stewed meat 33
Thai bean 176
Thermometer(s) 13
  deep frying 48
  instant-read 42
  meat 35
  sugar 243
Tiger prawns 72
Timbales 52
Tins 16–17
Tofu 135
Tomatillos 189
Tomato(es) 186–7
  peeling 22, 187
Tongue *see* Offal
Truffles 200

Turkey 106–7
  carving 50
  escalopes 45
  roasting times 37
Turnip 166

Ugli fruit 215

Vanilla, preparing 233
Veal 86–87
  breast roast, carving 51
  roasting times 36
Vegetable(s) 157–85
  baking and roasting 38
  barbecuing 43
  blanching times 23
  boiling 26, 27
  braising 32
  brunoise 32
  carved 53
  fat 122
  mirepoix 32
  preparing for stir-frying 47
  steaming 30, 31
  stuffing 25
  see also names of vegetables; Salads
Venison 115
Vinaigrette 191
Vinegar(s) 236–7

Wakame 201
Watercress 192
Watermelon 221
Wheat grain 139
Whipping cream 120, 121
Whitecurrants 211
Wok 46
Wood pigeon 112
Woodcock 112
Worcestershire sauce 238

Yams 168, 169
Yeast 149
Yogurt 120

Zest 212

acknowledgements

Contributors

Pat Alburey is an established and experienced food writer, contributing features, creating and testing recipes and styling food for many magazines. She is a cookery consultant, the author of several books and broadcasts on radio.

Chrissie Ingram worked as Cookery Editor for a leading magazine before becoming a freelance cookery writer and editor. She now writes for many magazines and publications and has written a number of cookery books.

Editor Jane Bamforth
Art editor Gilda Pacitti
Editorial assistant Charlotte Beech
Design assistant Ambrene Marghoob
Photographers David Murray, Jules Selmes
IT management Paul Stradling, Elisa Merino
Production manager Karol Davies
Production controller Nigel Reed
Picture researcher Richard Soar
Indexer Madeline Weston

Carroll & Brown would like to thank the following for supplying illustrations:

Cucina Direct
www.cucinadirect.co.uk
Telephone 020 8246 4311
p. 32 (bottom left)

Divertimenti
227–229 Brompton Road
London SW3 2EP
www.divertimenti.co.uk
Telephone 020 7581 8065
p. 11 (top right), p. 45 (bottom left), p. 131 (bottom left), p. 141 (bottom right), p. 151 (top right), p. 155 (bottom right), p. 186 (bottom right), p. 251 (bottom left).